EDWIN EE

© 1993 Edwin Ee

Published by
Heian International Inc.
1815 West 205th Street
Suite #301
Torrance, CA 90501
Web site: *www.heian.com*
E-mail address: *heianemail@heian.com*

Original edition published by SNP Publishing Pte Ltd, Singapore

All rights reserved. No part of this publication may be reproduced, stored in a retrieval system, or transmitted in any form or by any means, electronic, mechanical, photocopying, recording or otherwise, without prior permission of the publishers.

Cover design by Albert Tan
Illustrations by Alvin Ee, Kent Goh and Peh Soh Hoon

First American Edition 1998

98 99 00 01 02 9 8 7 6 5 4 3 2 1

ISBN 0-89346-861-4

Printed in Singapore by Chong Moh Offset Printing Pte Ltd

For Shan

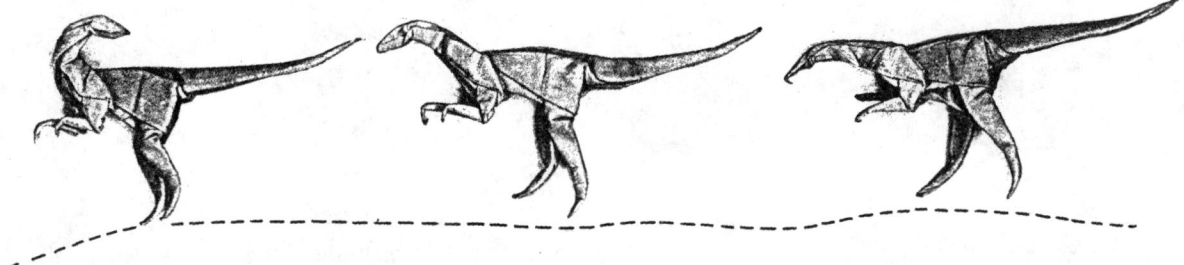

Preface

All of us, whether young or old, are enthralled by dinosaurs. We are fascinated by them, even when we can't tell a *Diplodocus* from a *Brachiosaurus*. However, thanks to numerous dinosaur books out there and films like *Jurassic Park*, we are slowly being exposed to, and educated about (usually much later than our children), the work of palaeontologists and their astonishing insights as to how dinosaurs may have lived and died.

I hope this book will in some way add to the interest in these "terrible lizards" which once roamed the earth 65 million years ago.

Contents

Introduction	1
Getting Started	2
Basic Folds and Bases	
Folding Symbols	7
Valley Fold	8
Mountain Fold	8
Reverse Fold (1)	8
Reverse Fold (2)	8
Crimp Fold (1)	9
Crimp Fold (2)	9
Crimp Fold (3)	9
Crimp Fold (4)	10
Crimp Fold (5)	10
Crimp Fold (6)	11
Rabbit-ear Fold	12
Sink Fold (1)	13
Sink Fold (2)	14
Squash Fold	15
Petal Fold	16
Preliminary Base	17
Offset Preliminary Base	18
Bird Base	19
Frog Fold	20
Frog Base	22
Box Fold	23
Tail Base	25
Hadrosaur Base	29

Dinosaur Models

- *Tyrannosaurus* — 35
- *Compsognathus* — 44
- *Diplodocus and Apatosaurus* — 57
- *Ceratosaurus* — 66
- *Allosaurus* — 72
- *Megalosaurus* — 79
- *Deinonychus* — 85
- *Coelophysis* — 90
- *Velociraptor* — 96
- *Brachiosaurus* — 103
- *Camarasaurus* — 110
- *Triceratops* — 115
- *Stegosaurus* — 123
- *Saurolophus* — 131
- *Parasaurolophus* — 139
- *Lambeosaurus* — 146
- *Iguanodon* — 149
- *Stegoceras* — 156
- *Pteranodon* — 162
- *Dimetrodon* — 170

Making Your Own Dinosaur Park — 177

Approximate Dinosaur Dimensions — 181

Paper Size to Use — 182

References — 183

Introduction

Jurassic Origami covers 20 of the more popular dinosaurs and reptiles living during the Jurassic and Cretaceous periods. All 20 models are original works and some of them require a bit more practice before you can get them right. By making slight modifications to the models in this book you should be able to make many more of your own dinosaur models to add to your collection.

As most dinosaurs look alike (e.g. *Tyrannosaurus*, *Allosaurus* and *Ceratosaurus*), you should pay careful attention to minor details when making them, e.g. shape of the head, thickness of the jaw, length of the tail and body posture. Some background knowledge about the dinosaur, e.g. whether it is a vicious hunter or docile vegetarian, large and lumbering or small and speedy, will help tremendously. I strongly recommend that you invest in some dinosaur books (preferably those with plenty of pictures) for reference. That way you can compare your completed work of joy with the picture in the book and, in doing so, perhaps understand why your *Tyrannosaurus* looks like a sad-looking *Hadrosaurus* instead of the fierce flesh-eating theropod it was meant to be.

In creating my models, my emphasis is to make them realistic. I think this is a very important point if we are to encourage the art of origami. People lose interest if you show them an ambiguous-looking model and call it a *Triceratops* just because it has three horns. A consequence of this attempt at realism is that most of my models are made with two pieces of square paper rather than a single piece. This enables me to give the models a three-dimensional profile and to include minor details which make the models so much more realistic. Purists may cry foul at this practice, but I think that as long as you are able to fold a model with just paper to start with and have enjoyed yourself in the process, then the essence of origami has been captured.

With this, I wish you good luck in your folding endeavours. May your *Iguanodon* look like an *Iguanodon* and your *Tyrannosaurus* a *Tyrannosaurus*. Most of all ... don't forget to enjoy yourself.

Getting Started

If you are a beginner at origami, I strongly suggest that you read through *Basic Folds and Bases* (pages 7 to 31) to get acquainted with the various folds before attempting the models. It is frustrating when you are halfway making a model and have to refer back to the basic steps to see how a fold is executed. Once you can intuitively do a reverse fold, crimp fold and sink fold, you will enjoy making the models, which is what origami is about — fun!

For the experienced paper folder, just skim through the *Basic Folds and Bases* section to see if there are any folds or bases that are not familiar to you. In all likelihood you will be familiar with folds but know them by different names.

What Type of Paper to Use

Any type of paper is fine. For practice purposes, I suggest you use the junk mail that you get in your letterbox. Rummage through your study. You might find old photocopied notes which are A4 size (210 x 297 mm). Just tear them into 21-cm squares (which is what I use mostly throughout this book).

When making a dinosaur park, use thick coloured paper (vanguard sheets are way too thick). Never mind if it is coloured on one side only. Thick paper, although harder to fold, will give your models more "body" and the three-dimensional effect is definitely easier to achieve. The stiffness of the paper will allow your models to stand on their feet, with the tails off the ground. Wipe the paper with a damp cloth to soften it if you find it too hard to fold.

Nearly all the dinosaur models in this book are made from two pieces of square paper. One piece is used to make the head. The other piece is used to make the body and tail. The head is usually made from a smaller piece of paper than the tail (with the exception of *Brachiosaurus*). The different paper sizes are important if you want to make a model that is proportionate.

Making Your Dinosaur Models

It is important that you make these three models first:
- *Tyrannosaurus*
- *Compsognathus*
- *Diplodocus*

These models cover all the types of folds that you are likely to encounter. Since the other dinosaur models are based on these three models, you will find the instructions easier to follow once you have mastered making these three models.

The Dinosaur Head

If you look closely at pictures of dinosaurs, you will find that they all share similar body shapes. The difference is in the head. Pay careful attention to details like the length of the head, shape of the head, thickness of the neck and thickness of the lower jaw. They make a lot of difference to the final appearance of your model.

Getting the details correct depends a lot on the positions and angles of your folds. When making any fold (e.g. a reverse fold or crimp fold), look closely at where the fold is to be made. Analyse your result and ask yourself, "Does the head look too long? Are the legs too thin?", and so on.

The Dinosaur Body and Tail

The bodies of dinosaurs (for this matter, even animals) are very similar. Certain groups share similar characteristics.

The bodies of large theropods, e.g. *Tyrannosaurus*, *Allosaurus*, *Ceratosaurus* and *Megalosaurus*, are similar: strong backs, powerful legs and tails.

The large sauropods, e.g. *Diplodocus*, *Apatosaurus*, *Camarasaurus* and *Brachiosaurus*, have bulky bodies, elephantine legs and very long tails.

The ornithopods, e.g. *Parasaurolophus*, *Saurolophus*, *Lambeosaurus* and *Iguanodon*, have similar body shapes to the large theropods except for the hunched backs and different body postures.

The small theropods have thin bodies, flattish backs, thin bird-like legs and tails that give them an air of fleet-footedness.

In this book, the bodies of nearly all the dinosaur models are made following certain standard steps. I have outlined these steps in the *Tyrannosaurus* model (representing the large theropods and ornithopods), the *Compsognathus* model (representing the small theropods) and the *Diplodocus* model (representing the sauropods). When making the bodies of the other models, you will be referred to any one of these three models.

Basic Folds and Bases

Folding Symbols

— · — · — · — · — Mountain fold

- - - - - - - - - - - Valley fold

———————— Creases from previous fold(s)

Fold in that direction

Fold behind

Fold and unfold

- - - - - - - - - - - - - Hidden portion of model

Turn model over

Lift or pull

Press, push in, squash or sink

✂ - - - - - x Cut along dotted line

Valley Fold

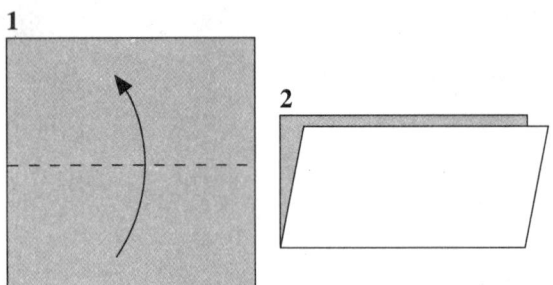

Mountain Fold

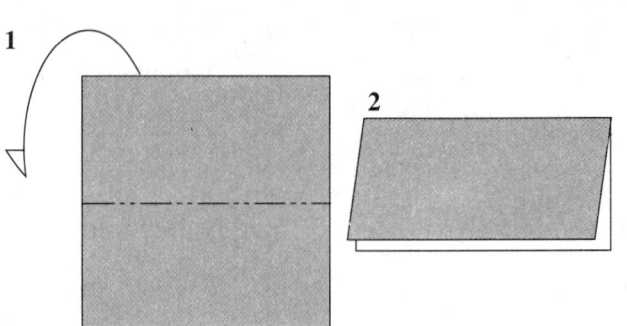

Reverse Fold (1)

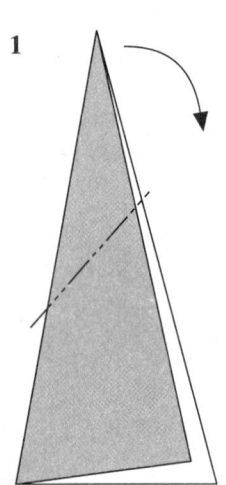

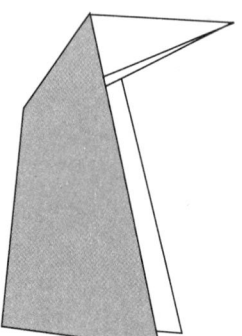

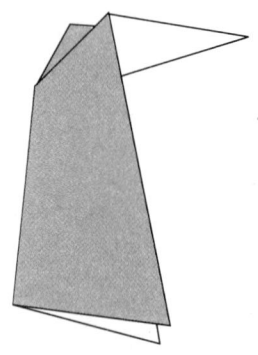

Reverse Fold (2)

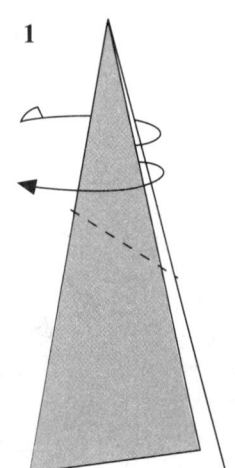

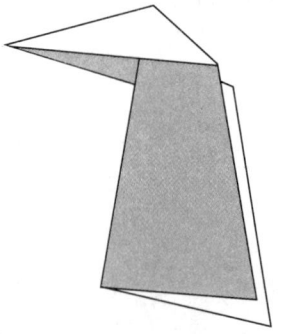

Crimp Fold (1)

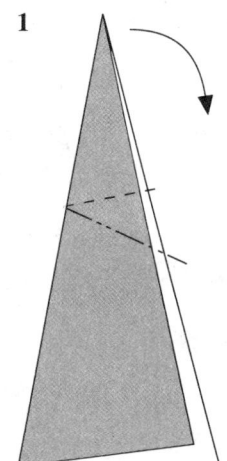
1

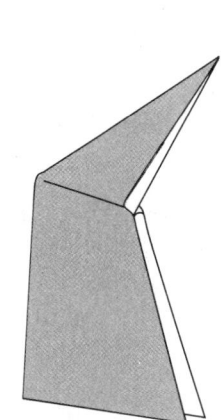
2

Crimp Fold (2)

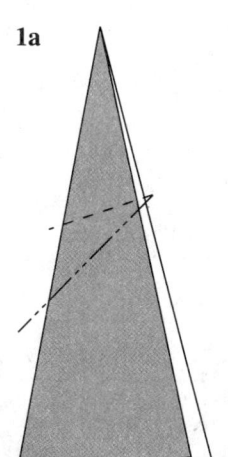
1a

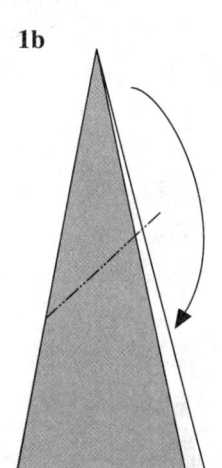
1b

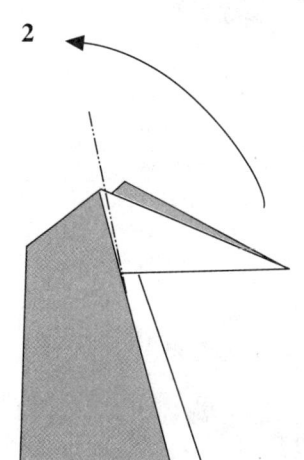
2

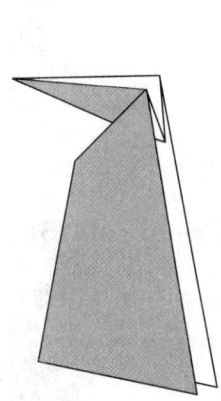
3

Crimp Fold (3)

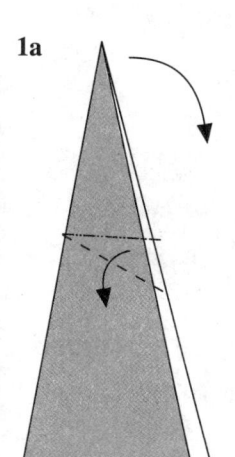
1a

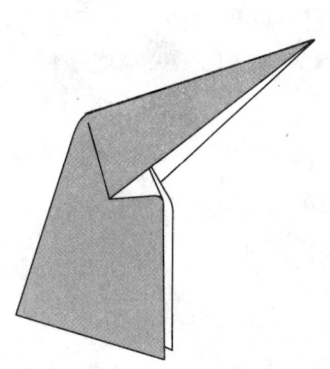
2a

2b

Crimp Fold (4)

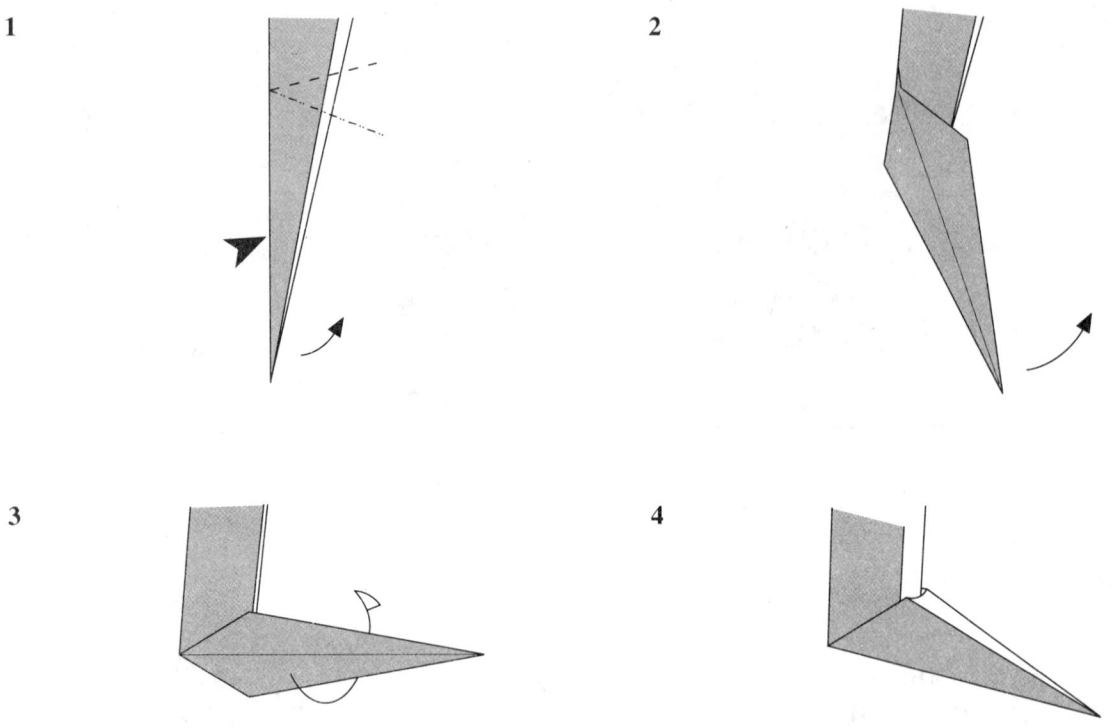

Crimp Fold (5)

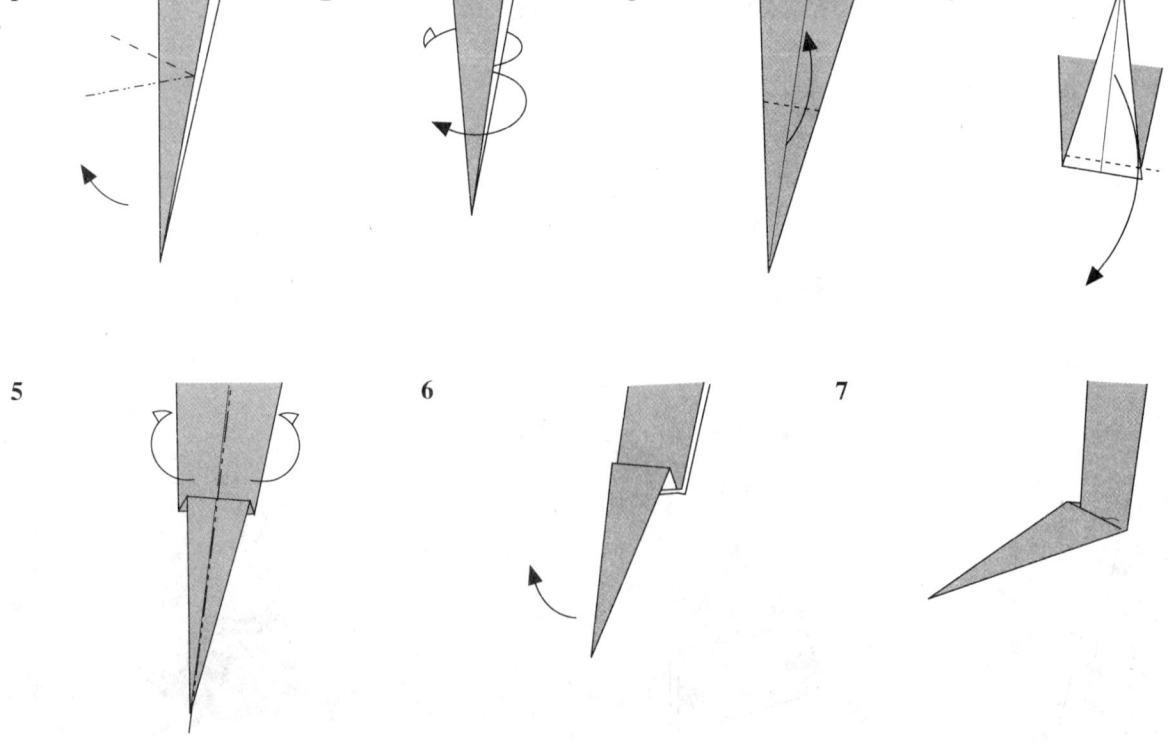

Crimp Fold (6)

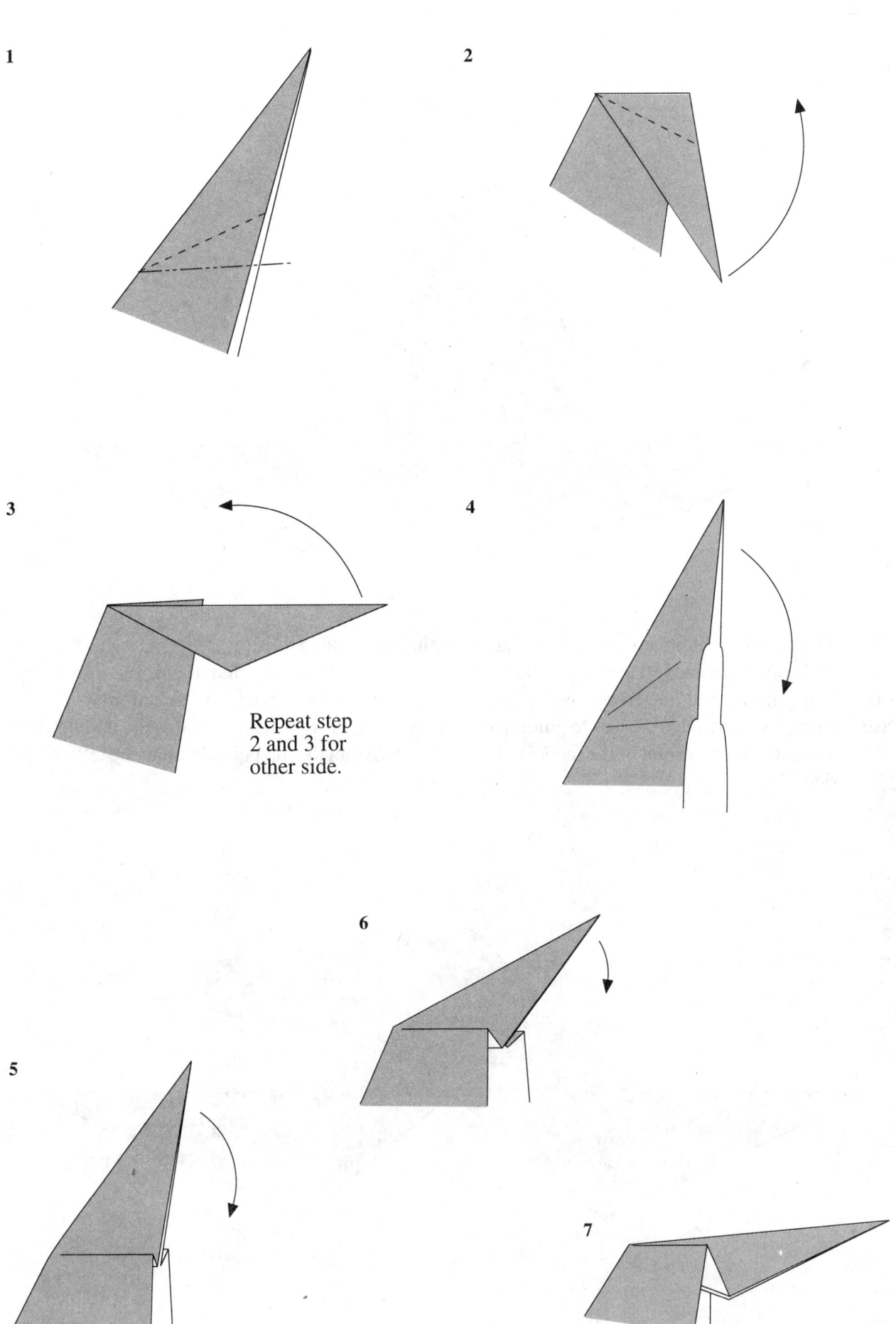

Repeat step 2 and 3 for other side.

Rabbit-ear Fold

1

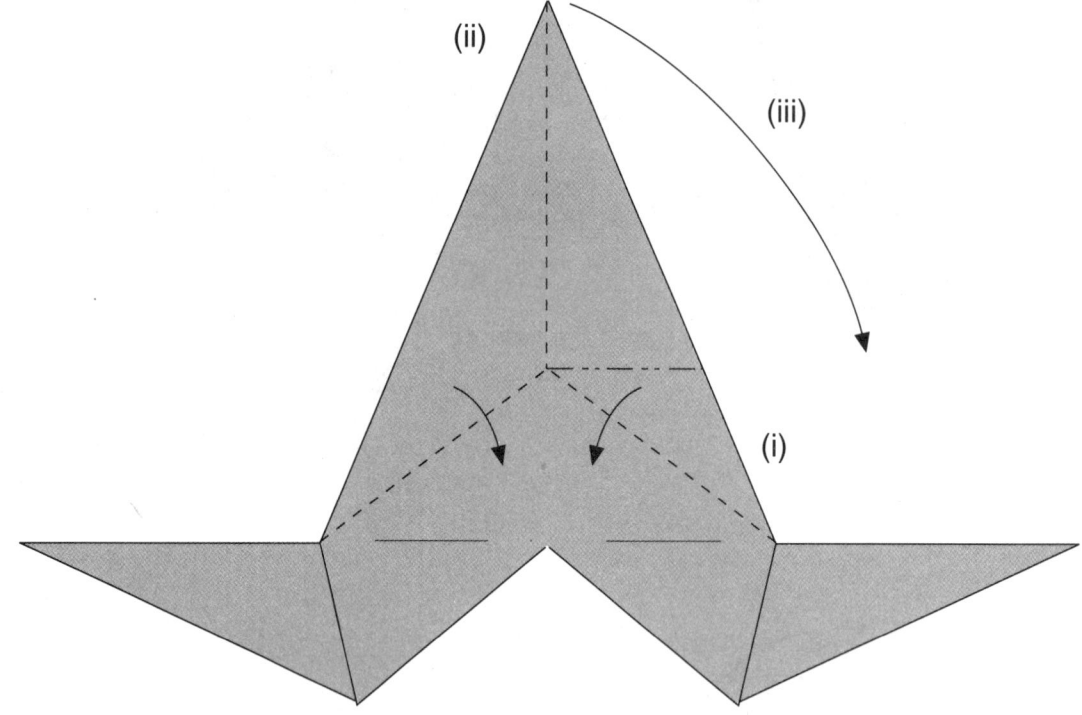

This fold is carried out on any triangular shaped portion of the model.
  (i) Make the right and left creases by doing valley folds and then unfolding them.
  (ii) Make the vertical line crease by folding the top portion of the model in half. Unfold it.
  (iii) Using the pre-folded creases to guide you, fold the left and right edges towards the middle. This will cause the top point of the model to lift vertically. Bring the top point down to the left or right side.

2

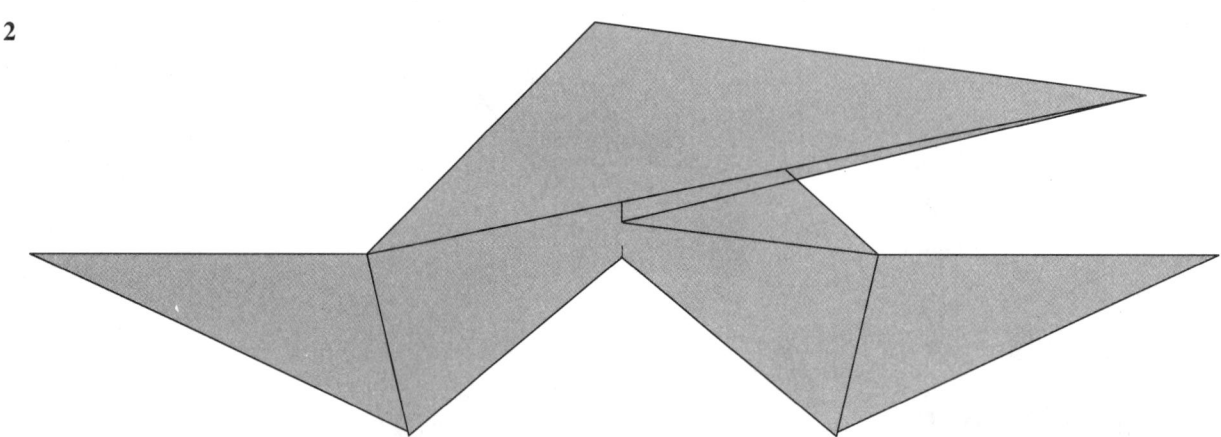

Sink fold (1)

In this fold, a portion of the model is "squashed" inwards.

1

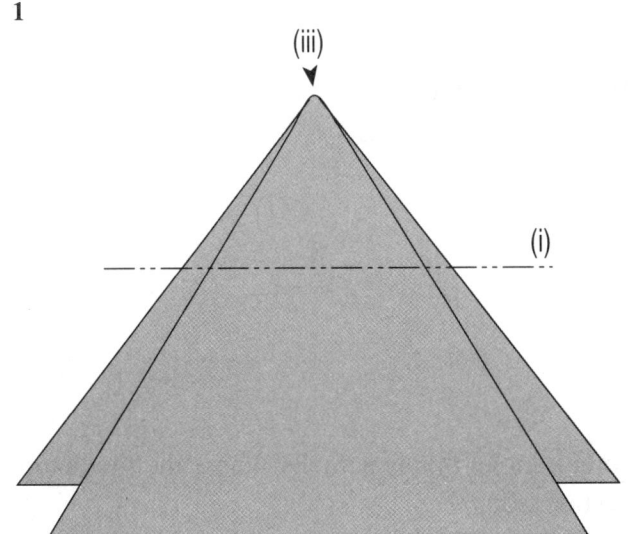

(i) Fold the paper forward and then backwards along the crease line. Crease as hard as you can. Unfold it.
(ii) You may have to open the model slightly apart.
(iii) Press from the top and depress the top portion inside the rest of the model.

2

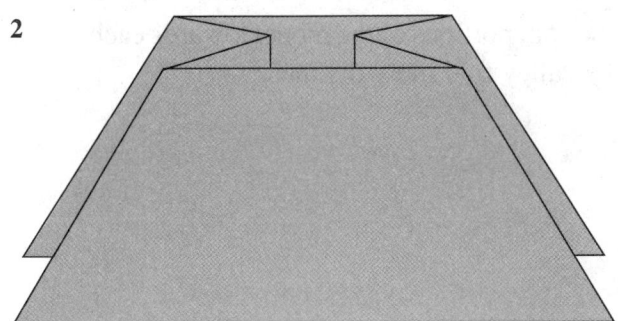

Sink fold (2)

In this fold, part of the model is dented in to give it a three-dimensional effect.

1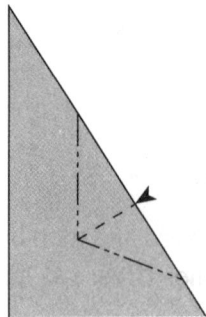

Mountain fold creases shown to be dented in.

2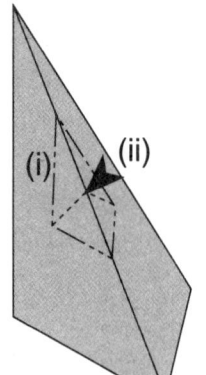

Viewed from another angle, this is actually where the mountain fold creases are to be made.
  (i) Make the mountain fold creases by pinching the paper a bit at a time along where the creases should lie.
  (ii) "Dent" in the paper at where the valley fold crease should be.

3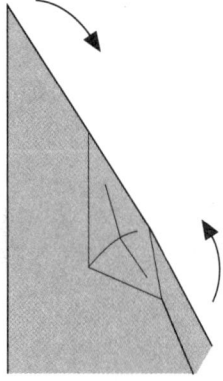

Bend the top and bottom portions of the model towards each other. This will make the valley fold more distinct.

4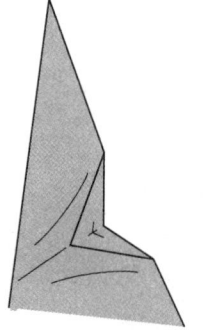

Shape your model, ensuring that the dent is confined only to the area within the mountain fold creases.

Squash Fold

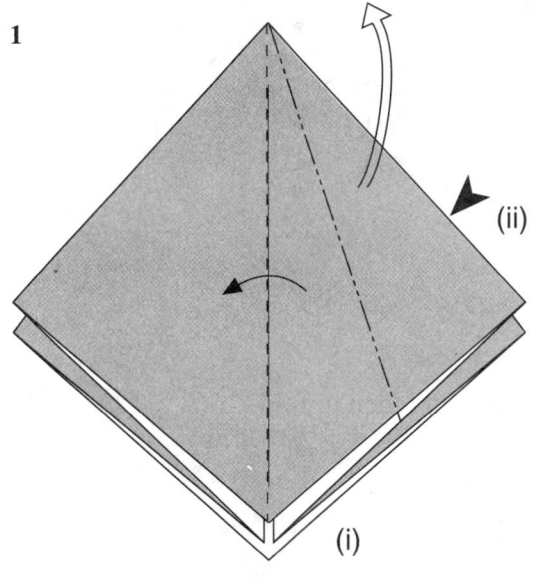
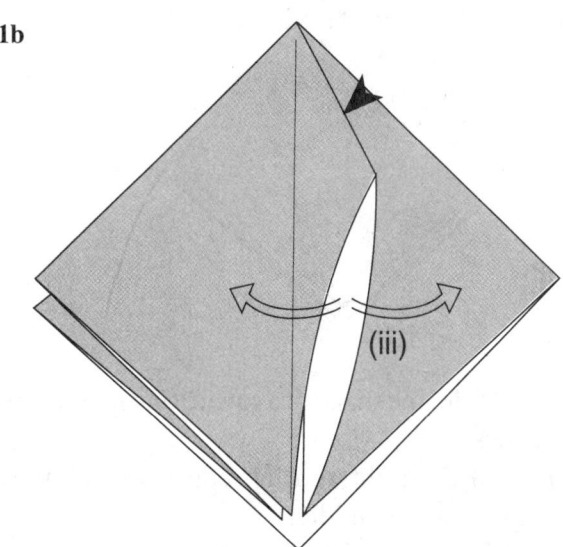

(i) Make creases along the two lines shown.
(ii) Lift up one flap vertically.

(iii) Open the vertical flap slightly apart.

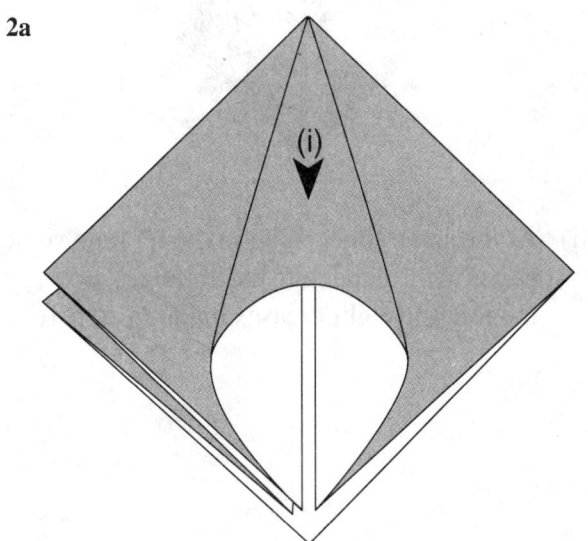
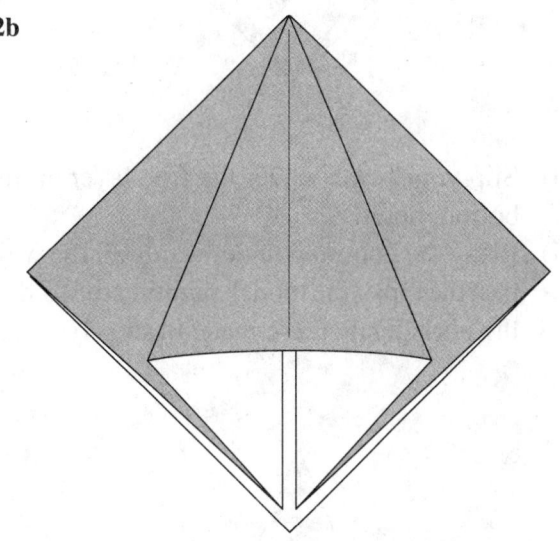

(i) Press the vertical flap downwards to the middle, squashing the vertical flap such that half of it is squashed to the left and the other half is squashed to the right.

15

Petal Fold

1

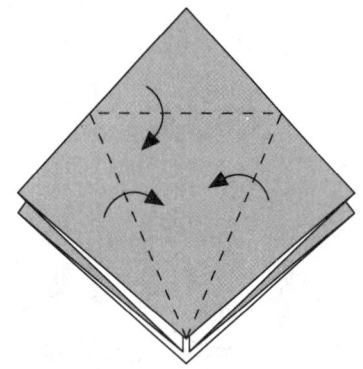

In a petal fold, the shape of a square flap is changed as follows:
  (i) Fold the right and left edges so that they meet in the middle.
  (ii) Fold the top triangle downwards to make a horizontal crease.

2

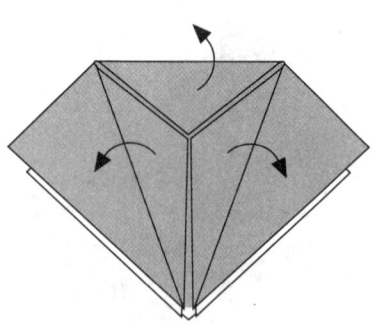

Crease well and then unfold.

3a

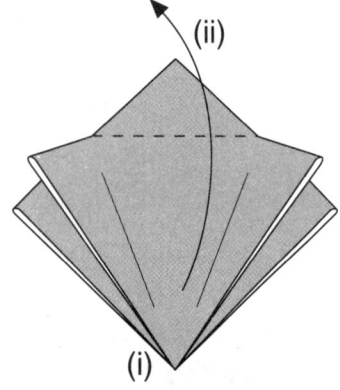

  (i) Slip your finger under the first layer at the bottom point.
  (ii) Bring the bottom point upwards all the way past the top of the model, pivoting the fold at the horizontal crease made in step 1(ii).

3b

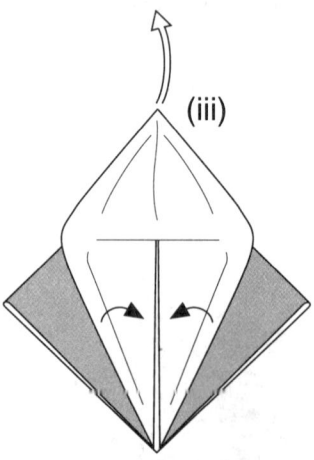

  (iii) At the same time, bring in the left and right edges of the paper into the middle, following the left and right creases made in step 1(i).

4

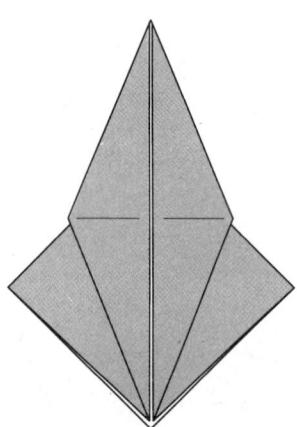

The completed petal fold

Preliminary Base

1

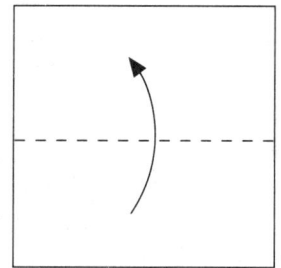

Valley fold the square piece of paper in half, bringing the bottom half to the top half.

2

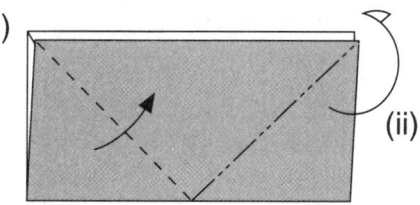

(i) Fold the bottom left corner forward to meet with the centre top of the model.
(ii) Fold the bottom right corner backwards to meet with the centre top of the model. One fold should be on one side of the model and the other fold on the other side.

3

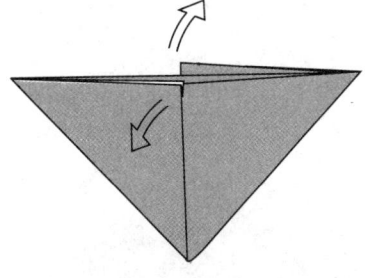

Open up the model, as shown in step 4, by pulling the centre layers apart.

4

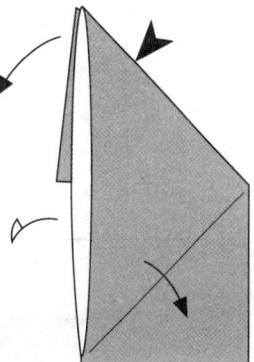

Squash the paper vertically down from the top, making sure that half is squashed to the left and the other half to the right.

5

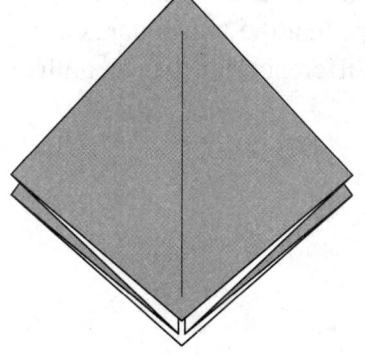

The completed preliminary base

Offset Preliminary Base

1

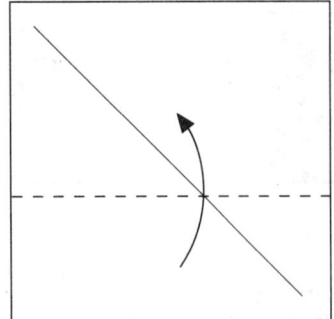

Valley fold the bottom half of the paper upwards. The bottom edge does not meet with the top edge. Instead there is a gap called the "offset". Whenever the "offset" is referred to, the length of this gap is meant.

2

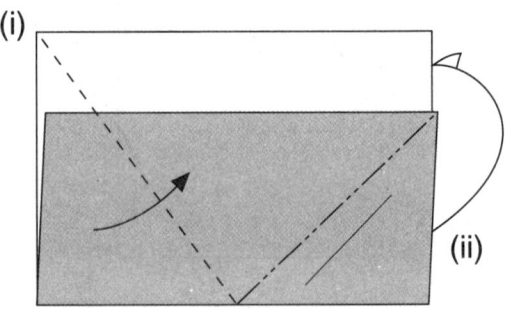

(i) Fold the left side towards the front.
(ii) Fold the right side towards the back.

3

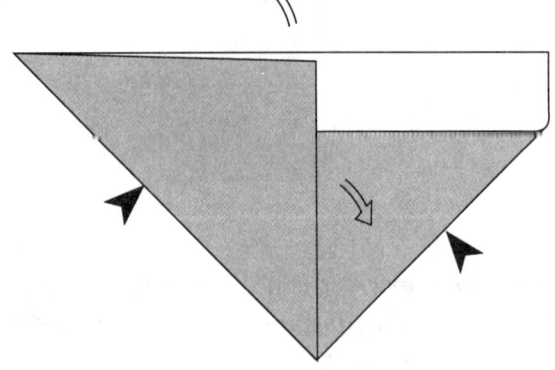

Sqread the centre apart and squash fold.

4

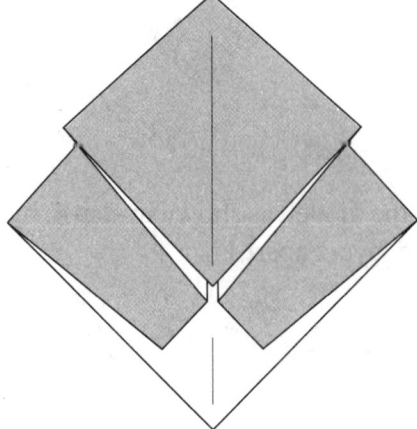

The completed base looks like the preliminary base except that the two squares are of different sizes, the difference due to the length of the offset.

Bird Base

1

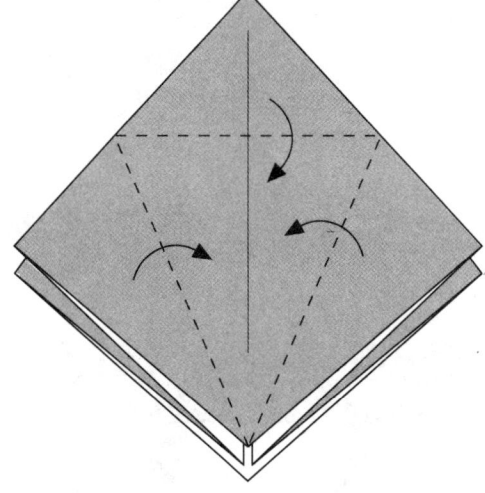

Fold a preliminary base.
Do a petal fold to get to the diagram shown in step 2.

2

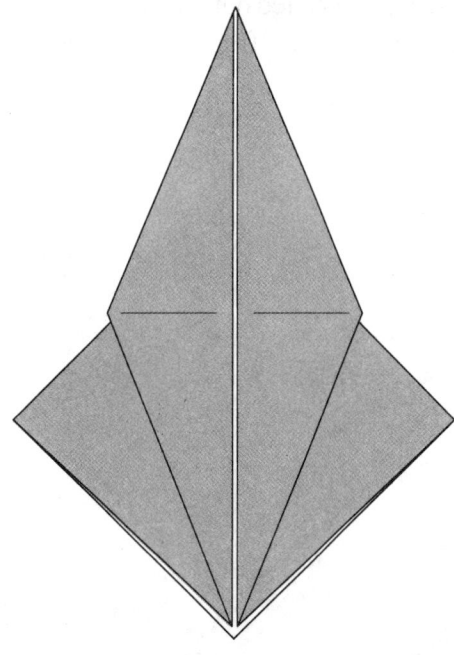

Turn the model over and do a petal fold as well.

3

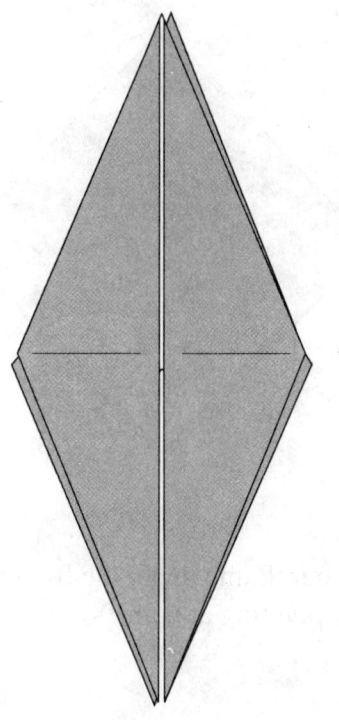

The completed bird base

Frog Fold

This fold can be carried out on any square surface flaps similar to the flaps found on a preliminary base. The steps show how a frog fold is done from a preliminary base.

1

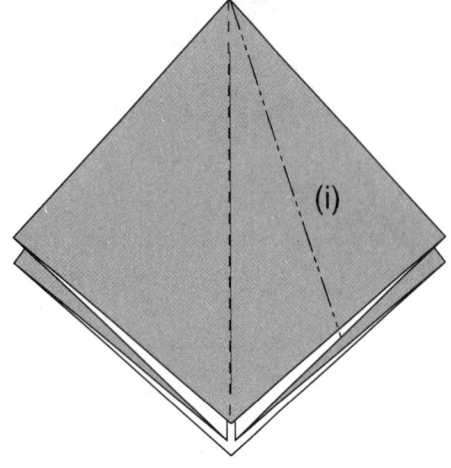

(i) Lift up the right flap and do a squash fold.

2

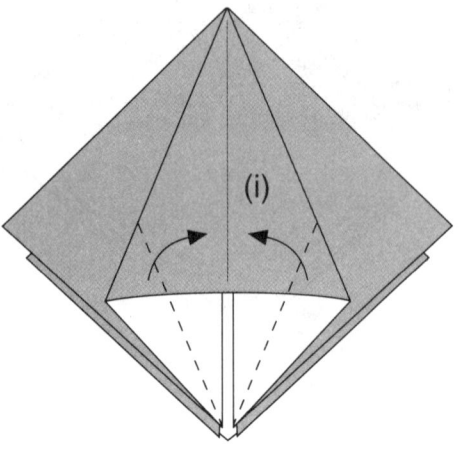

(i) Fold the right and left edges to meet in the middle.

3

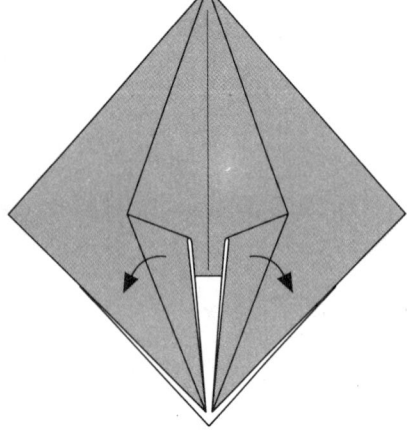

Unfold the folds made in step 2.

4a

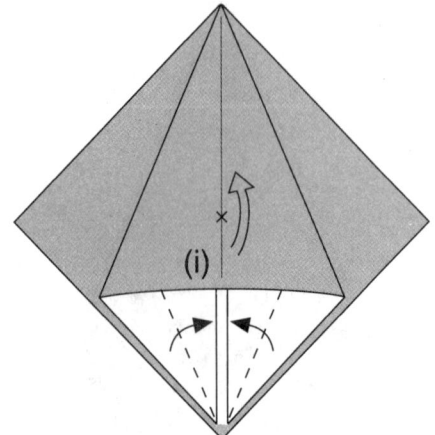

(i) Put your thumb under the front flap and lift it up, pivoting at point X.

20

4b

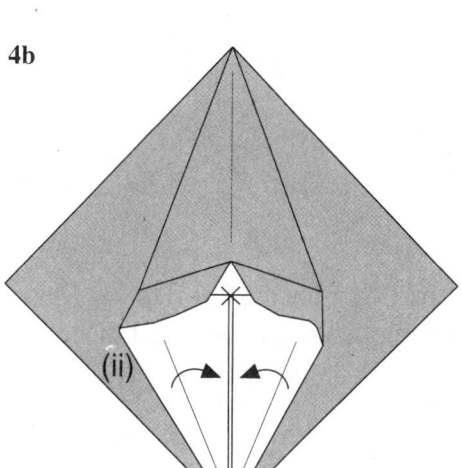

(ii) Fold the left and right edges inwards to meet each other as in step 5.

5

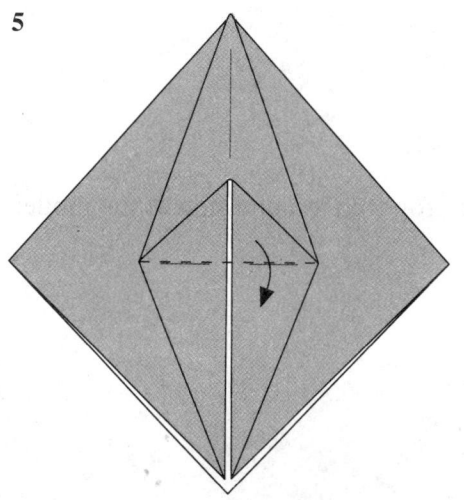

Fold the triangular flap downwards.

6

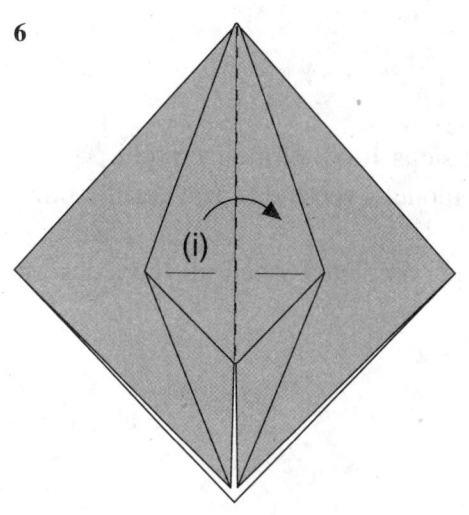

(i) Fold the left triangular portion over to the right-hand side.

7

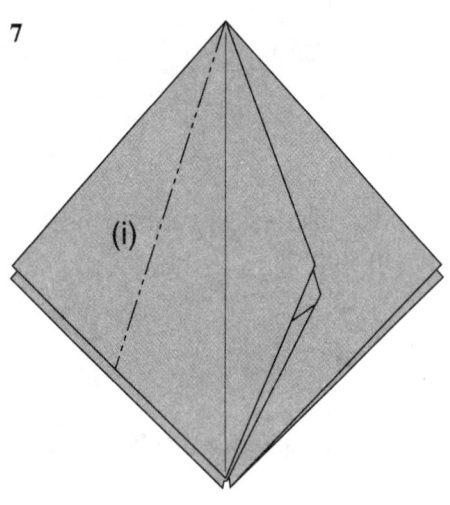

(i) Repeat steps 1 to 5 for the left flap.
(iii) Arrange the model to look like that in step 8.

8

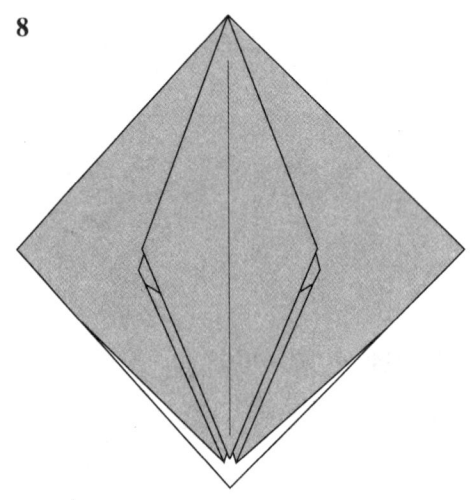

The completed frog fold on one side of the model

Frog Base

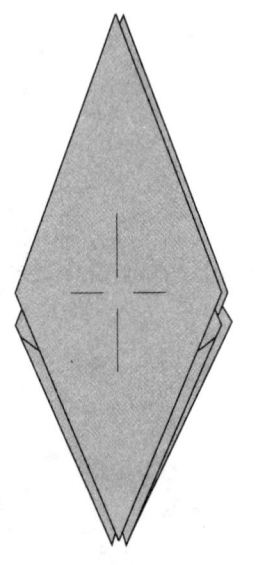

Do a preliminary base.
(i) Carry out steps 1 to 8 of the frog fold.
(ii) Turn the model over and repeat for the other side.

The frog base is completed when all the sides are folded.

Box Fold

This fold gives a frog fold a different shape.

1

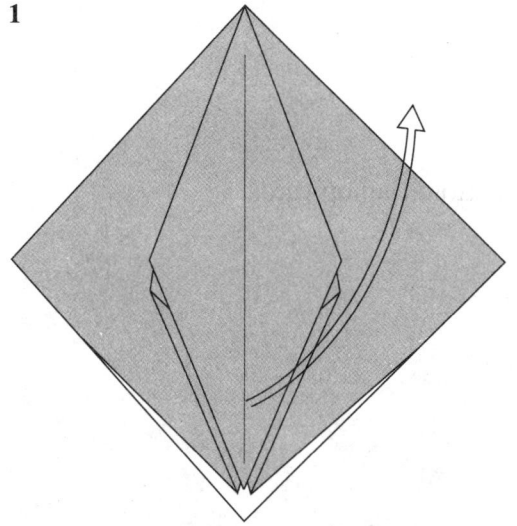

Starting from a frog fold, lift the bottom flap upwards.

2

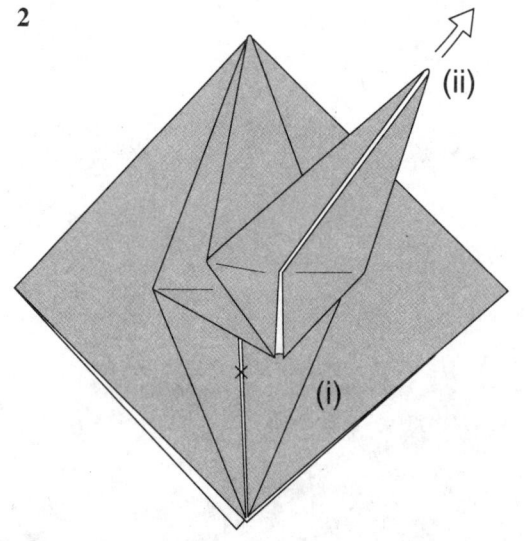

(i) Place one finger at point X.
(ii) Pull the flap as far up as you can go. The flap will straighten to give a box-like appearance in the centre.

3

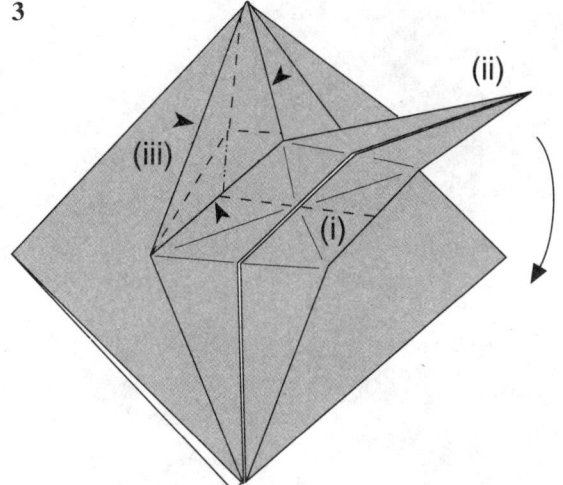

(i) Crease the two side edges of the box well.
(ii) Pull the lifted flap downwards.
(iii) Press the three points together on the right and left-hand sides. The box will be folded in half.

23

4

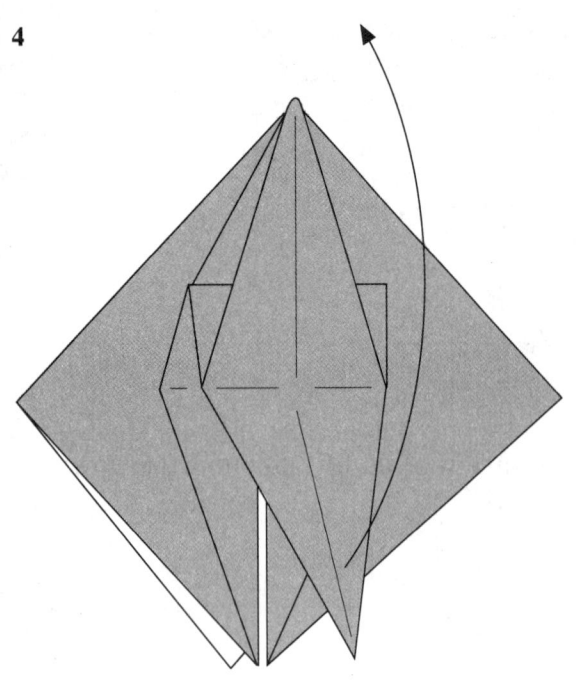

Fold the bottom flap upwards.

5

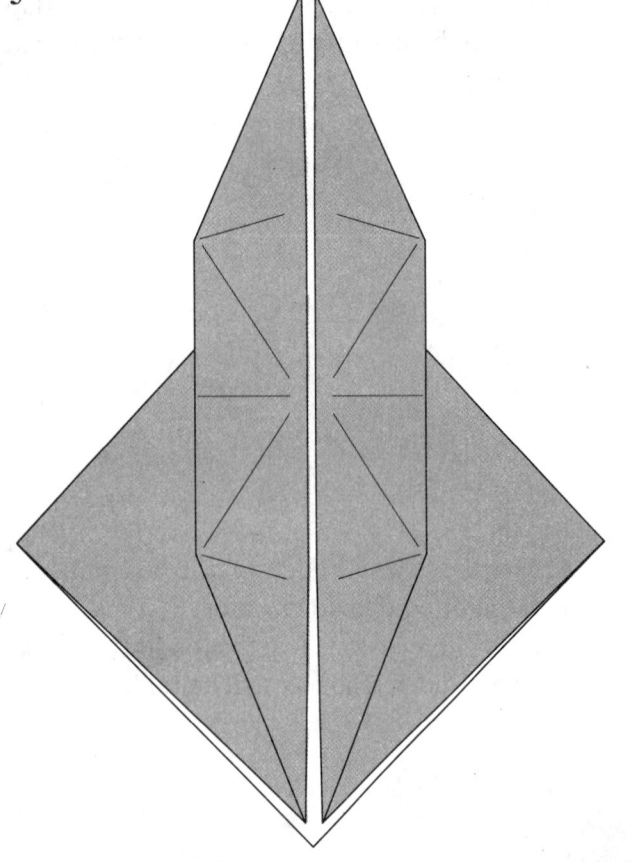

The completed box fold

24

Tail Base

This is the most used base in this book. I strongly encourage you to practise making this base. Nearly all the bodies of the dinosaur models in this book are made from the tail base.

Note: When making this base, your model steps may not appear exactly as shown in these diagrams. This is because the offset preliminary base that you are using can be for a larger or smaller offset than what is shown here. It is more important for you to know what is being achieved at each step rather than try to make your model look like what is shown in the diagrams.

Tail Base A

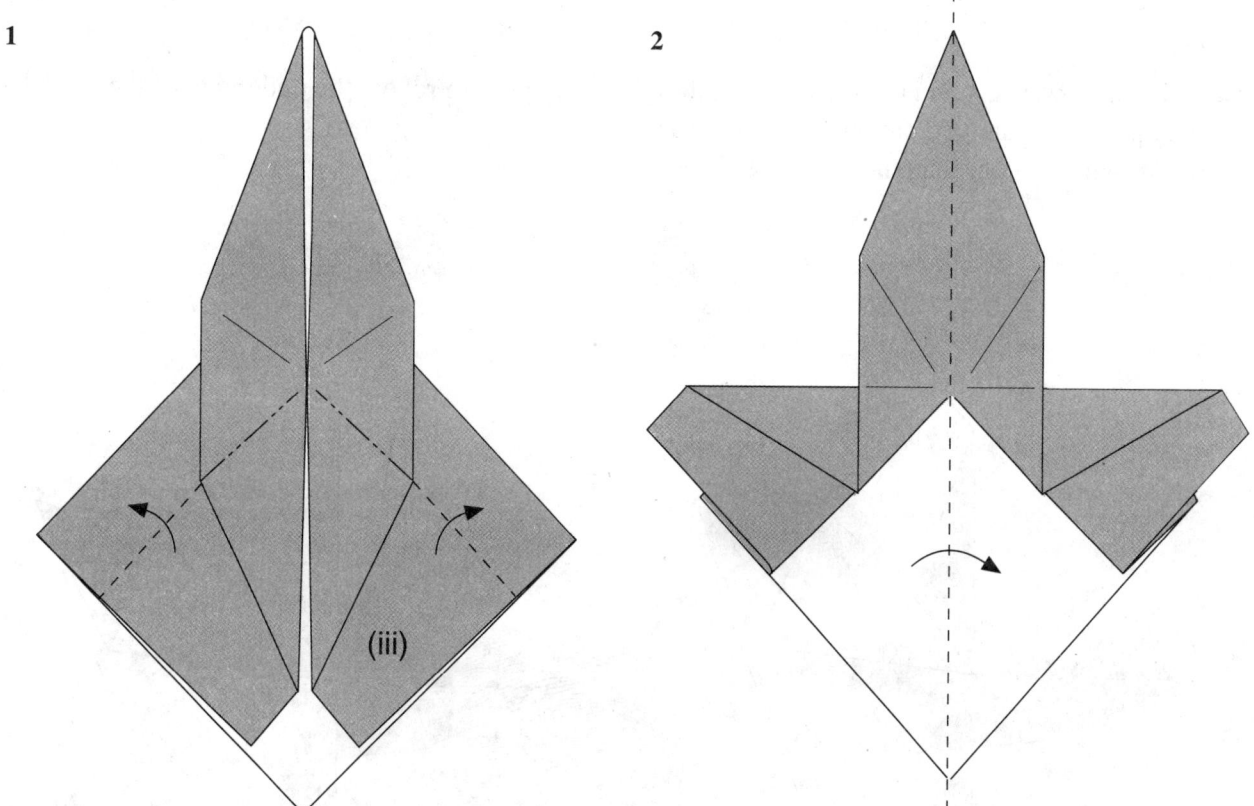

(i) Start with an offset preliminary base.
(ii) Do a frog fold, followed by a box fold to get to the model shown in this step.
(iii) Reverse fold the right and left flaps 90 degrees upwards.

Fold the model in half.

3

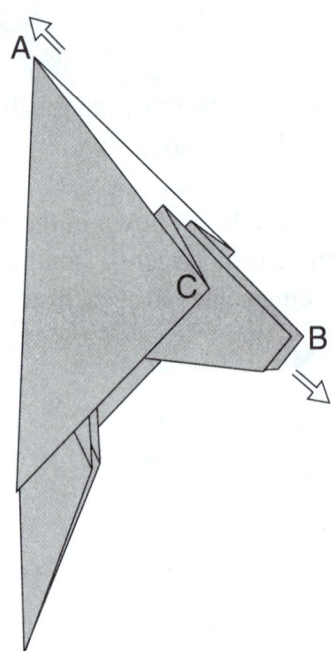

Hold down at points A and B shown and pull the model apart as far as you can go. A new crease mark (D) will be seen. Flatten the crease.

4

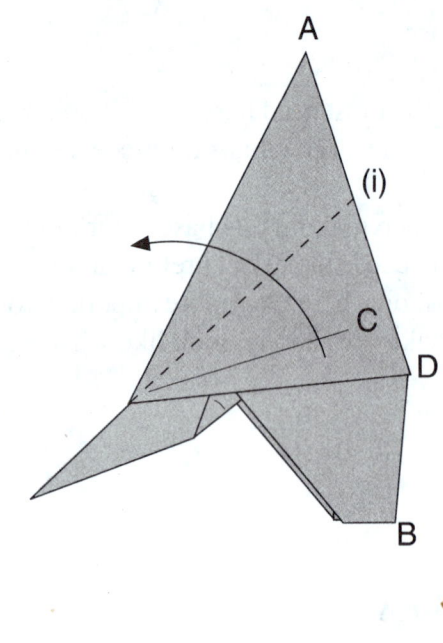

(i) Fold to reveal the underside of the model.

5

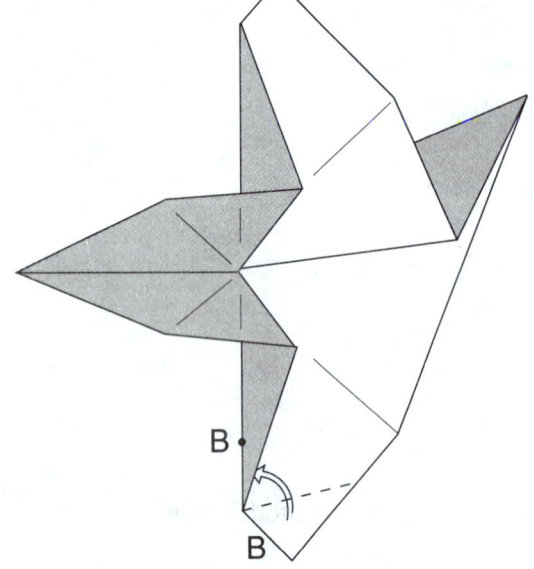

Fold and tuck in. The bottom B edge must be folded such that it lies at the new B position.

6

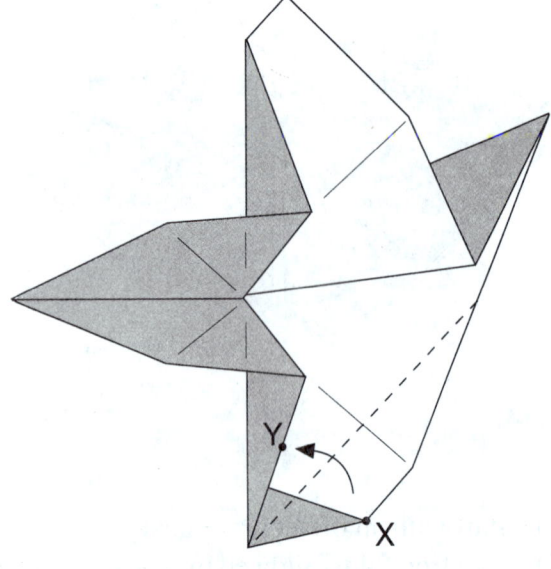

Fold X to Y.

26

7

8

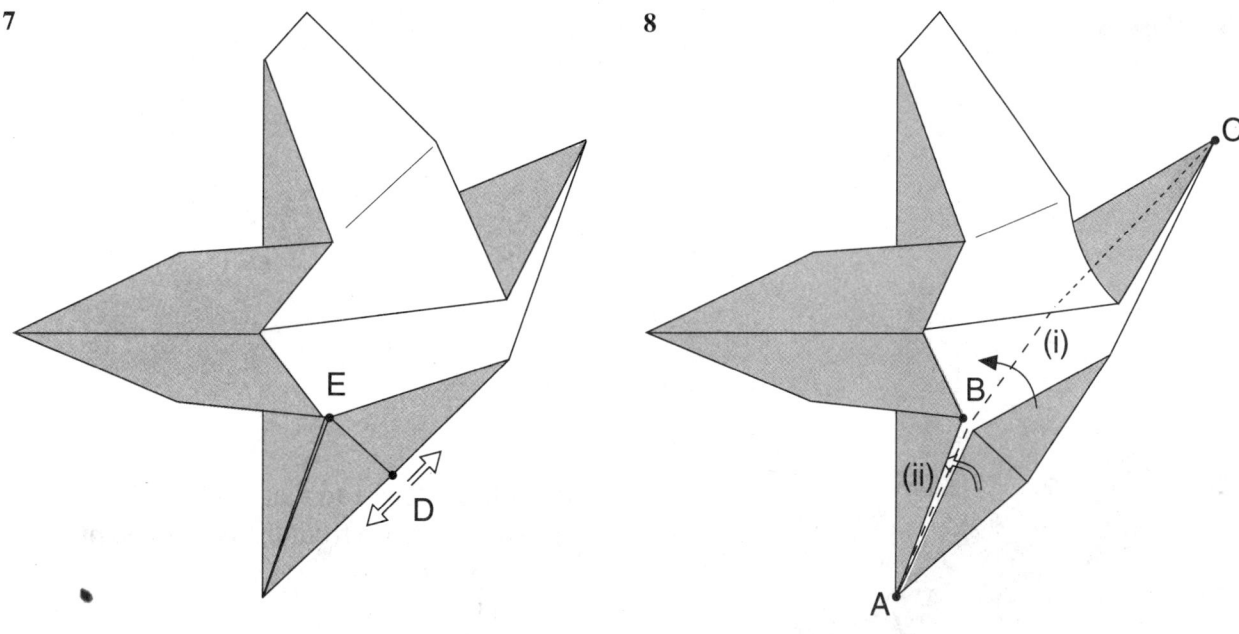

Gently pull point D apart to give the model a bent outer edge as seen in step 8. (Take care not to pull at point E.)
Note : For small offsets, this may not be apparent.

(i) Make a crease from A to B to C. Fold inwards.
(ii) Between A and B, tuck the outside flap underneath.

9

10

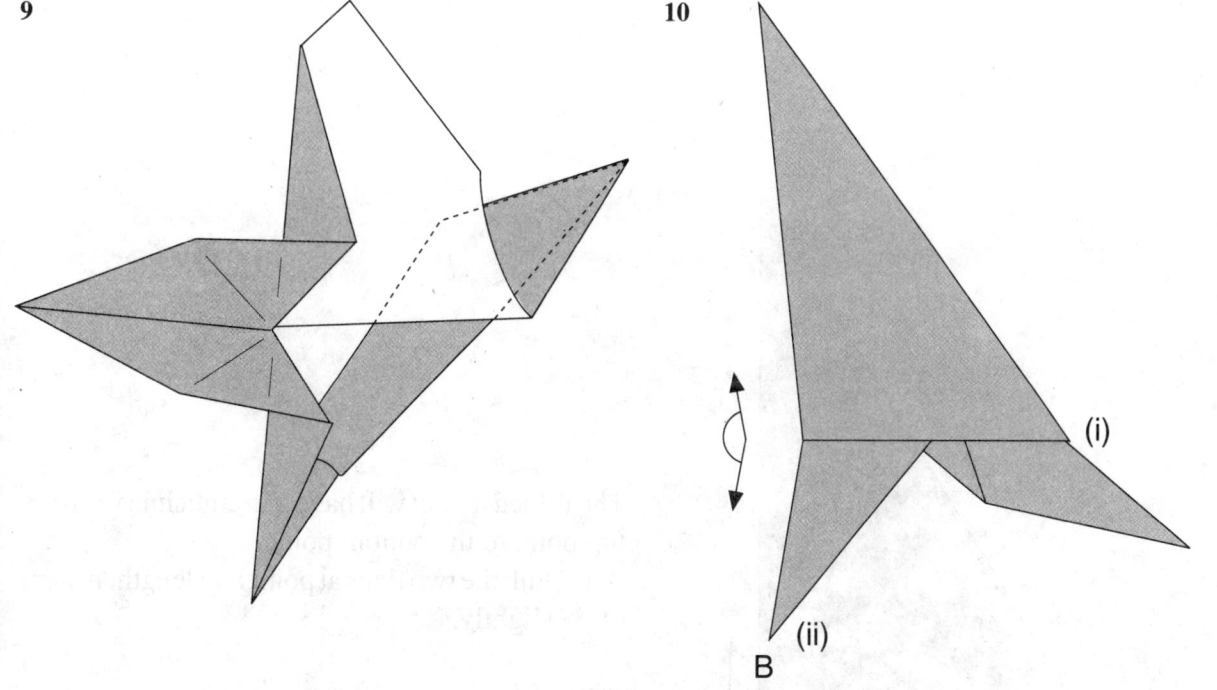

Diagram showing completed step 8. Repeat from step 5 onwards for the other side.

(i) If your model is folded correctly you should have a slight angle from the top point to the bottom point.
Note : For small offsets, this may not be apparent.
(ii) Pull the two flaps at point B to lengthen them slightly.

Tail Base B

1

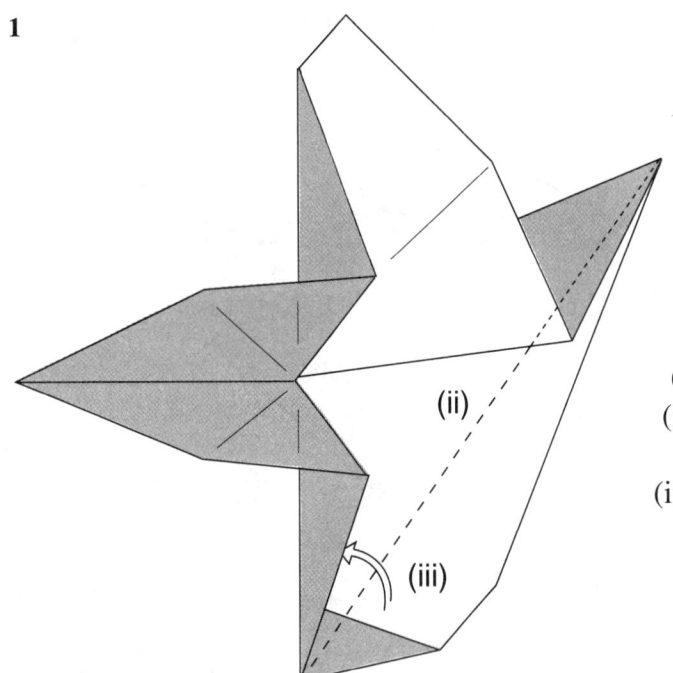

(i) Follow steps 1 to 5 of tail base A.
(ii) Mark a crease from the bottom point to the top point.
(iii) Fold and tuck in.

2

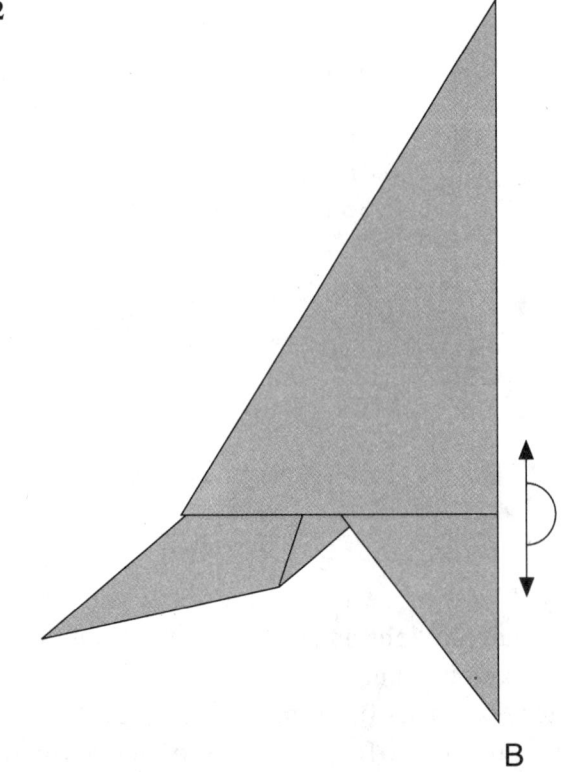

The folded model will have a straight line from the top point to the bottom point.
(i) Pull the two flaps at point B to lengthen them slightly.

Hadrosaur Base

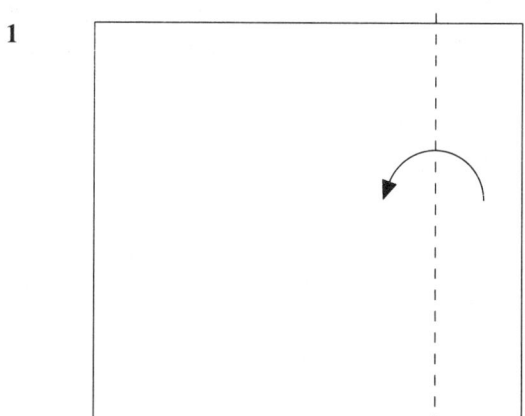

Fold the right edge of the paper inwards. The distance from the edge of the paper to where the fold is made will be called the "offset".

Fold to form a right angle triangle at the top right corner.

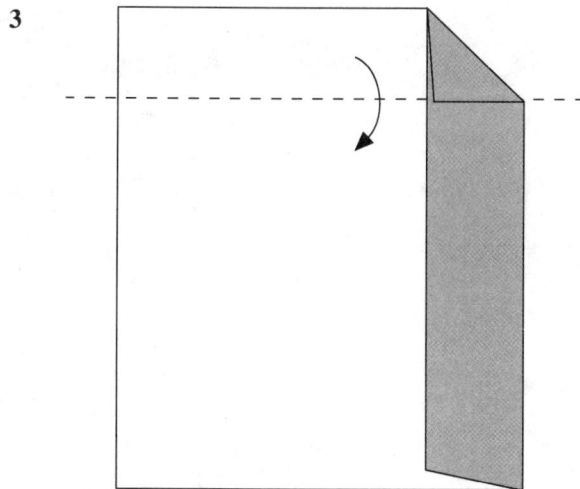

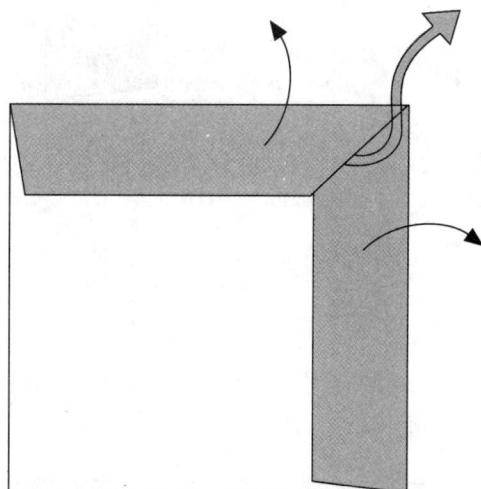

Fold the top edge downwards the same offset length as in step 1.

Lift the top right edge folds to pull out the hidden triangular flap.

5

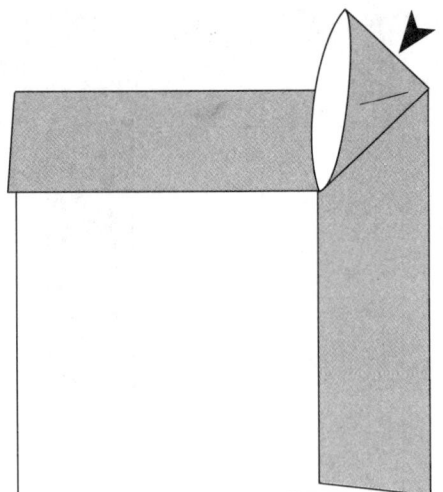

Do a squash fold.

6

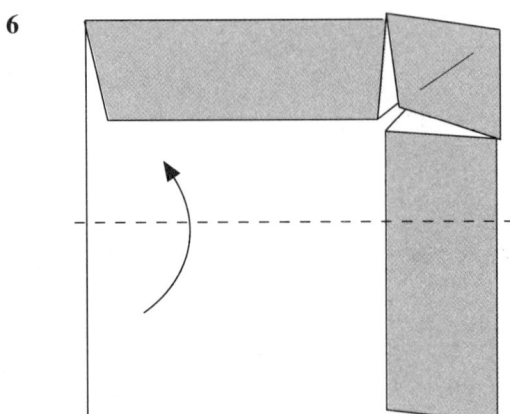

(i) Fold the bottom edge upwards.

7

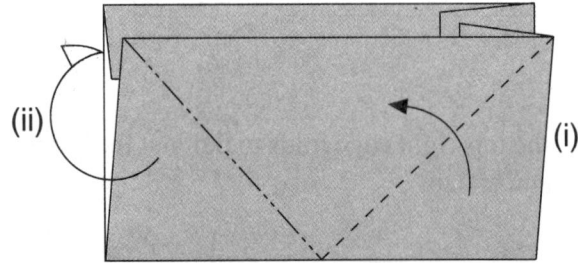

(i) Fold the bottom right corner forward towards the middle.
(ii) Fold the bottom left corner backwards towards the middle.

One fold should be on one side of the model and the other fold on the other side.

8

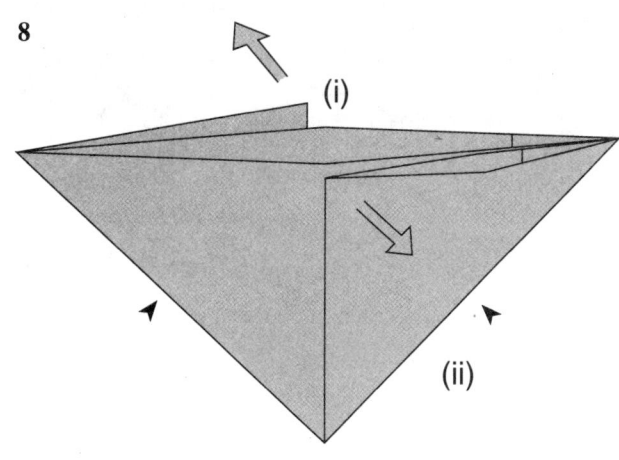

(i) Open up the model as shown by pulling the centre layers apart.
(ii) Press the left and right bottom edges to bring them together.

9

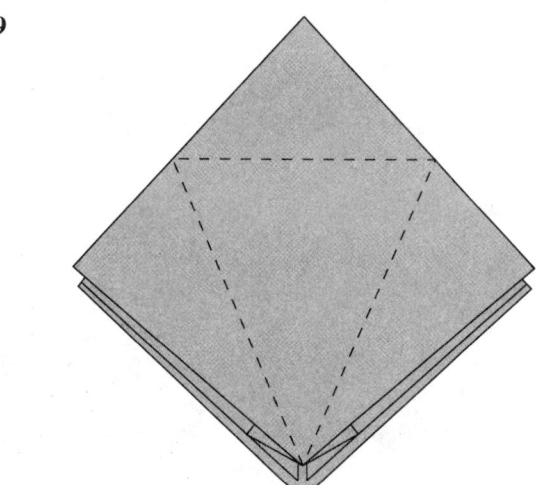

(i) Petal fold on both sides to get to the bird base.

10

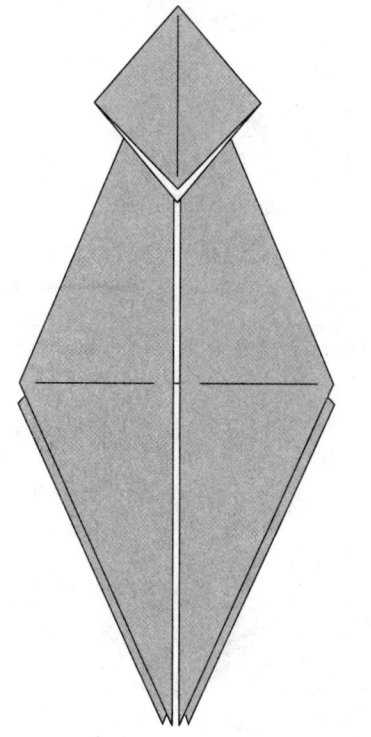

The completed hadrosaur base

Dinosaur Models

Tyrannosaurus

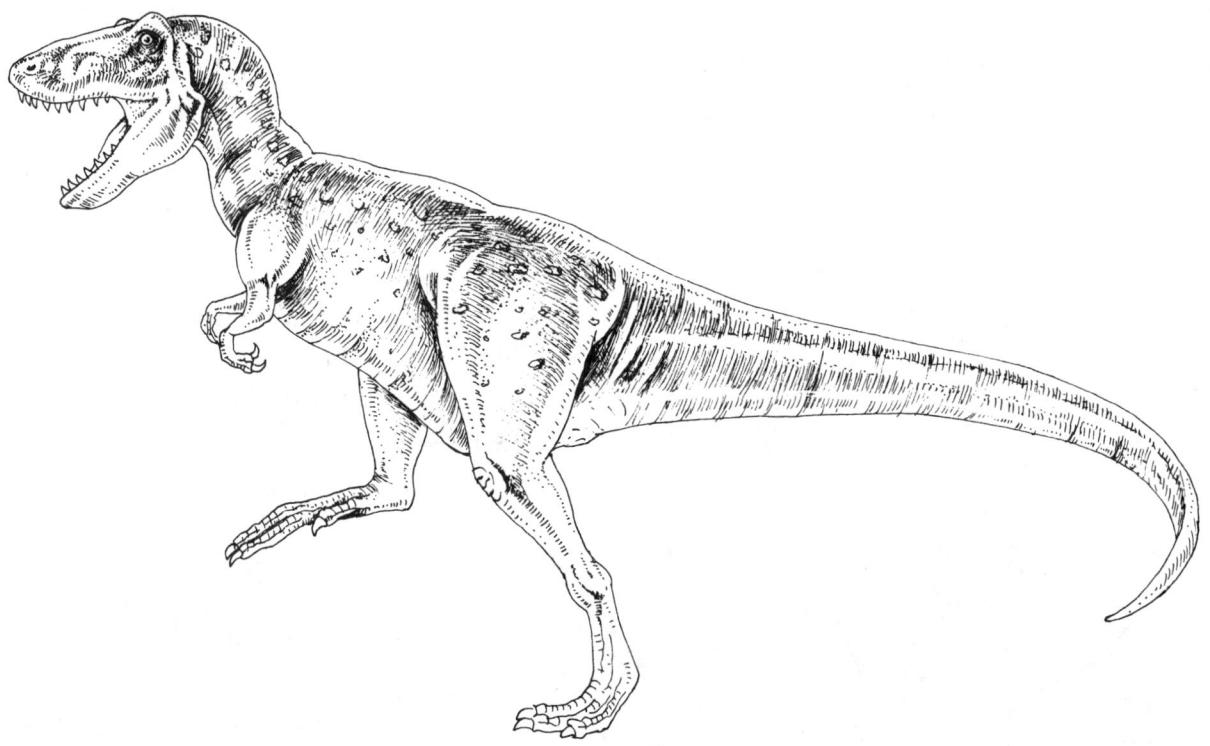

Tyrannosaurus is the largest (45 ft/13 m long) and most ferocious of all dinosaurs. It is as tall as a giraffe. This dinosaur has a massive head and powerful jaws lined with stake-like teeth about 7 in (17 cm) long! At the lower jaw there is an extra joint which allows it to open its mouth very wide to handle the very large prey. *Tyrannosaurus* is powerfully built, has a strong back, powerful legs and a strong tail. However, it has ridiculously short forelimbs that have two claws each.

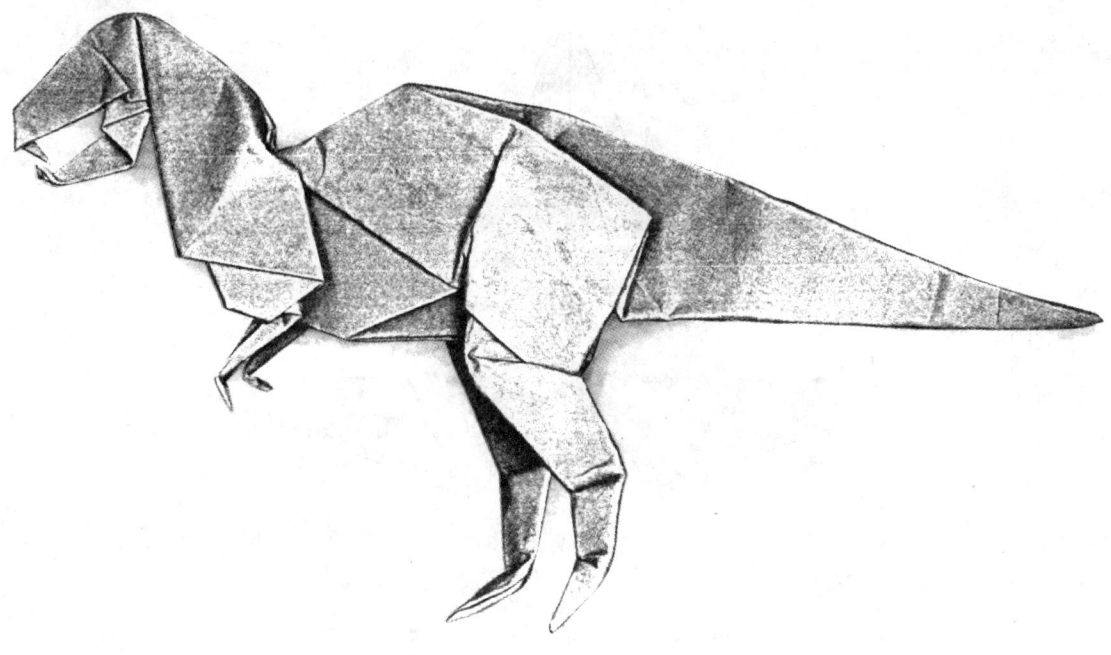

The *Tyrannosaurus* head

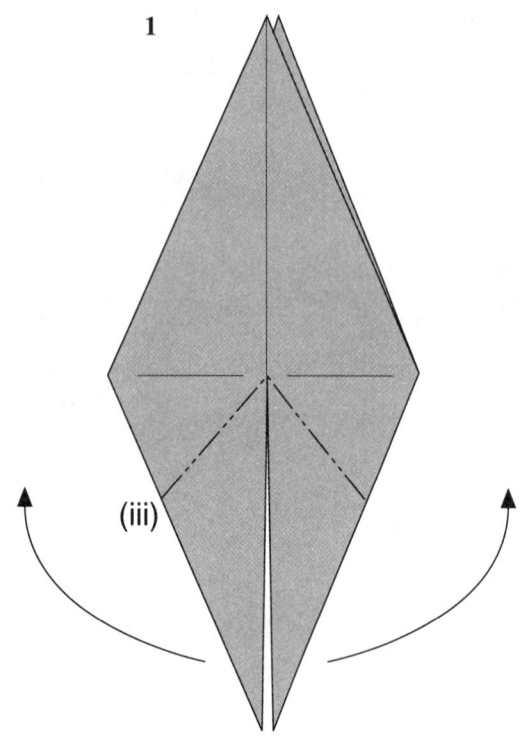

(i) Use a piece of 15 cm square paper.
(ii) Start from the bird base.
(iii) Reverse fold the two flaps upwards to form the forelimbs.

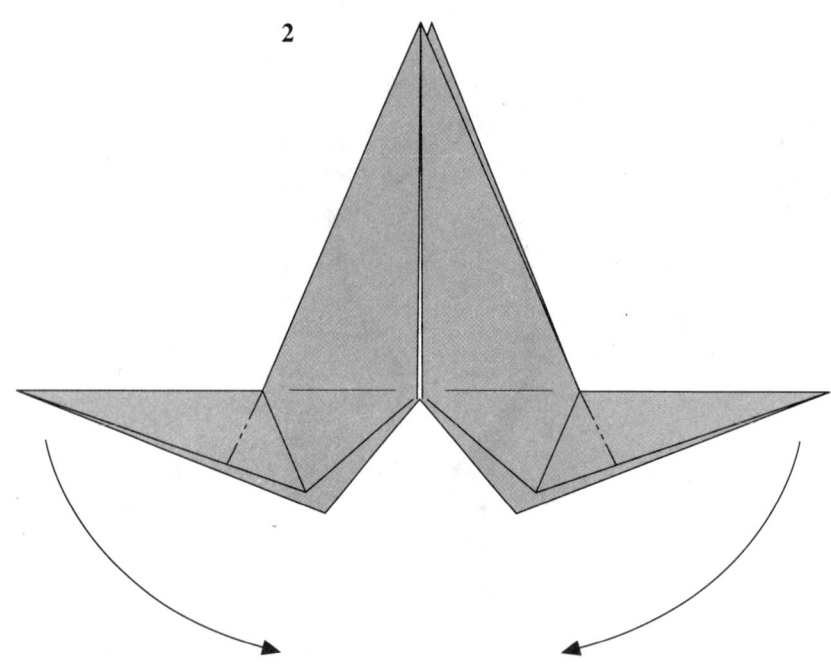

Reverse fold downwards.

3

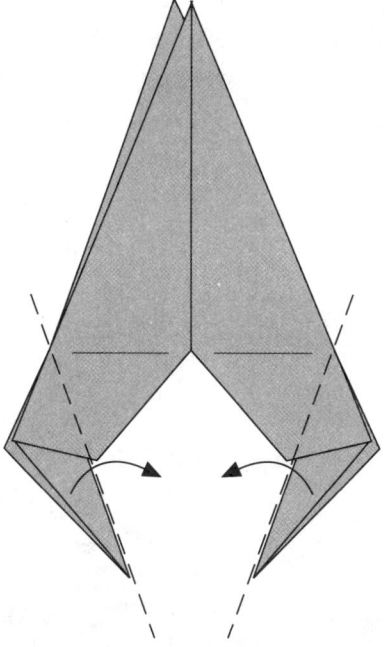

Open up the two flaps.

4

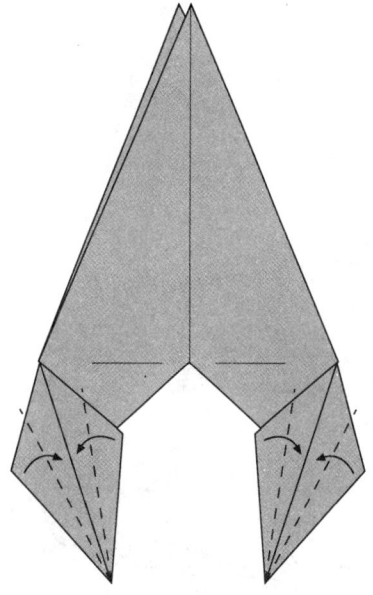

Fold inwards to make the forelimbs thinner.

5

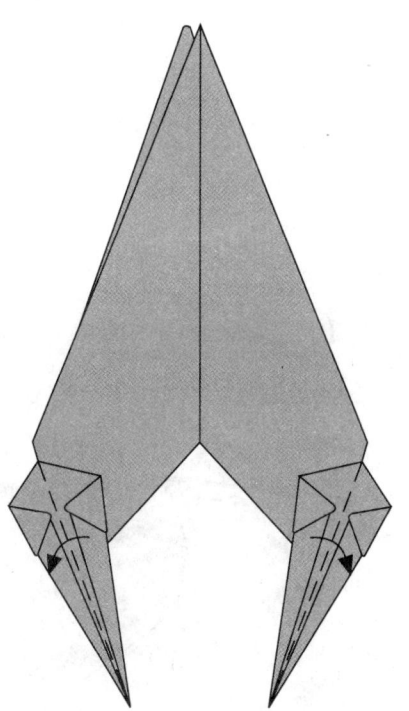

Fold over.

6a

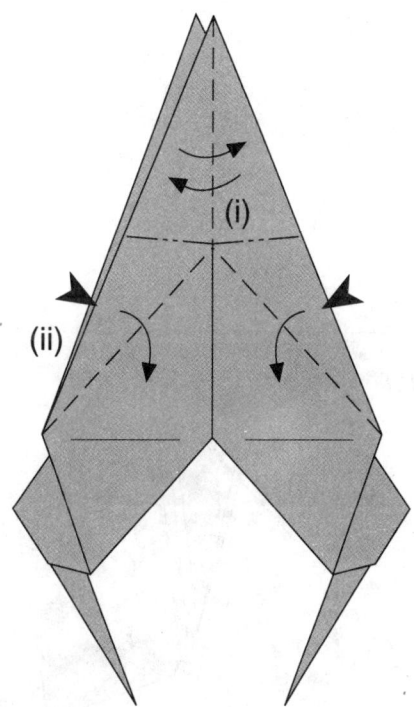

(i) Look between the front and back flaps of the top portion. You will see a triangular section. The tip of the triangular section is where you want your creases to meet.

(ii) Valley fold to the right and left to make the left and right creases. The creases should meet at the position in (i).

(iii) Fold (both layers) the right and left edges inwards along the creases made in (ii). The upper portion will lift as in 6b.

6b

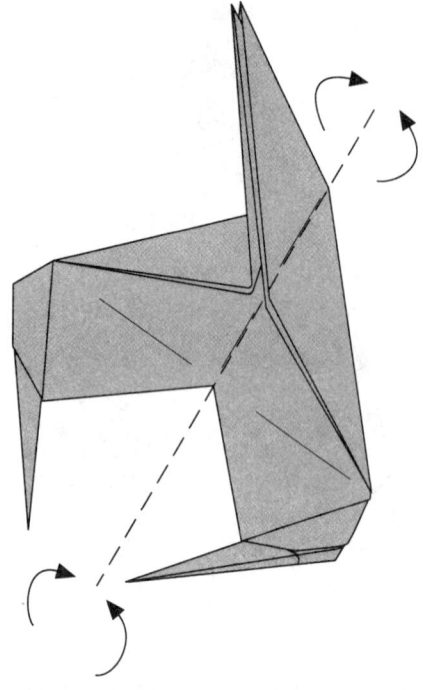

Fold the model in half.

7

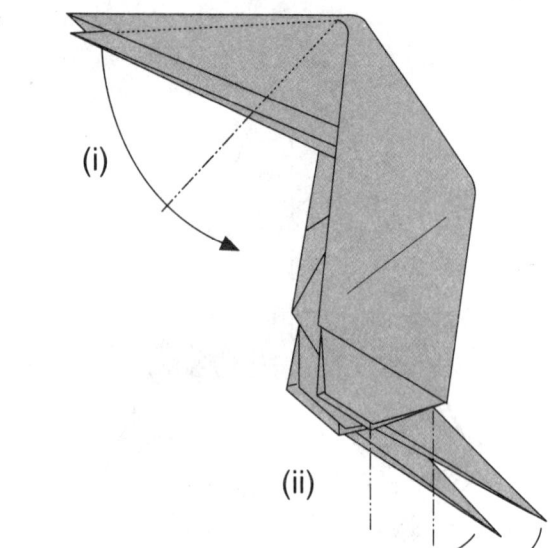

(i) Reverse fold the lower jaw downwards.
(ii) Reverse fold the forelimbs forward.

8

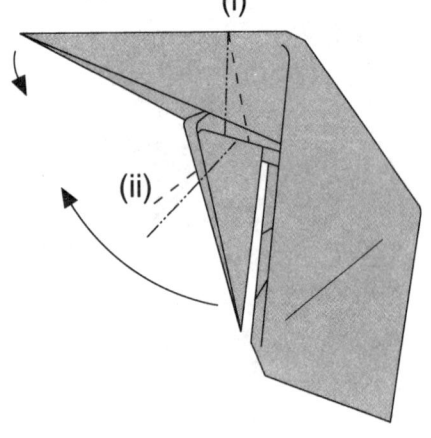

(i) Crimp fold the upper jaw to form the cheeks.
(ii) Reverse fold the lower jaw upwards.
(iii) Adjust the lower jaw position by pulling it downwards slightly.

9

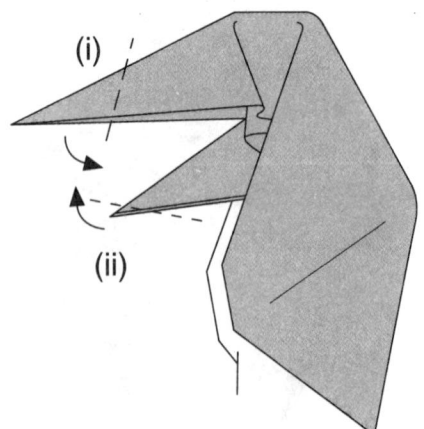

(i) Reverse fold the upper jaw downwards to form the upper teeth.
(ii) Reverse fold the tip of the lower jaw upwards to form the lower teeth.

10

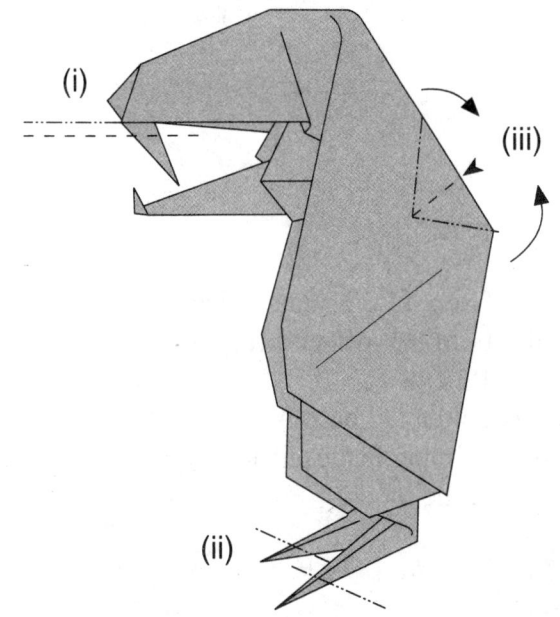

(i) Shorten the upper teeth by folding it upwards and then downwards.
(ii) Fold the wrists downwards to form the hands.
(iii) Sink fold the area at the back of the head. This forms the neck and shoulders.

11

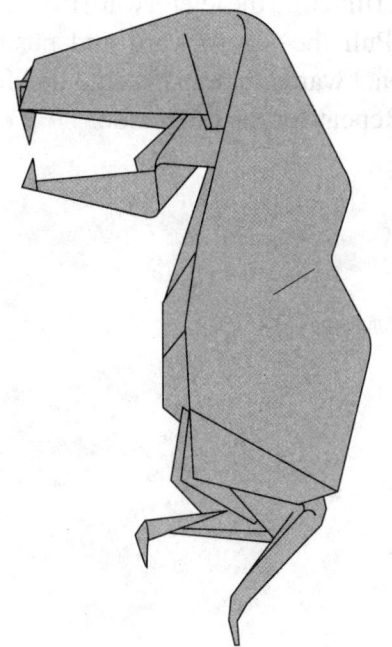

The completed *Tyrannosaurus* head

The *Tyrannosaurus* body and tail

12

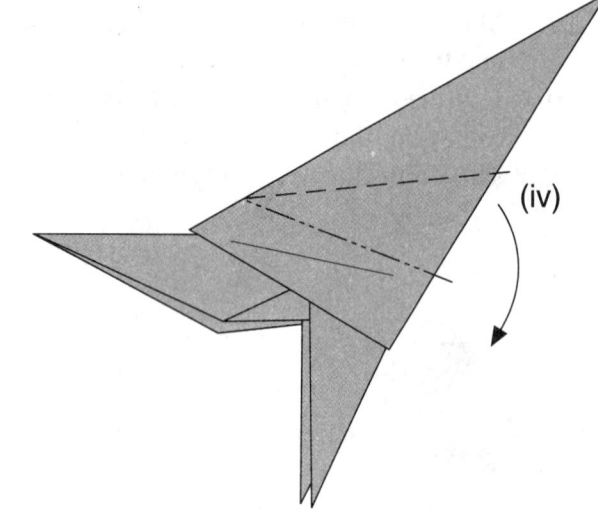

(i) Use a 21 cm square piece of paper.
(ii) Fold an offset preliminary base, offset 1.5 cm.
(iii) Fold a tail base A.
(iv) Crimp fold the tail downwards on both sides of the model.

13

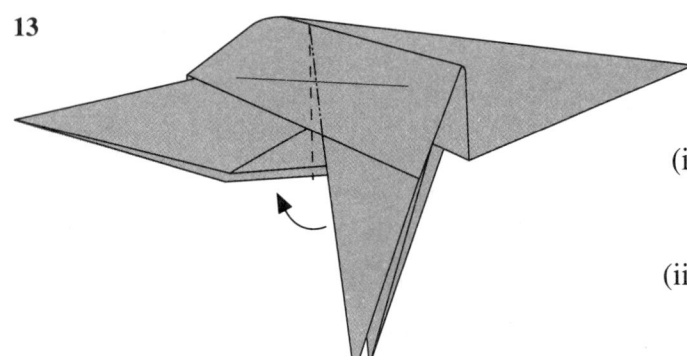

(i) Crimp fold the leg forward to form the thigh. (Pull the leg forward and push the body backwards to help execute this fold.)
(ii) Repeat for the other side.

14

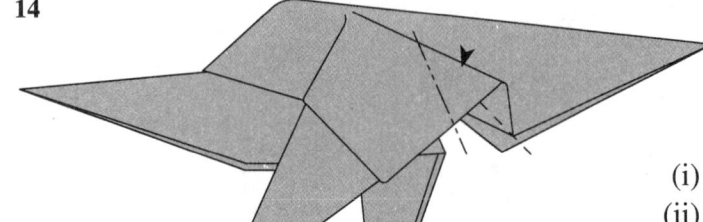

(i) Reverse fold the back of the thigh inwards.
(ii) Repeat for the other side.

15

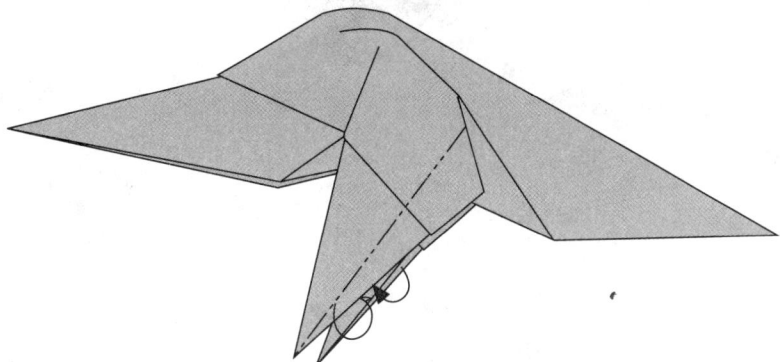

(i) Fold the legs inwards to make them proportionately thinner.
(ii) Fold the inside flap of each leg also.
(iii) Repeat for the other side.

16a

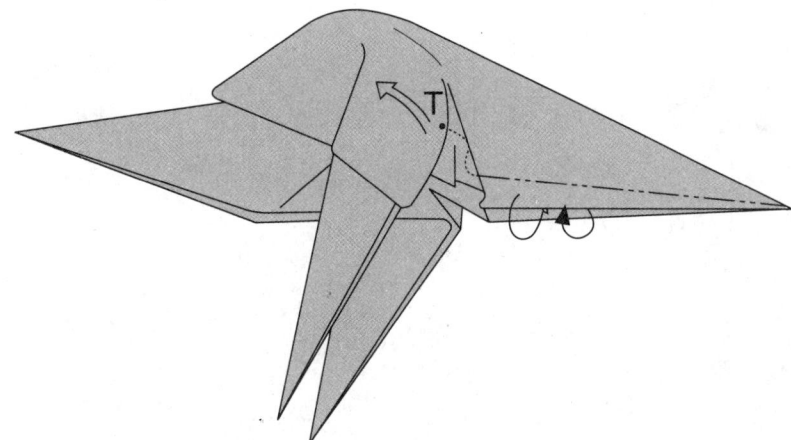

(i) Fold the tail inwards to make it proportionately thinner. (This is a tricky step. You have to lift the back of the thigh and make the mountain fold up to the point T. See also *Compsognathus* steps 24 to 26.)
(ii) Repeat for the other side.

16b

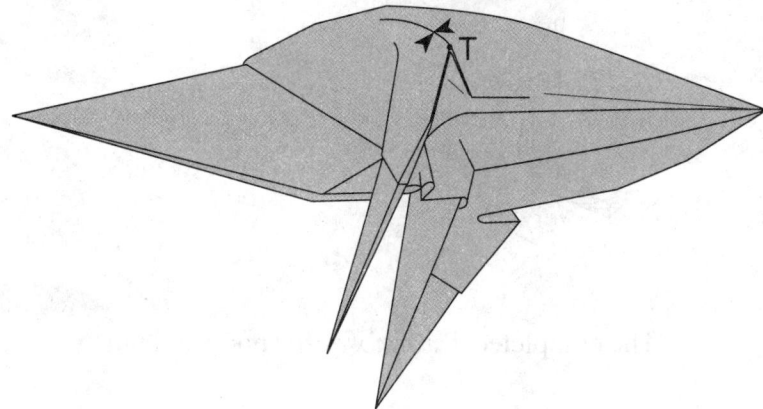

(i) Pinch the T-junction and then press the thigh against the tail to flatten it. Pull the tail downwards to help execute this fold.
(ii) Repeat for the other side.

17

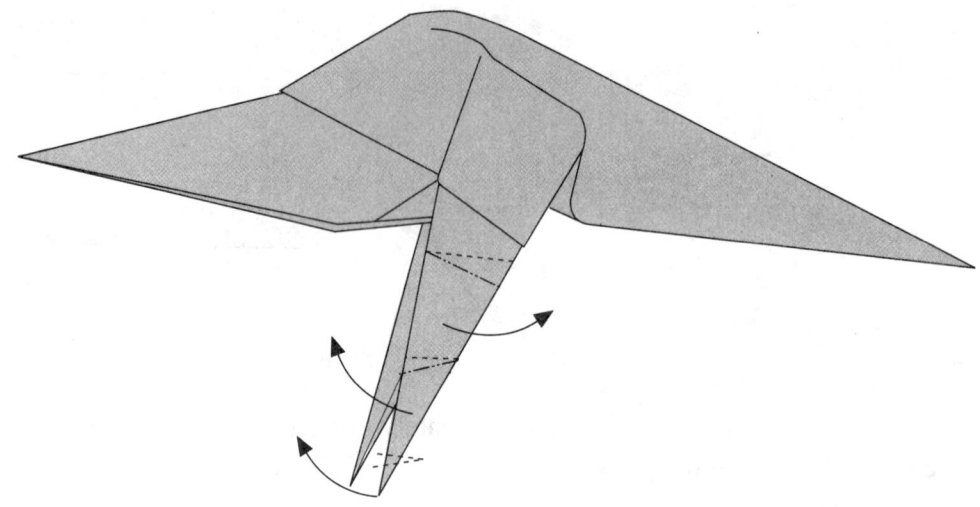

Crimp fold both legs to form the knees, ankles and feet.

18

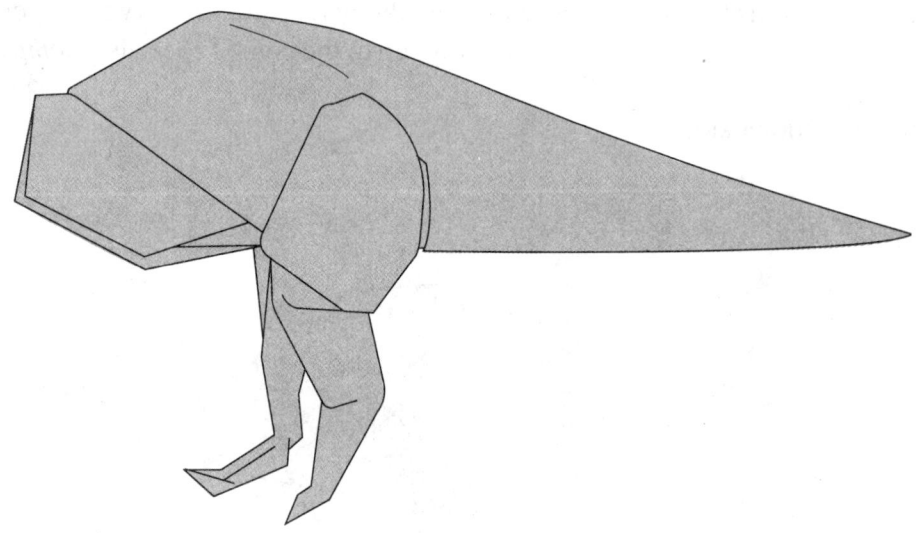

The completed *Tyrannosaurus* body and tail.

19

The completed *Tyrannosaurus* model

Join the head and body together, using glue. Pay careful attention to the posture it should adopt. To avoid giving it a stiff look, bend its head and tail to one side, open its jaws wider and position the legs such that its knees are facing outwards on both sides.

Compsognathus

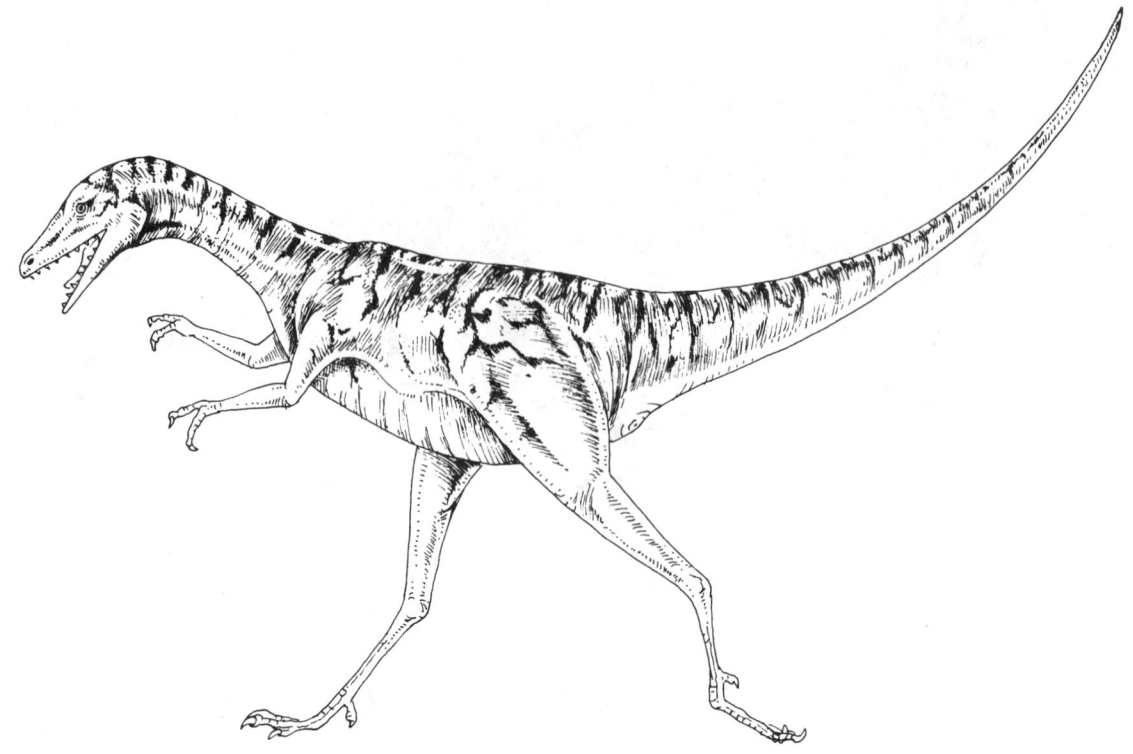

Compsognathus is one of the smallest theropods, about the size of a chicken (2 ft /60 cm long). It lived on lizards and insects and roamed about in the Jurassic period in packs. *Compsognathus* has a narrow head, long thin legs, a thin tail, and on its forelimbs, two claws like *Tyrannosaurus*.

The *Compsognathus* head

1

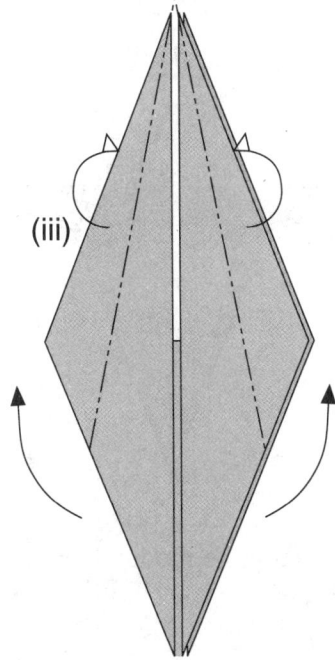

(i) Use a piece of 15 cm thin square paper.
(ii) Start by folding a bird base.
(iii) Fold the left and right edges backwards for the top flap only.

2

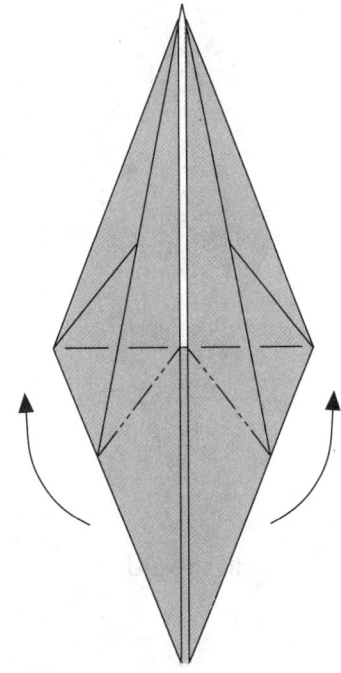

Reverse fold 90 degrees upwards to form the forelimbs.

3

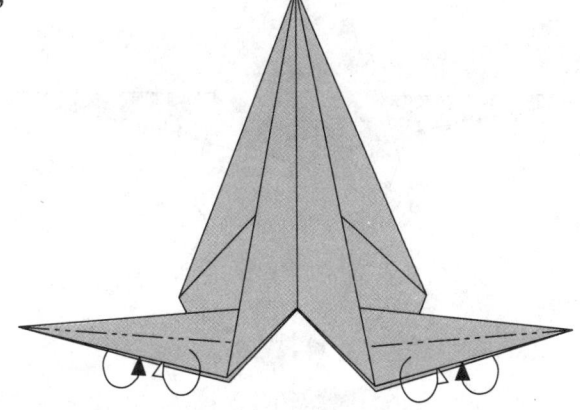

Fold inwards to make the forelimbs thinner. This fold determines the thickness of the forelimbs.

4

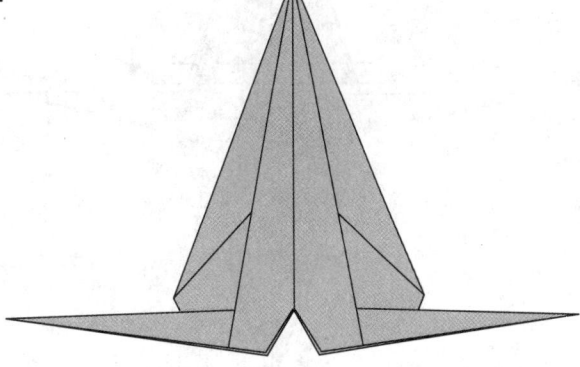

Turn the model over and fold the top flap down to get to step 5.

5

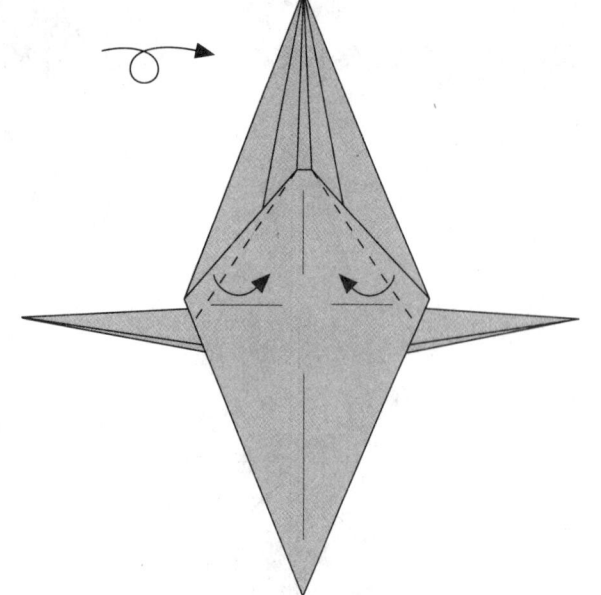

Fold inwards.

6

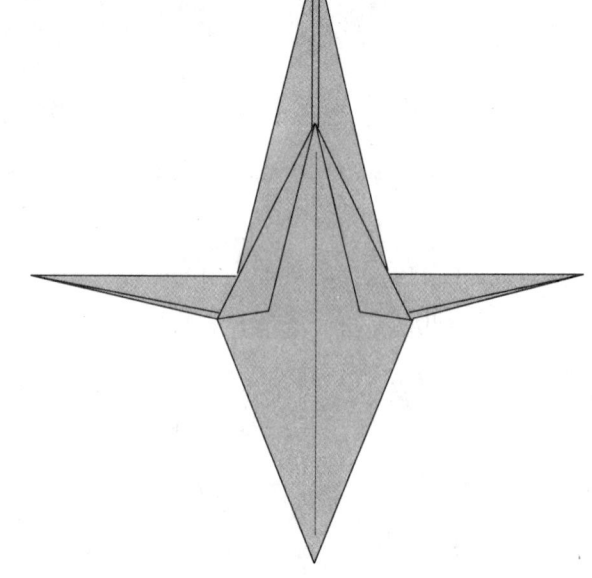

Turn the model over.

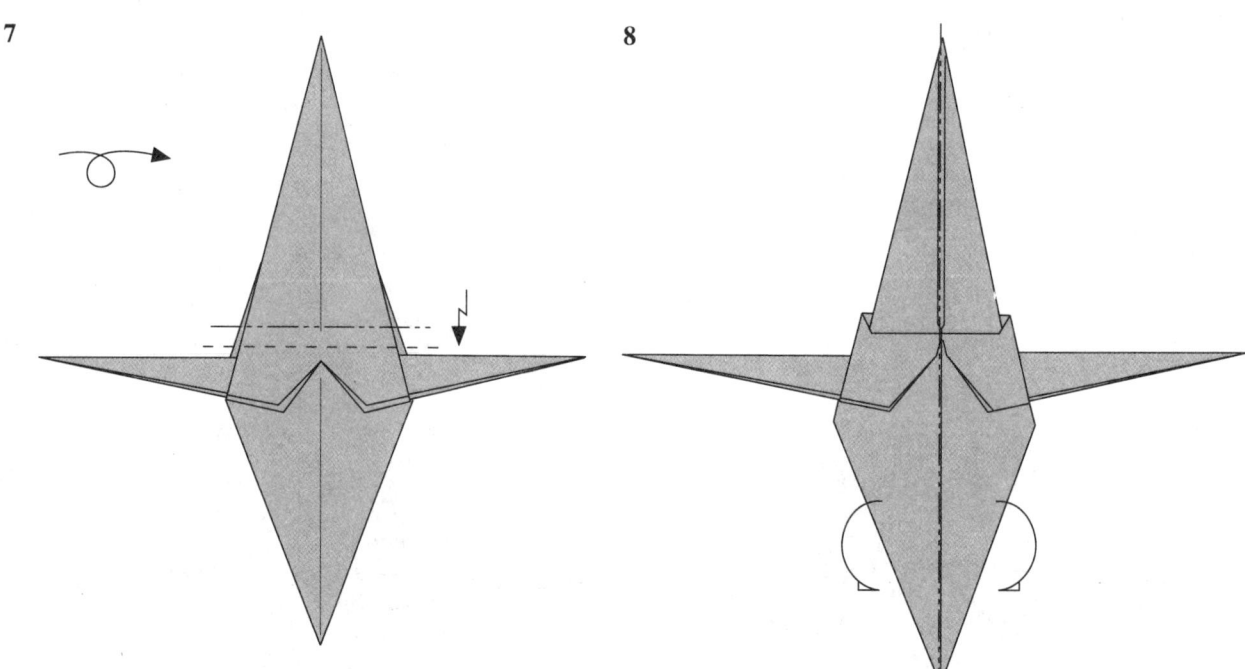

7

Fold downwards and then upwards in a pleat to form the neck and shoulders.

8

Fold the model in half.

9

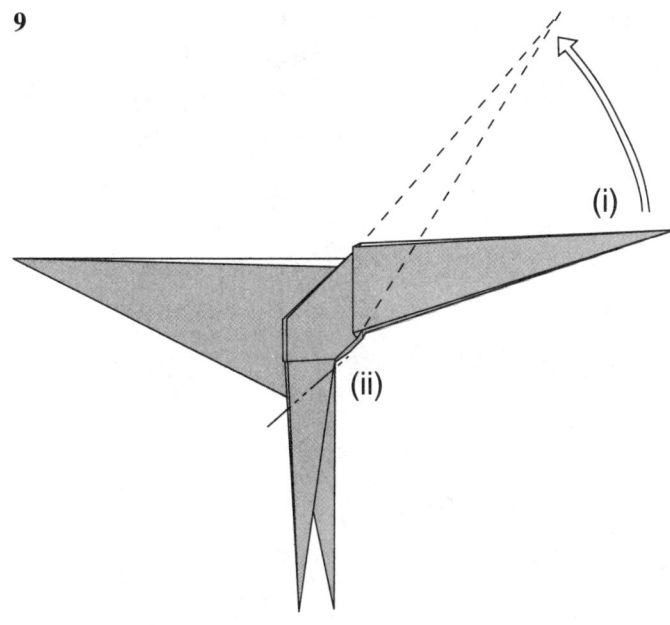

(i) Angle the neck upwards.
(ii) Reverse fold the forelimbs backwards.

10

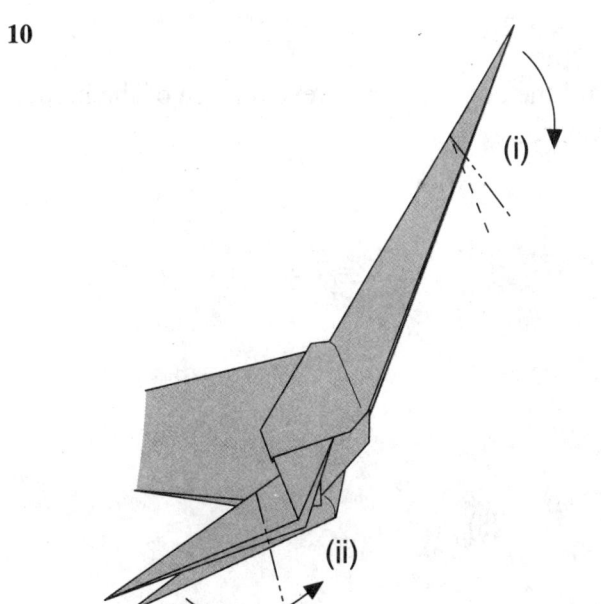

(i) Crimp fold downwards to form the head.
(ii) Reverse fold the forelimbs forward to form the elbows.

11

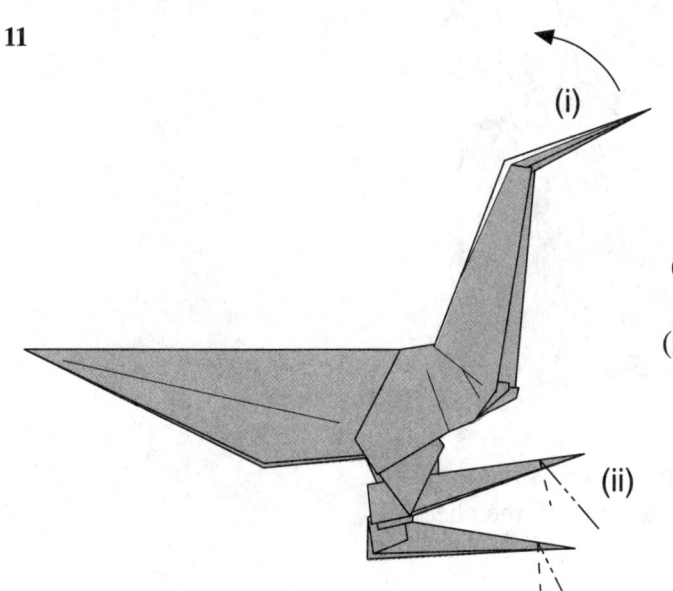

(i) Straighten the head back to the position in 10(i).
(ii) Crimp fold to form the hands.

12

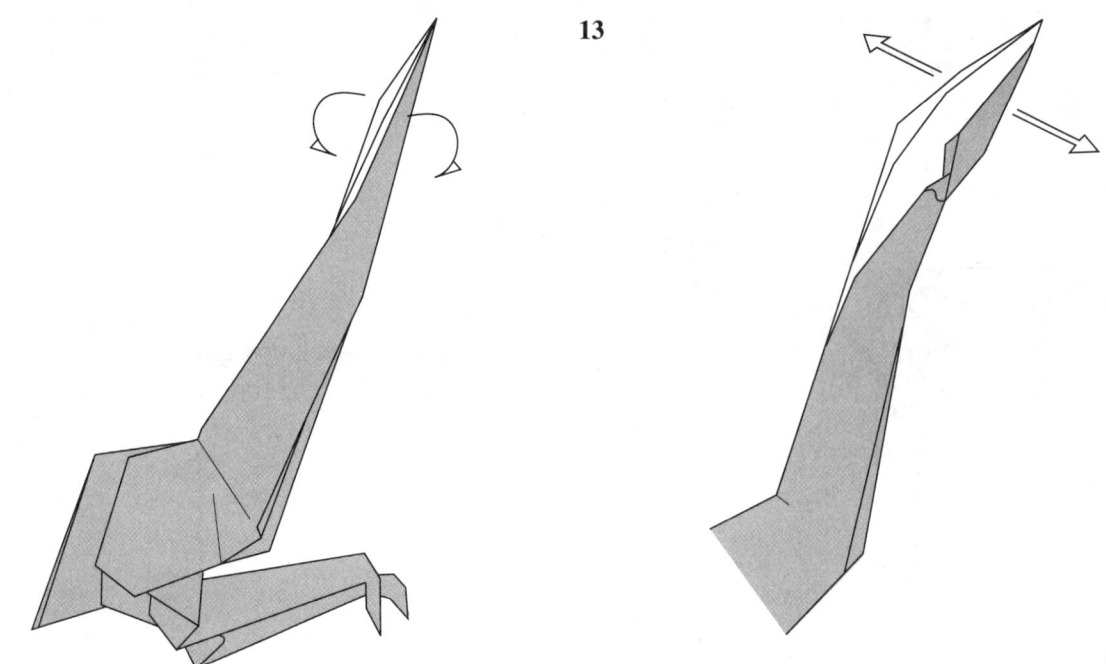

To shape the head, lift the two paper edges at the top of the head and invert them.

13

Pull the edges apart to reveal more of the hidden paper.

14

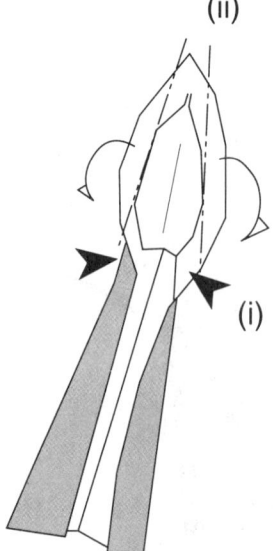

(i) Pinch the base of the head where the crimp fold was made earlier.
(ii) Fold downwards along the sides of the head to form the cheeks.

15a

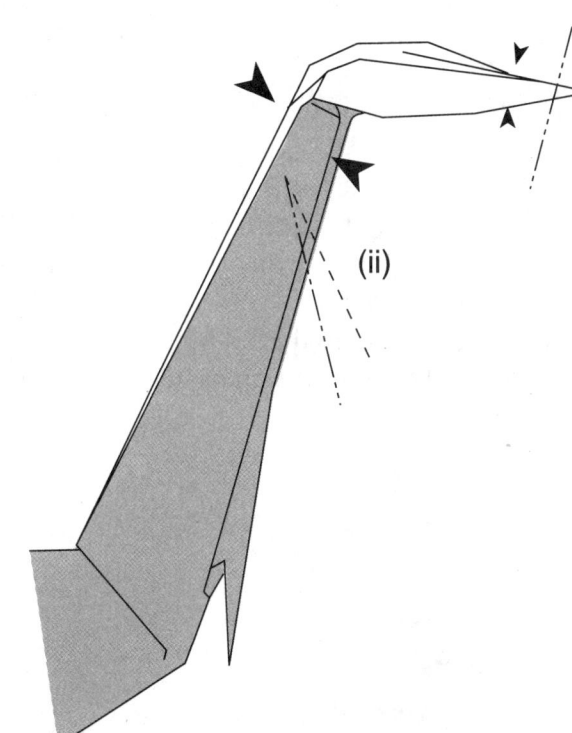

(i) Still pinching the base of the head, tuck in the tip of the head and pinch to shape the mouth and snout.

(ii) Crimp fold the neck to give it a slight curve.

15b

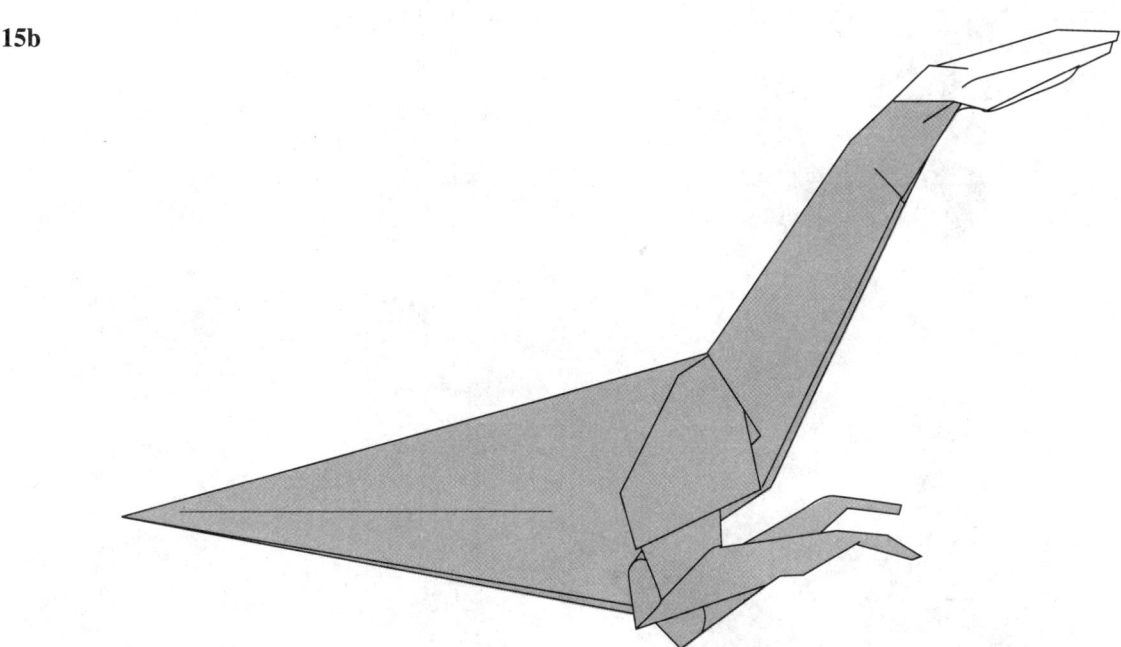

The completed *Compsognathus* head

You can vary the posture of the head by interchanging the position of the valley and mountain folds in step 7. You can also turn the neck to make the model look backwards over its shoulder.

The *Compsognathus* Body

16

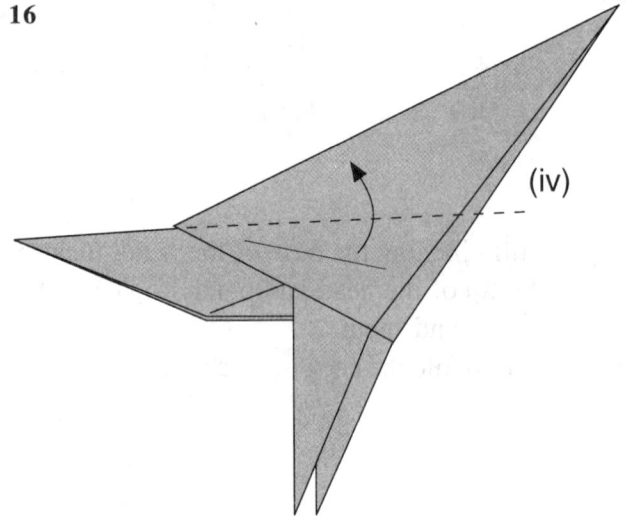

(i) Use a 21 cm square piece of paper.
(ii) Start by folding an offset preliminary base, offset 2.3 cm.
(iii) Proceed to fold a tail base A.
(iv) Fold to show the underside of the model.

17

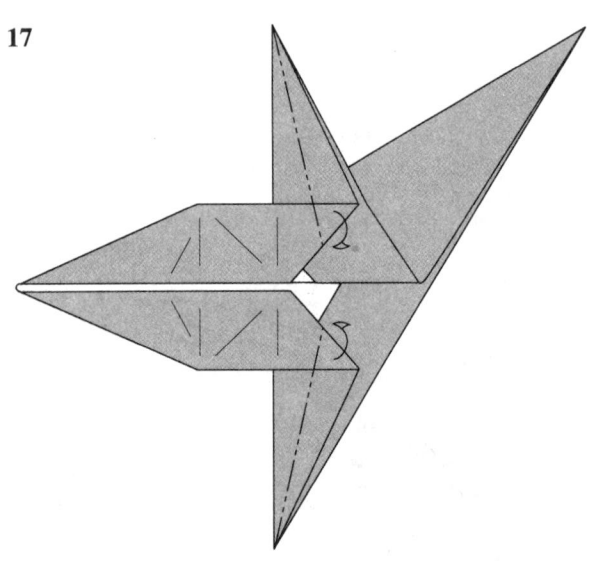

Fold the two flaps inwards. This will help to give your model thinner legs.

18

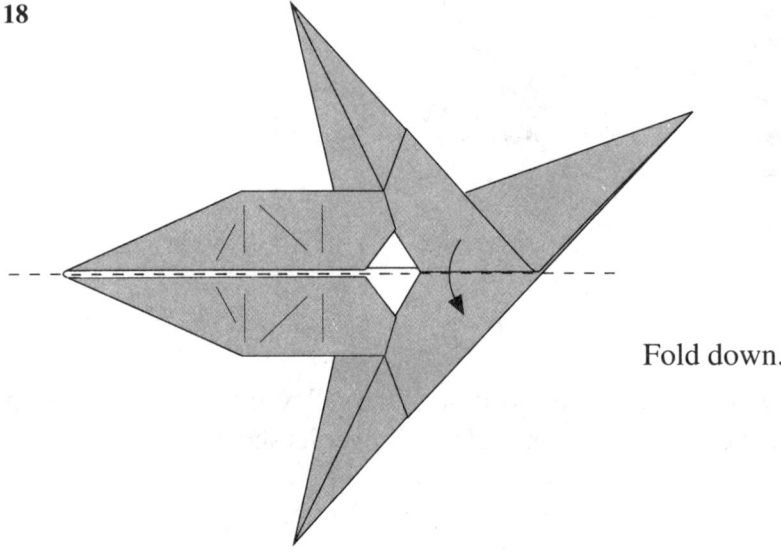

Fold down.

19

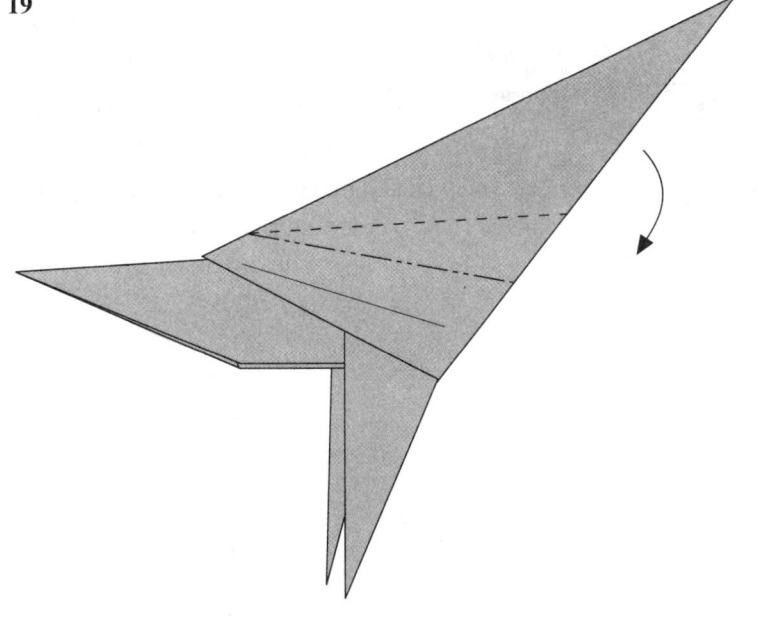

Crimp fold downwards to form the back. Pay attention to the angles of your folds. They determine the shape of the back. A generally thin and flattish back is required for *Compsognathus*.

20

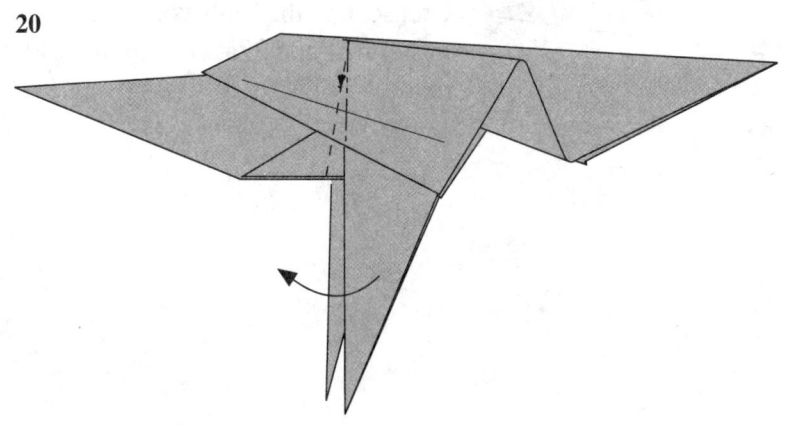

Crimp fold to form the shape of the thigh. (Pull the legs forward and push the body backwards to help you execute this fold.)

21

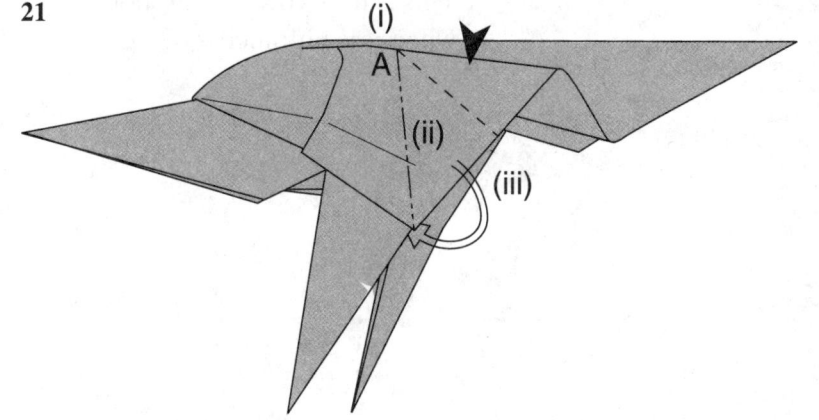

(i) Slip your finger inside the model to point A.
(ii) Make a mountain fold crease from point A downwards. Where you start to crease will determine the thickness of the thigh.
(iii) Fold inwards.

22a

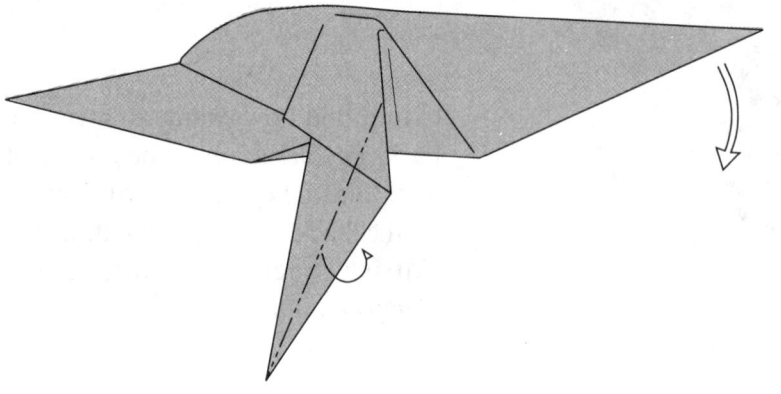

(i) Fold inwards to make the legs thinner.
(ii) The edge of the inside leg flap (see step 17) should more or less line up with the outside leg flap edge.

22b

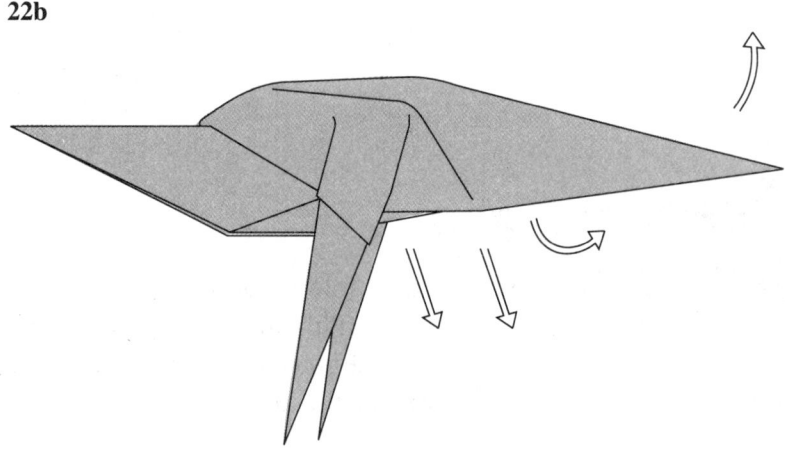

Crease hard the folds you have made in steps 21 and 22a. Unfold the folds made.

23

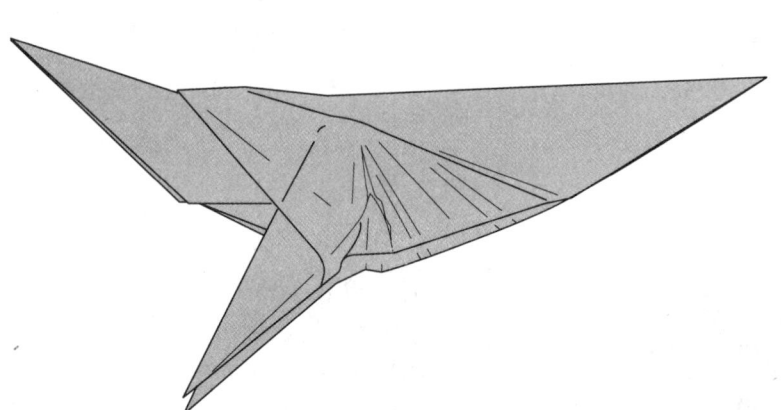

This is how your model should look when it is unfolded.

24

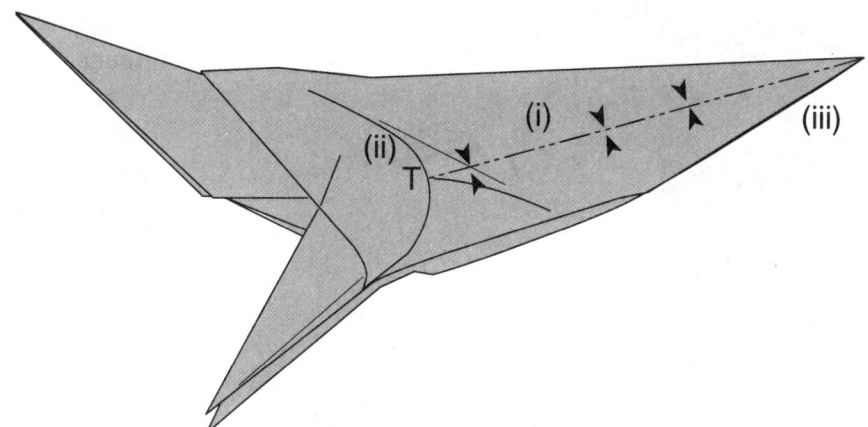

To make the tail thinner:
 (i) Make a mountain fold crease along the tail, starting from the end of the tail and working towards the body. Do this by pinching the fold bit by bit along the tail or by folding the whole tail inwards and then unfolding it.
 (ii) Continue to make the crease for the tail right up to the T-junction. (It is important that the crease lines meet in a form of a T or Y-junction.)
 (iii) Fold the tail inwards to make it thinner, starting from the end of the tail.

25

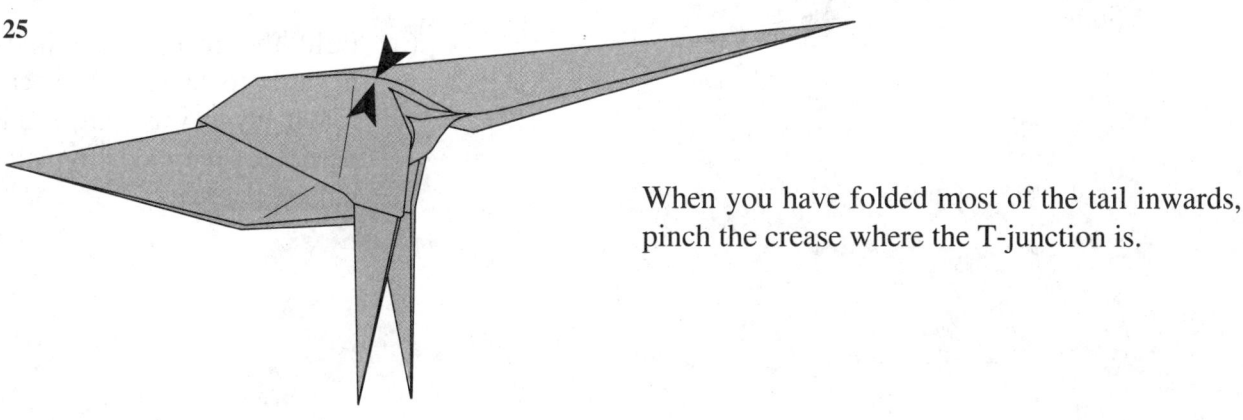

When you have folded most of the tail inwards, pinch the crease where the T-junction is.

26

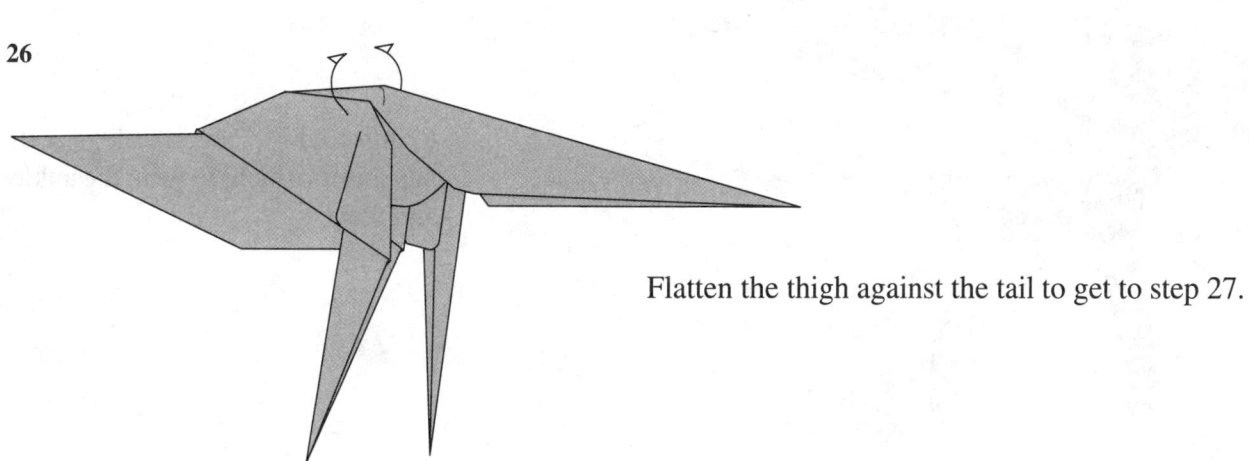

Flatten the thigh against the tail to get to step 27.

27

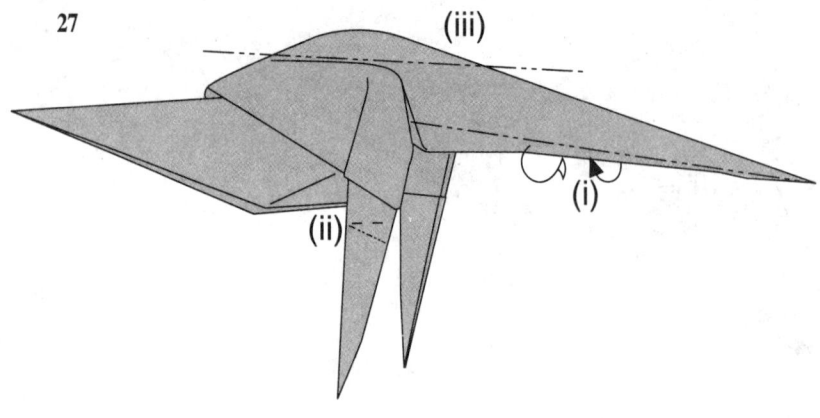

(i) Fold inwards to make the tail thinner.
(ii) Crimp fold the legs backwards to form the knee.
(iii) Flatten the hump on the back by pulling the tail and folding in more paper at the crease outlining the back (made in step 19).

28

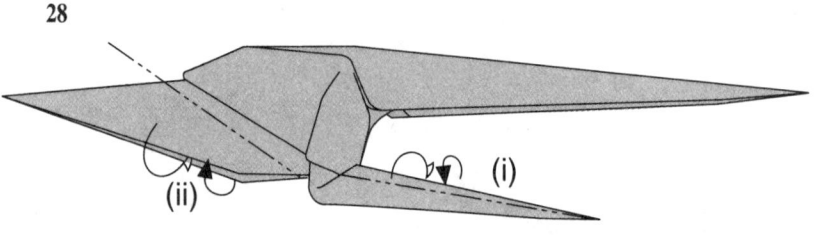

(i) Fold both sides of each leg inwards to make it even thinner. (If you are using fairly thick paper, this may not be possible.) The legs are now fairly compact.
(ii) Fold the rest of the body inwards to hide it. You can fold it any way as long as this portion of the model remains hidden.

29

Crimp fold (or bend the legs if the paper is too thick) to form the ankles and feet.

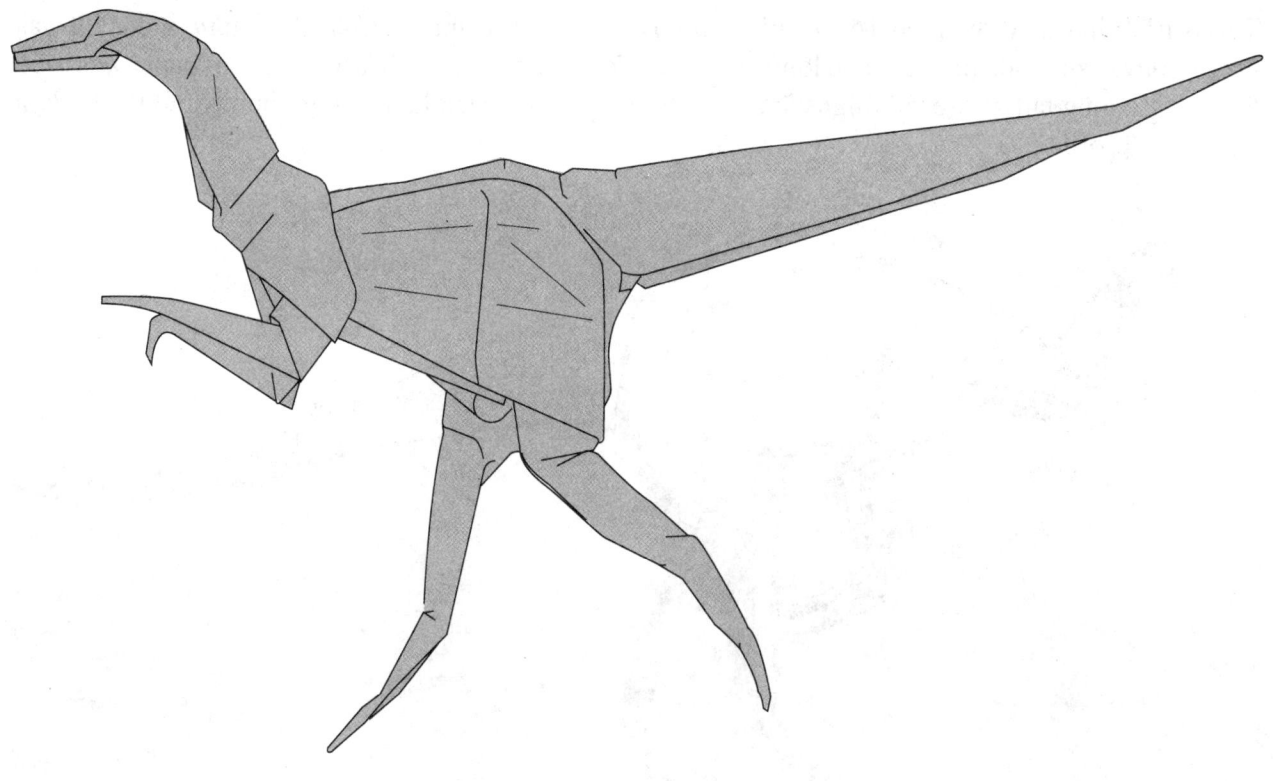

The completed *Compsognathus* model

Join the head and body together using glue. You can put it in a running position by holding the tail up high, positioning the legs in a stride and keeping its head down low.

Invent Your Own Dinosaur

This ostrich-like dinosaur model of "*Ornithomimus*" was made using the *Compsognathus* model. It was given a bird-like head, thin neck and long thin arms. For the body, a much larger piece of paper was used to give it a long tail, powerful thighs and very thin legs. The back had a slight hump and the body a triangular profile.

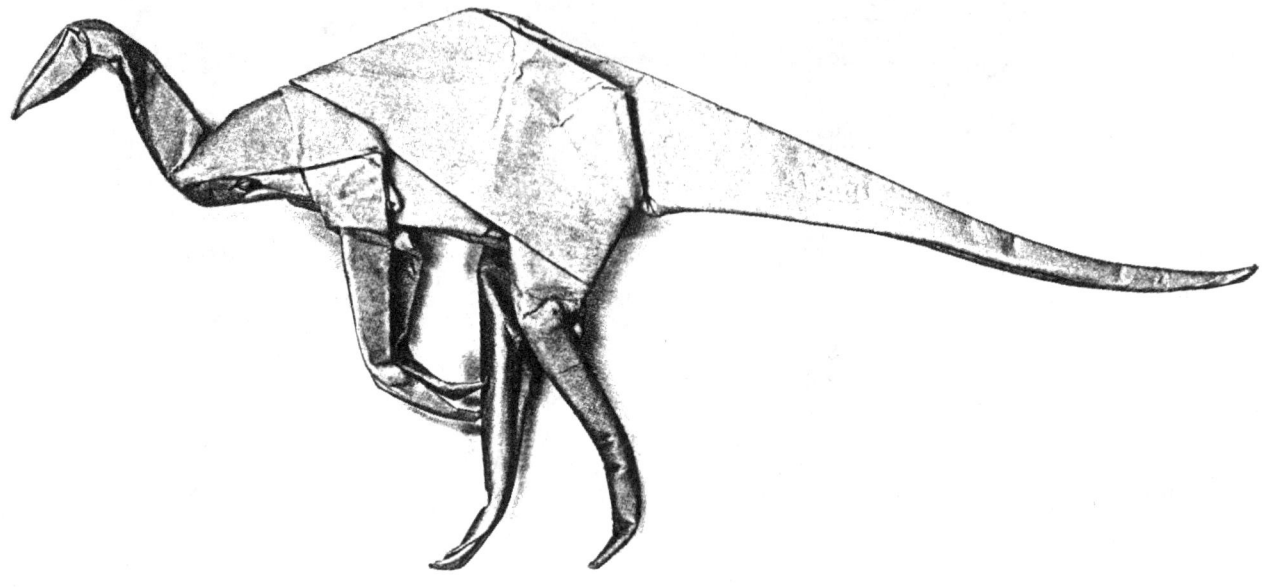

Diplodocus and Apatosaurus

Diplodocus (meaning "double beam") is the longest sauropod, reaching a length of 88 ft (27 m). Its whip-like tail is 45 ft (14 m) long and its slender neck about 26 ft (8 m). For such a large-sized dinosaur, *Diplodocus* weighs a surprising 10 tonnes only. It lived during the Late Jurassic period.

Apatosaurus was three times heavier than *Diplodocus* despite being only about 70 ft (21 m) long. It was initially called *Brontosaurus* (meaning "thunder lizard") because the ground shook whenever it walked. Compared to *Diplodocus*, it has a shorter and thicker neck and tail.

Diplodocus

The *Diplodocus* body

1

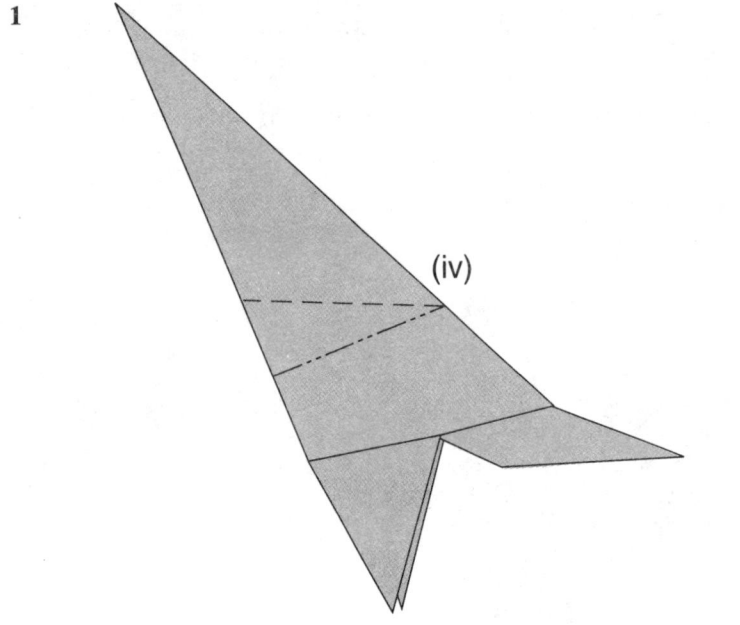

(i) Use a 26 cm square piece of paper.
(ii) Start by folding an offset preliminary base, offset 7.4 cm.
(iii) Proceed to fold a tail base B.
(iv) Crimp fold to form the back and hump of the sauropod. This fold should be fairly high up since *Diplodocus* has a high back.

2

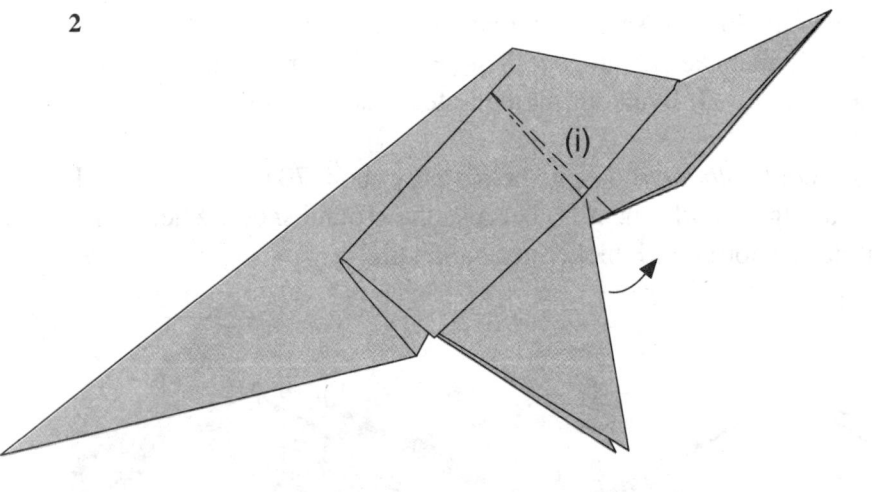

(i) Crimp fold the leg forward. (Pull the legs forward and push the body backwards to help you execute this fold.) Notice that the crease starts behind the highest point of the back. If you find this step difficult to execute, do it after you have completed the model.

3

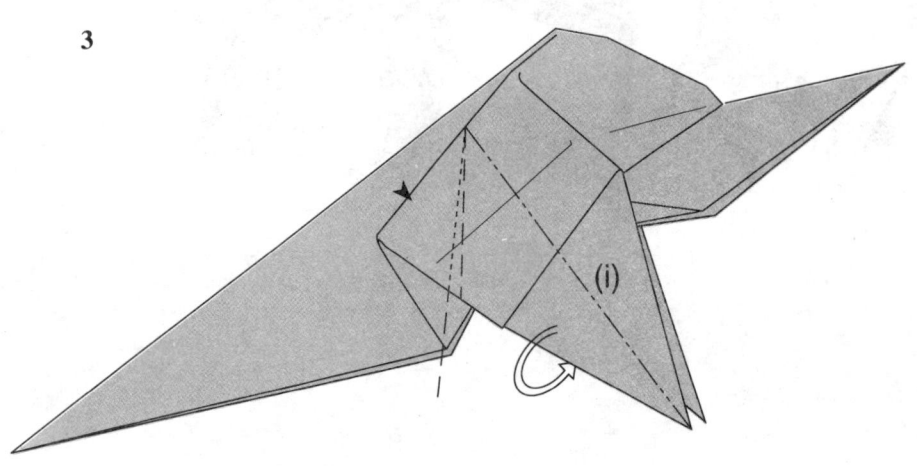

(i) Fold the outside of the leg inwards and tuck it under the inner (hidden) leg flap. To help you execute this fold, hold the leg at the tip and lift it upwards and forward.

4

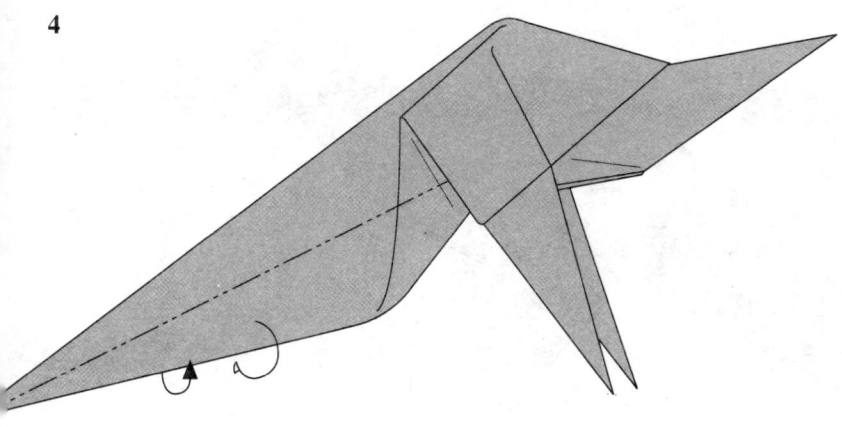

Fold the tail inwards to make it thinner.

5a

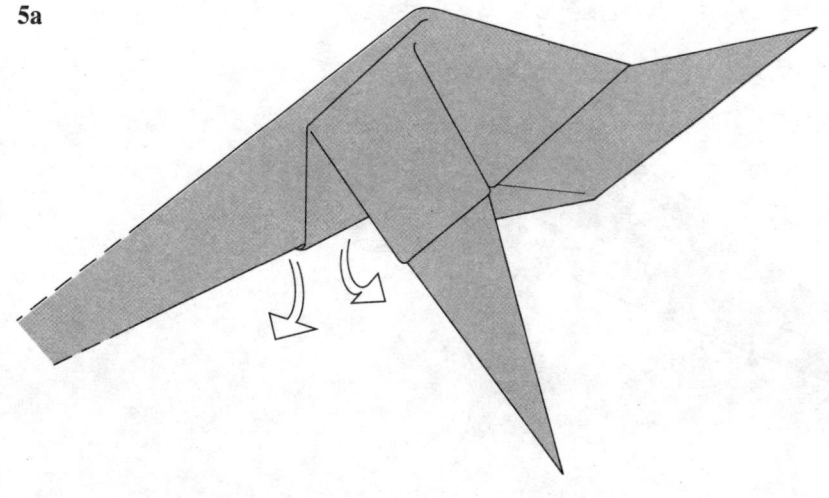

Near the leg end, unfold a bit of the tail folded in step 4.

5b

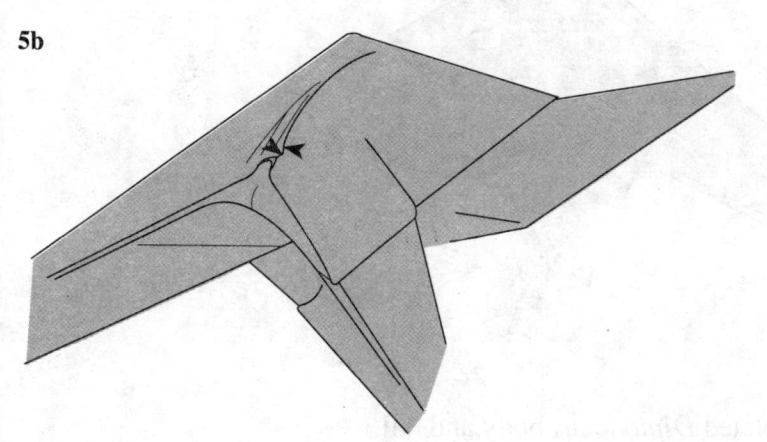

Form a crease mark from the tail to where the back and the leg meet. You should get a Y or T-junction crease mark. Pinch hard at the T-junction crease. The tail can now be folded back in place and the rest of the model flattened nicely.

6

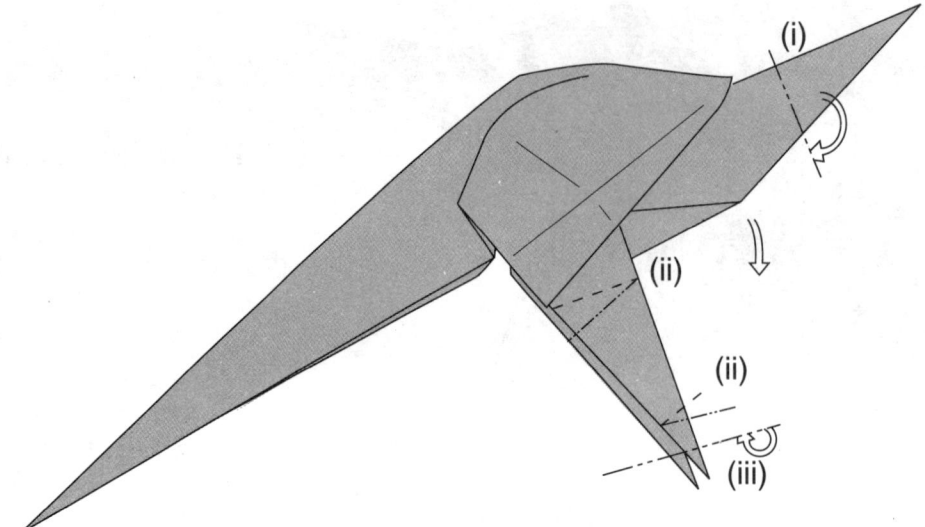

(i)   Tuck in to make the body length shorter.
(ii) Crimp fold to form the knees and ankles.
(iii) Tuck in the ends of the feet so that they are not pointed.
(At this stage, we have also made the bodies for *Apatosaurus* and *Camarasaurus*.)

7

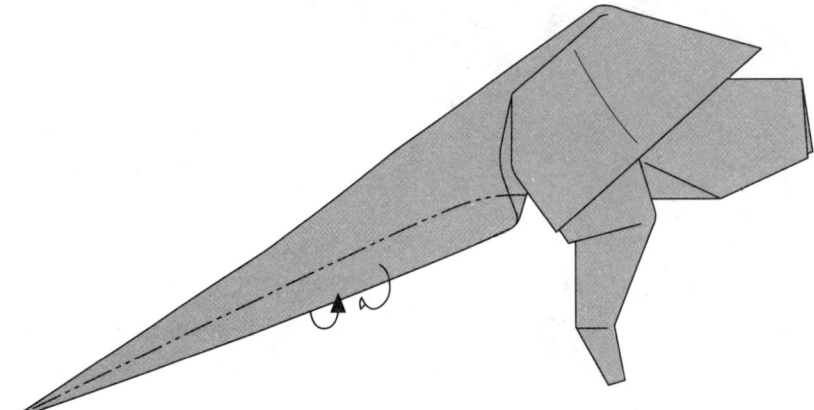

Fold the tail inwards to make it thinner.

8

The completed *Diplodocus* body and tail

The *Diplodocus* head

9

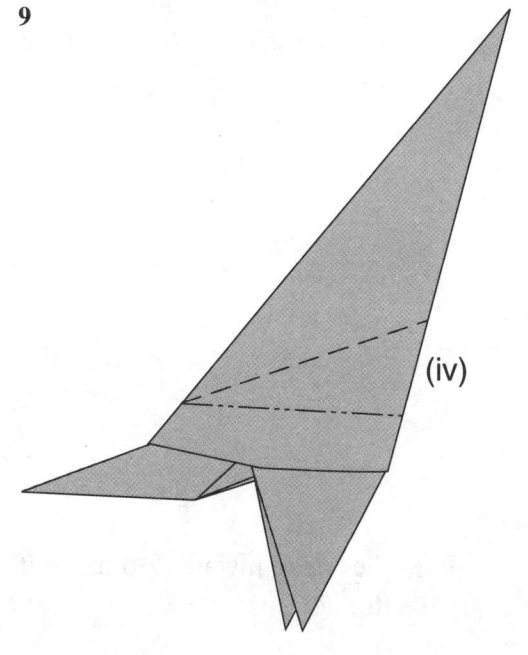

(i) Use a piece of 21 cm square paper.
(ii) Start by folding an offset preliminary base, offset 6.3 cm.
(iii) Fold a tail base B.
(iv) Crimp fold to form the shoulders and neck. Note the low position of the fold.

10

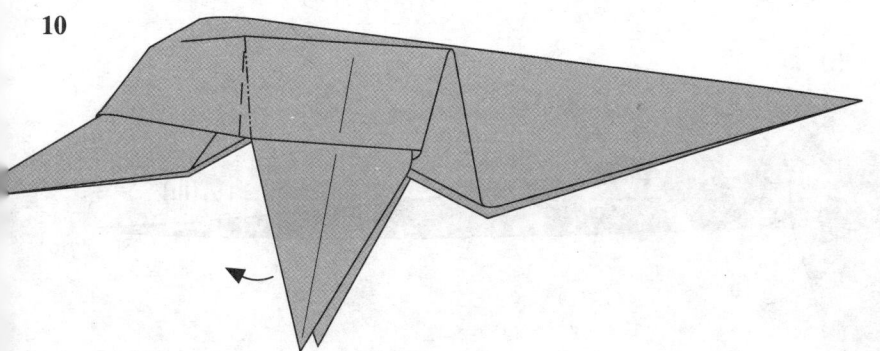

Crimp fold to form the back of the forelimbs. To execute this fold, move the forelimbs backwards to the left. This step may be left out or done after the rest of the steps have been completed.

11

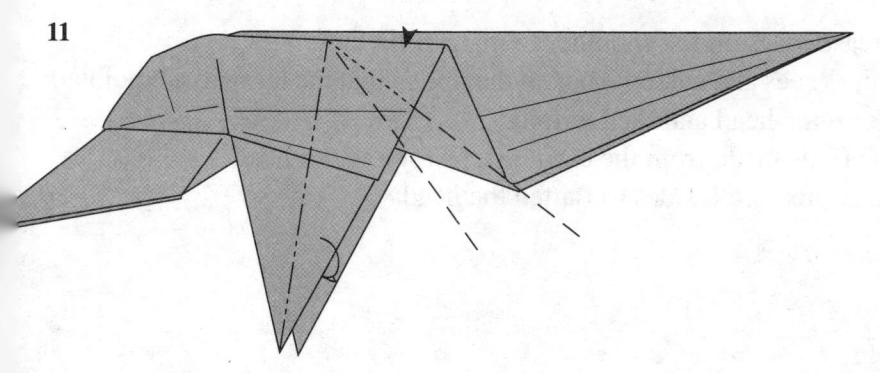

Halve the thickness of the forelimbs by folding the outer edge inwards. Lift the legs up and backwards (to the left) to help you execute this fold.

12

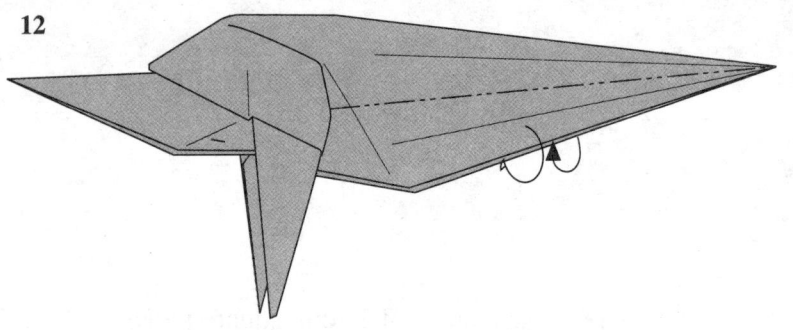

(i) Halve the thickness of the neck by folding it inwards.
(ii) Follow step 5 to fold the base of the neck properly.

13

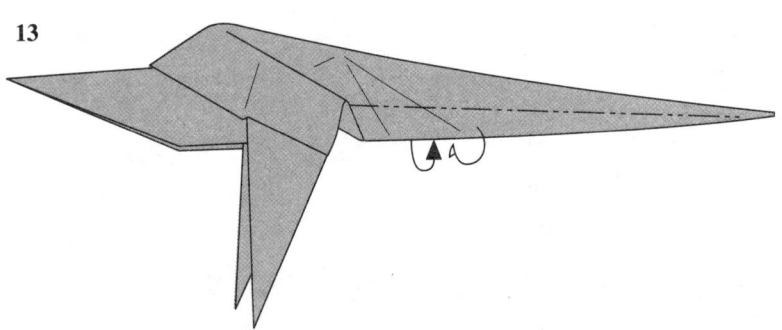

Fold the neck inwards to make it even thinner.

14

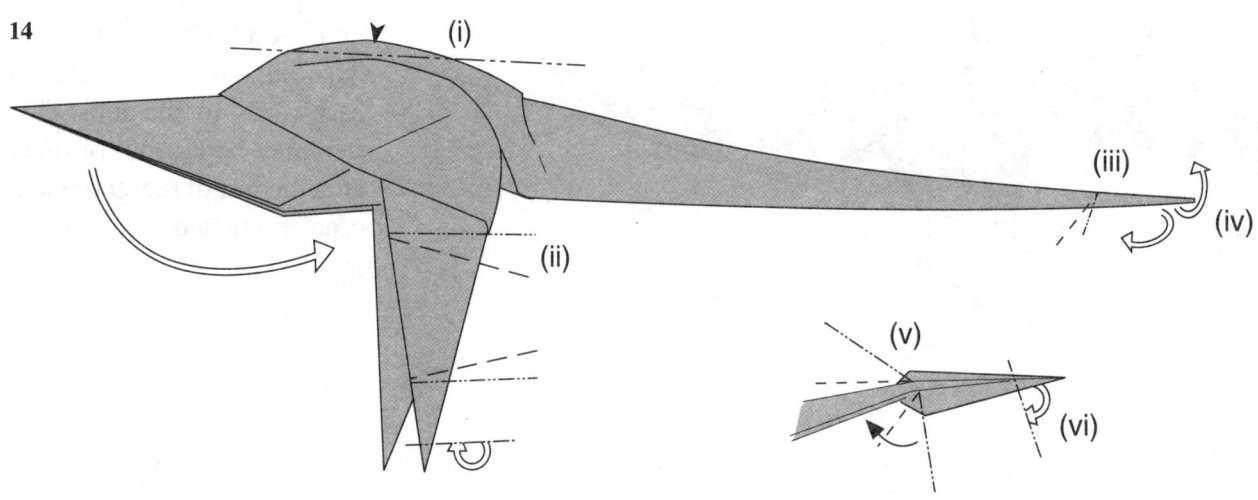

(i) Fold in more paper at the crease mark on the shoulder to make it flatter.
(ii) Crimp fold the legs to form the knees and ankles. Tuck in the tips so that the legs are not pointed.
(iii) Crimp fold downwards to form the head and then unfold.
(iv) Pull out from underneath the folds made from the earlier steps for a wider head.
(v) Pinch the base of the head and press both sides to flatten the head.
(vi) Tuck in the tip of the head.

15

Bend the neck to get a nice curve.

16

The completed *Diplodocus* model

Join the head and tail together in the position shown.

Apatosaurus (Brontosaurus)
The *Apatosaurus* head

(i) Use a 21 cm square piece of paper.
(ii) Start by folding an offset preliminary base, offset 5.9 cm.
(iii) Fold a tail base B.
(iv) Follow the steps for making the *Diplodocus* head. Skip step 13 as a thin neck is not wanted for *Apatosaurus*.

To shape the apatosaurus head:

1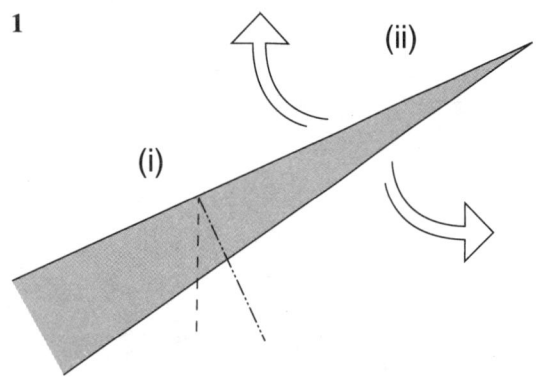

(i) Make a crimp fold and then unfold it.
(ii) Pull out from underneath the previously folded paper. Unfold past the crimp fold which marks the base of the head.

2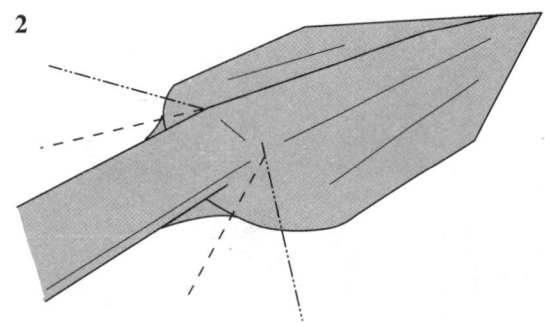

Pinch the base of the neck and then fold the sides inwards against the base of the head. This will form the jawline.

3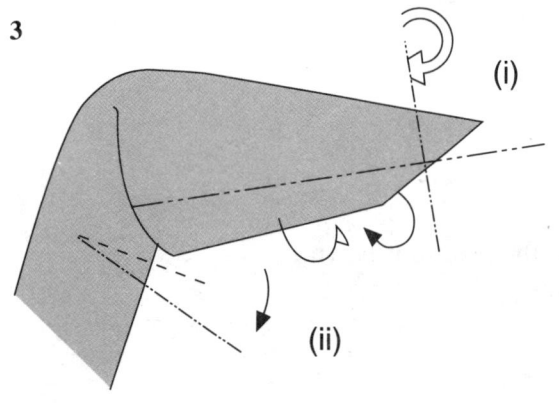

(i) Tuck inwards along the crease lines shown to give the head a triangular profile.
(ii) Crimp fold the neck near the base of the head to curve the head downwards even more.

The *Apatosaurus* body

4

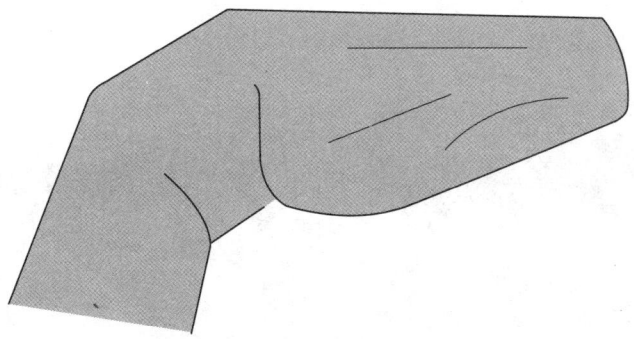

(i) Use a piece of 26 cm square paper.
(ii) Follow the steps for making the *Diplodocus* body.
(iii) Stop at step 7 since the tail of *Apatosaurus* is thicker.

5

The completed *Apatosaurus* model

Ceratosaurus

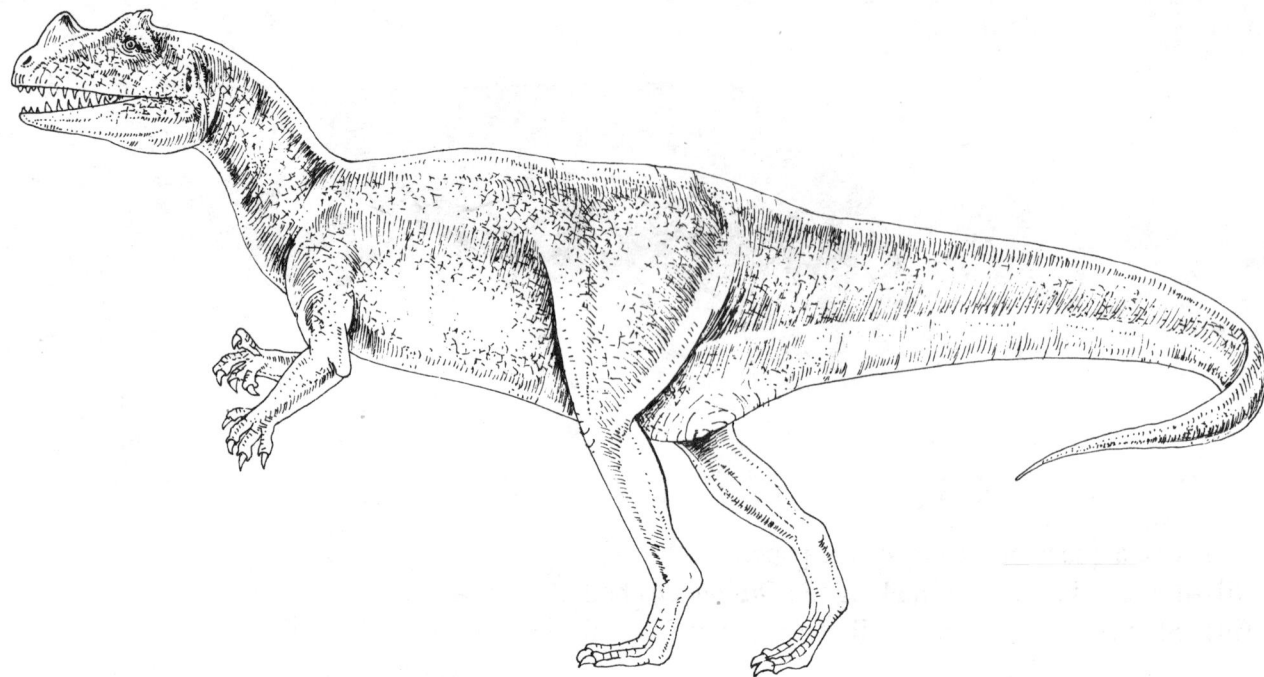

Ceratosaurus (horned lizard), a relatively large meat-eating theropod, lived during the Early Jurassic period. It measures about 20 ft (6 m) long. *Ceratosaurus* has a horn above its nose and eyes as well as scutes running down its back, thus giving it a fierce dragon-like appearance. On its powerful forelimbs are four-fingered hands. This dinosaur was a pack hunter.

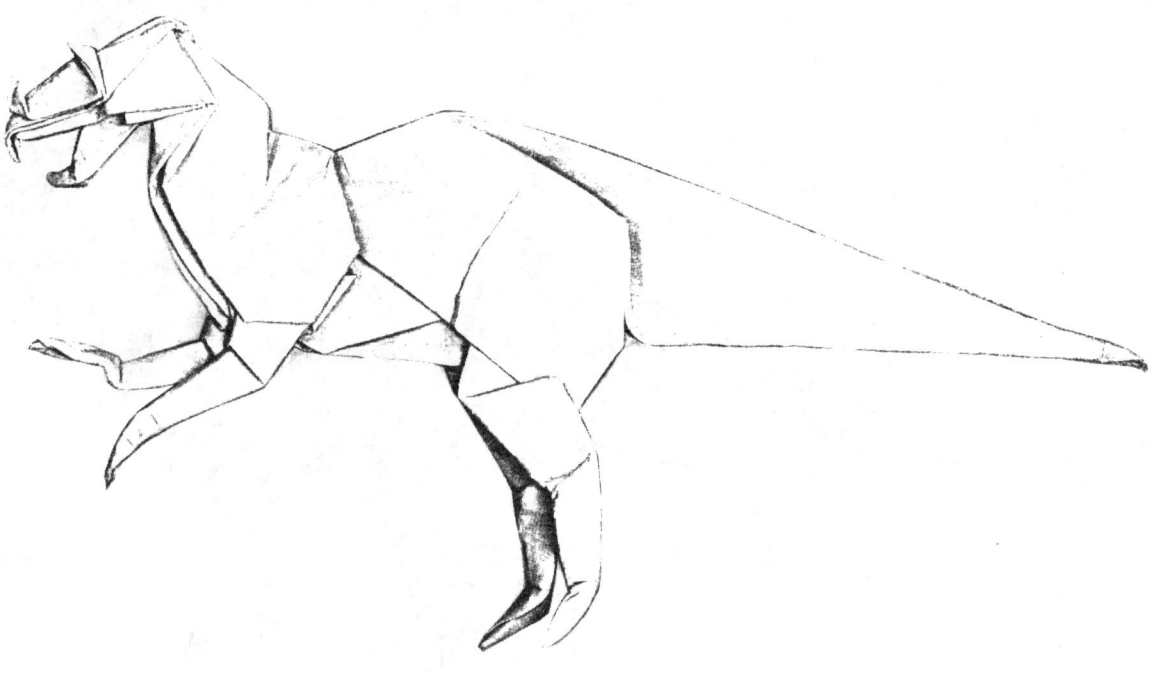

The *Ceratosaurus* head

1

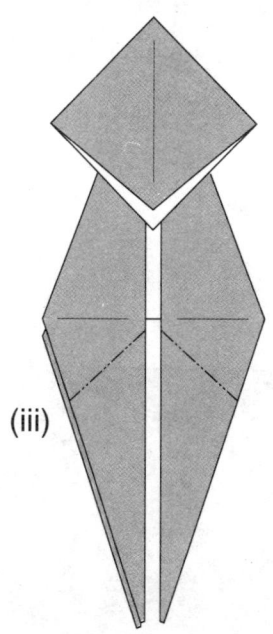

2

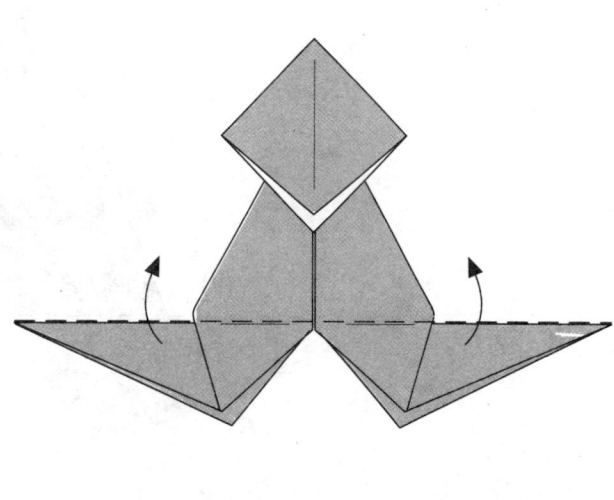

(i) Use a piece of 19 cm square paper.
(ii) Start by folding a hadrosaur base with an offset of 3 cm.
(iii) Reverse fold the two bottom flaps upwards to form the forelimbs.

Fold upwards.

3

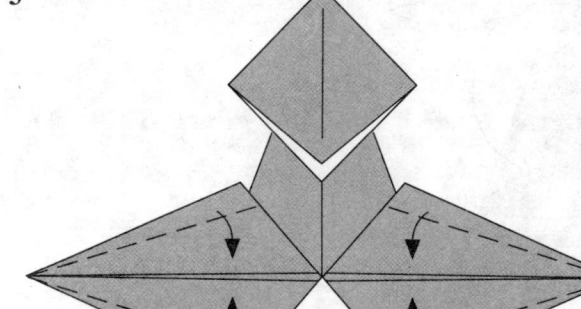

4

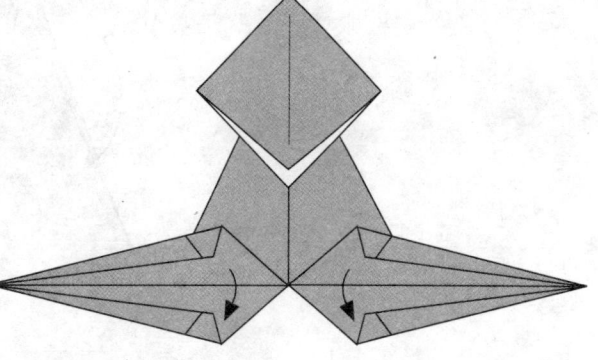

Fold inwards to make the forelimbs thinner. This fold will determine the thickness of the forelimbs. *Ceratosaurus* has powerful forelimbs unlike *Tyrannosaurus*.

Fold downwards.

5

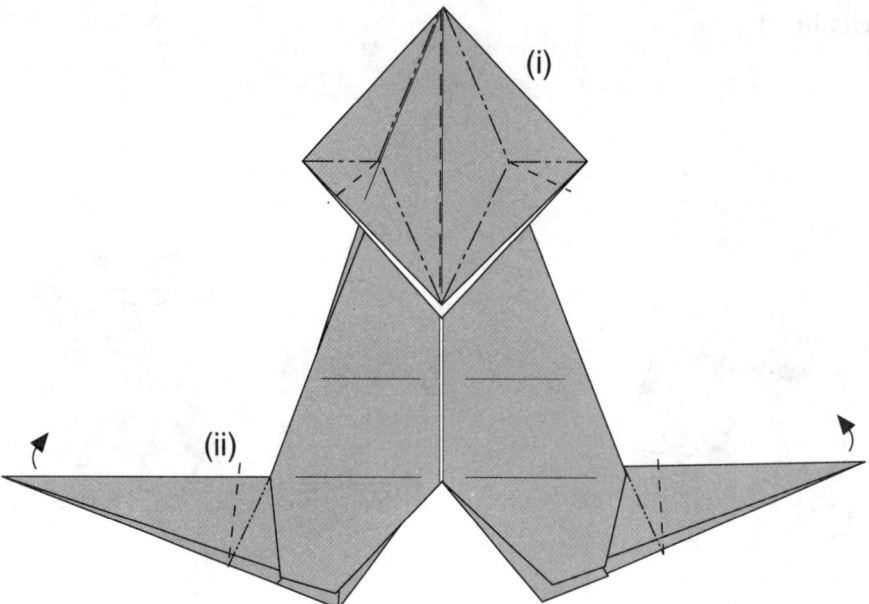

(i) Frog fold the small square portion at the top of the model.
(ii) Crimp fold to form the arms.

6

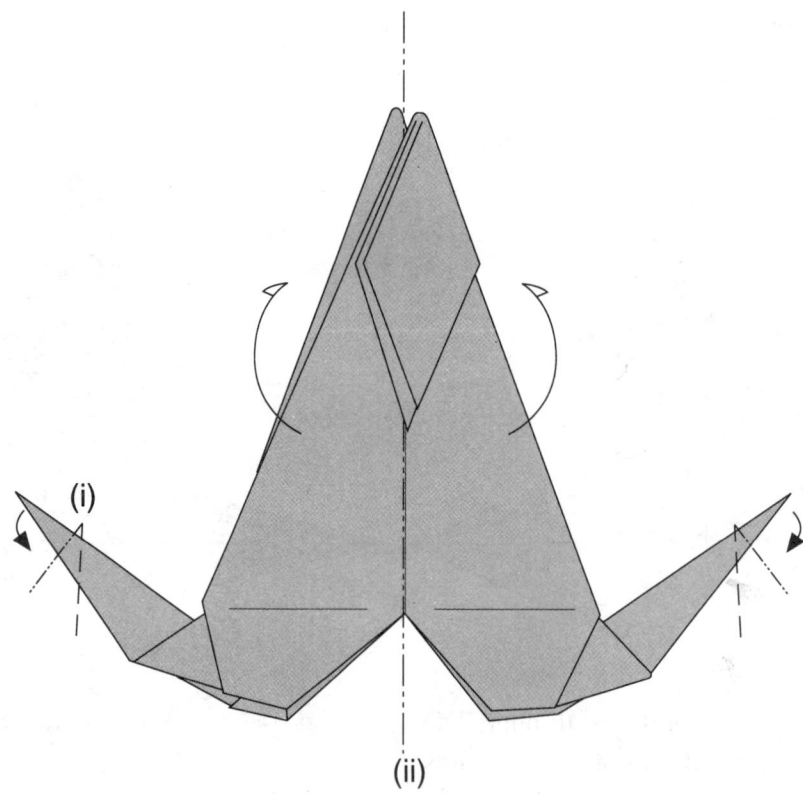

(i) Crimp fold to form the hands.
(ii) Fold the model in half.

7

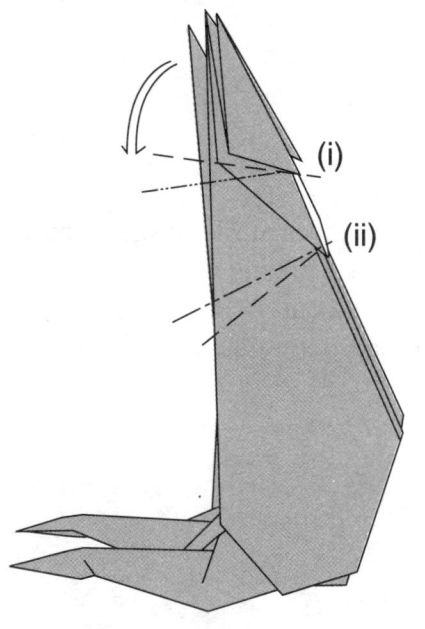

(i) Crimp fold downwards to form the cheeks.
(ii) Crimp fold downwards to form the head.

8

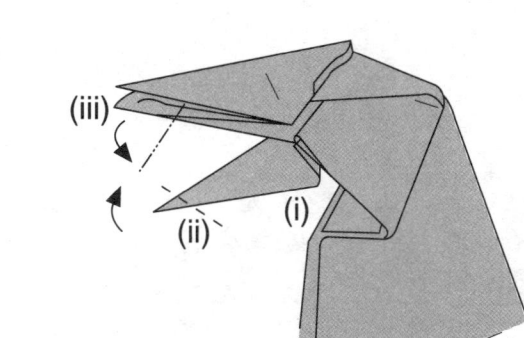

(i) Pull the lower flap slightly downwards to form the lower jaw.
(ii) Reverse fold the tip of the lower jaw to form the teeth.
(iii) Reverse fold the tip of the upper jaw to form the upper teeth.

9

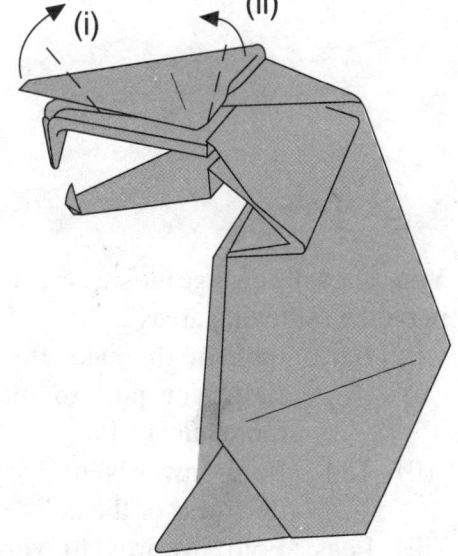

(i) Reverse fold the tip upwards to form the horn above the nose.
(ii) Fold the two triangular flaps forward to form the ridges above the eyes.

10

The completed *Ceratosaurus* head
Sink fold the area at the back of the head. (See *Tyrannosaurus* step 10(iii)) to form the neck and shoulders.

The *Ceratosaurus* body

11

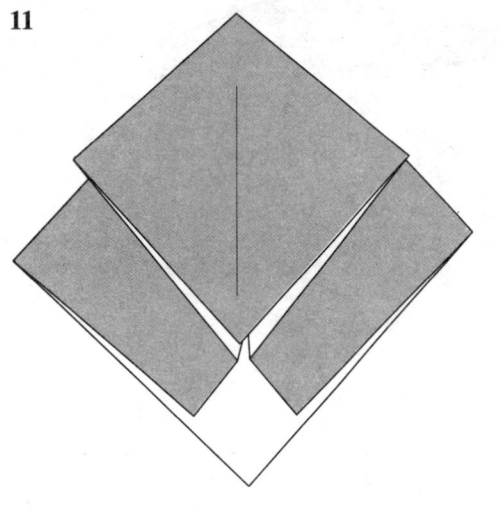

(i) Use a piece of 21 cm square piece of paper.
(ii) Start by folding an offset preliminary base, offset 2 cm.
(iii) Proceed to fold a tail base A.

12

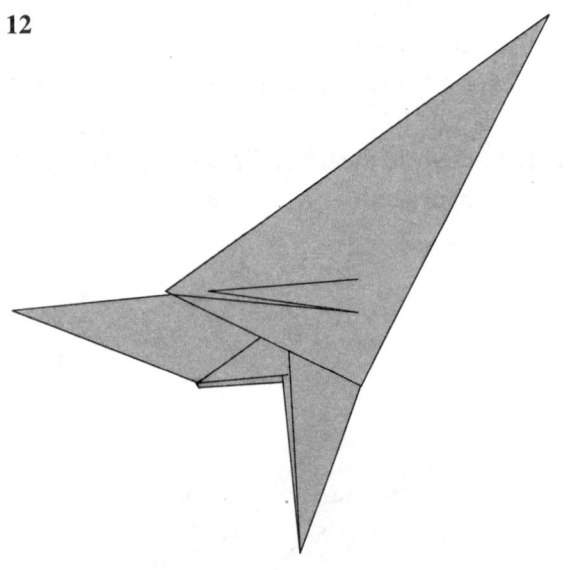

Follow steps 12(iv) to 17 of the *Tyrannosaurus* model. (Bear in mind that *Ceratosaurus* is less powerfully built than *Tyrannosaurus*, but it is a more agile hunter. You will want to make the thighs and legs slightly thinner and longer. The tail should be held high so as not to give it a sluggish appearance.)

The completed *Ceratosaurus* body and tail

13

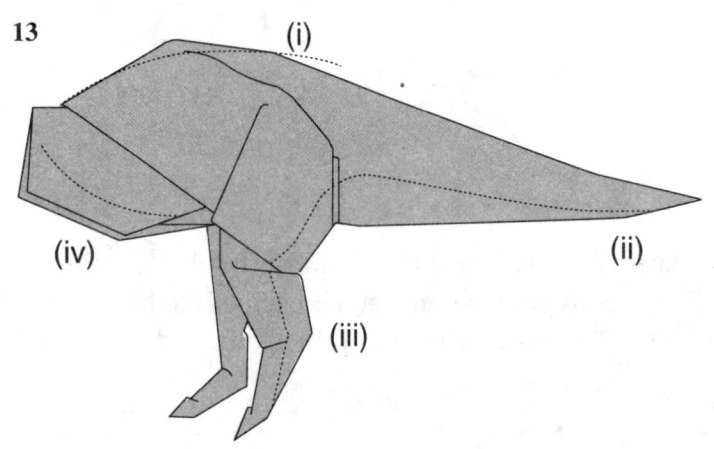

You can easily change the shape by folding in on the following areas :
  (i) Back : tuck in to make the back flatter or pull to make it more hunched.
  (ii) Tail : Fold inwards to vary the thickness of the tail.
  (iii) Legs : Fold inwards to vary the thickness of the leg.
       : Vary the positions of your leg folds to give them longer shins or longer thighs.
  (iv) Belly : Tuck in and shape the underbelly to give it a fatter or thinner body.

14

The completed *Ceratosaurus* model

Join the head and body using glue. The posture of *Ceratosaurus* is similar to the other large meat-eating dinosaurs like *Allosaurus* or *Tyrannosaurus*.

Allosaurus

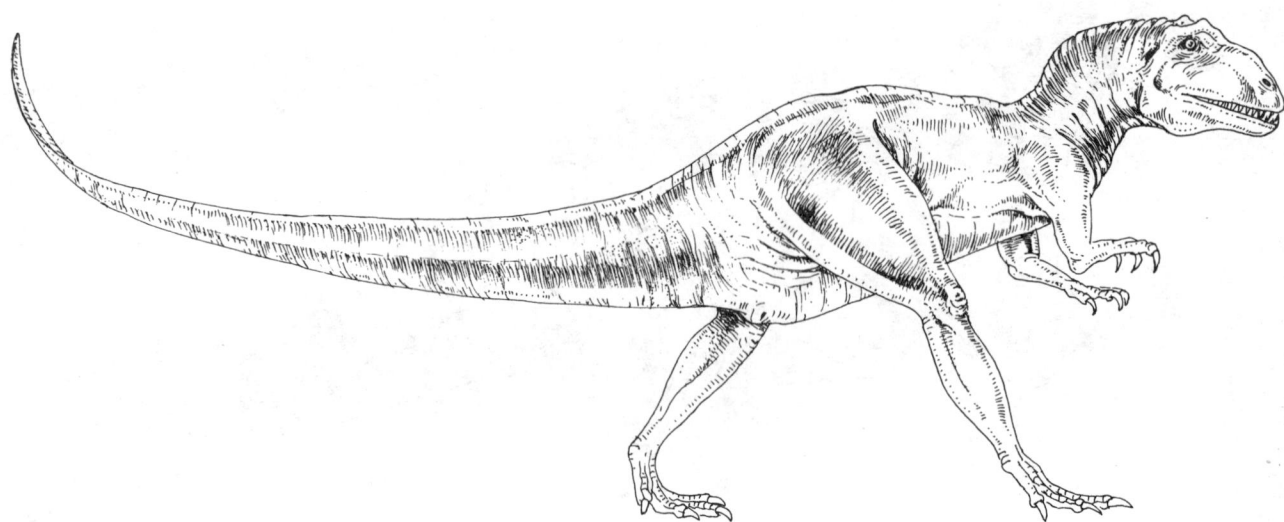

Next to *Tyrannosaurus*, *Allosaurus* is the second largest meat-eating dinosaur. At 36 ft (11 m), this two-legged theropod is as long as a school bus. At the top of its head are bony ridges and hornlets. It also has powerful jaws and powerful three-clawed forelimbs. *Allosaurus* may have hunted in packs, taking on large prey like the sauropods during the Jurassic period.

The *Allosaurus* head

1

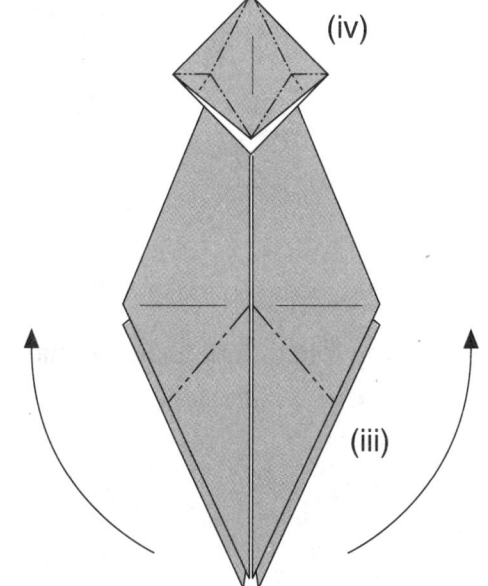

(i) Use a piece of 17 cm square paper.
(ii) Start by folding a hadrosaur base, offset of 2.7 cm.
(iii) Reverse fold the two bottom flaps upwards to form the forelimbs.
(iv) Frog fold the squares at the top of the model.

2

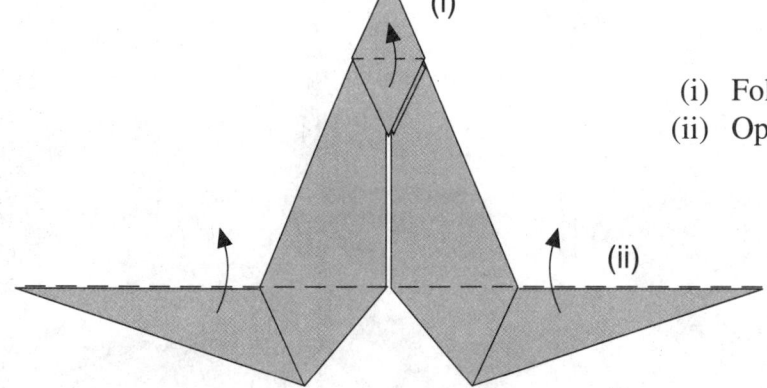

(i) Fold the small top triangular flap upwards.
(ii) Open up the two flaps of the forelimbs.

3

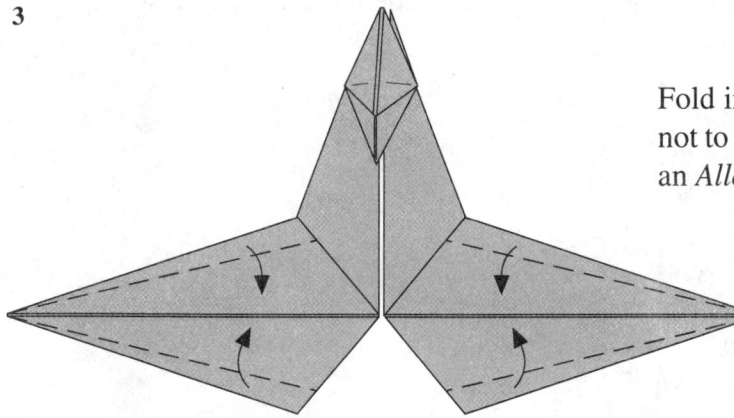

Fold inwards to make the forelimbs thinner. Try not to fold too thin or else you will end up having an *Allosaurus* with thin forelimbs.

4

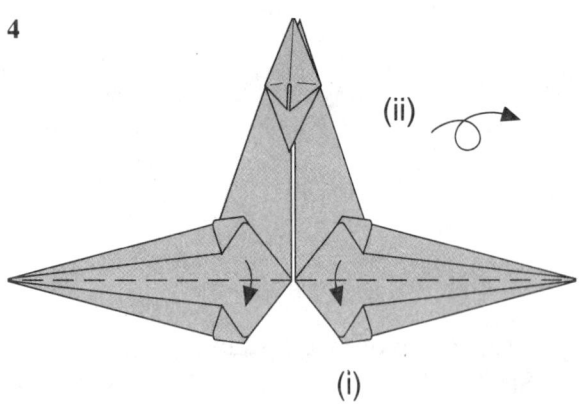

5

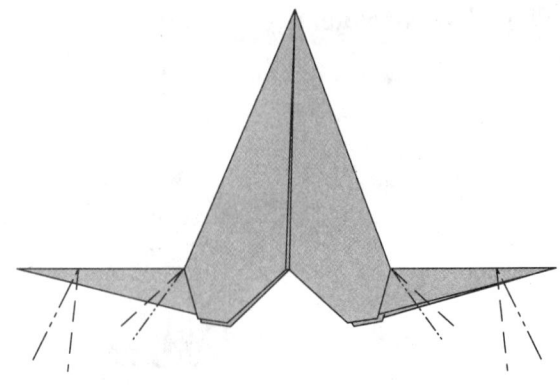

(i) Fold downwards.
(ii) Turn the model over.

Crimp fold to form the arms and hands.

6a **6b**

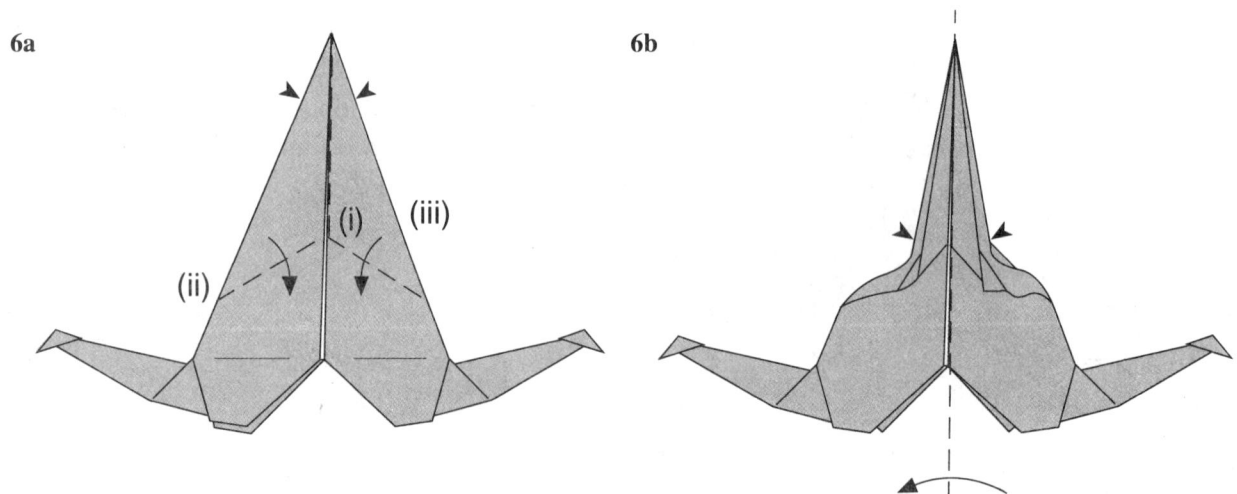

(i) Look between the front and back flaps of the top portion. You will see a triangular section. The tip of the triangular section is where you want your creases to meet.
(ii) Valley fold to the right and left to make the left and right creases. Make sure these creases meet at the position in (i).
(iii) Fold the right and left edges (both layers) inwards along the creases made in (ii). The upper portion will automatically lift (see step 6b).

Fold the model in half to get to step 7.

7

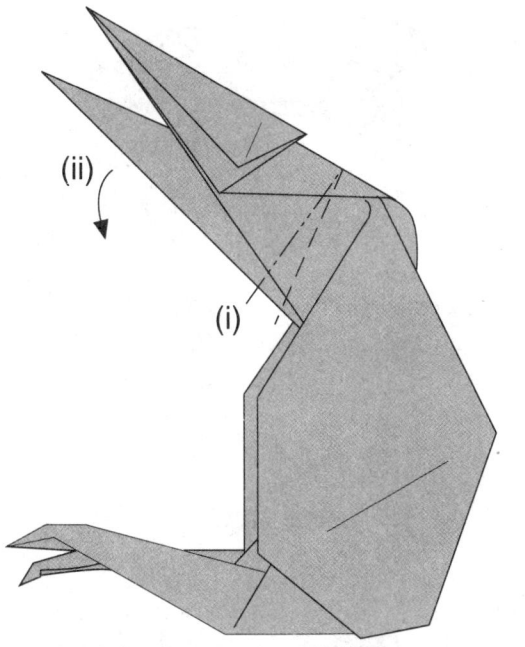

8

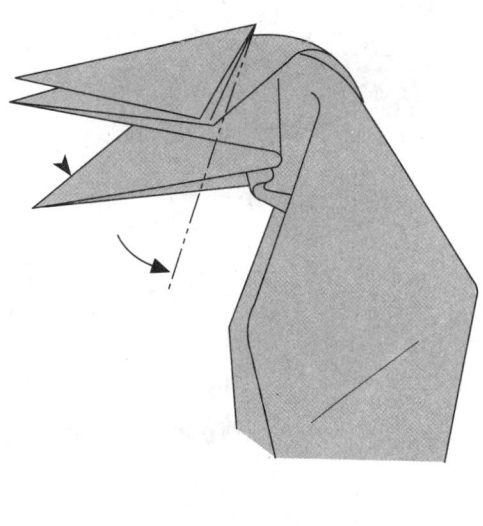

(i) Crimp fold both flaps downwards to form the cheeks.

(ii) Pull the lower flap slightly downwards to form the lower jaw.

Reverse fold the lower jaw downwards.

9

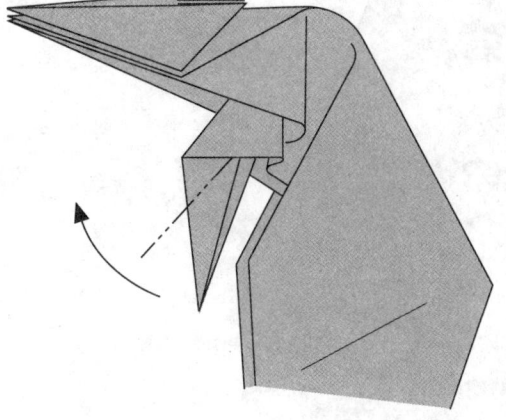

10

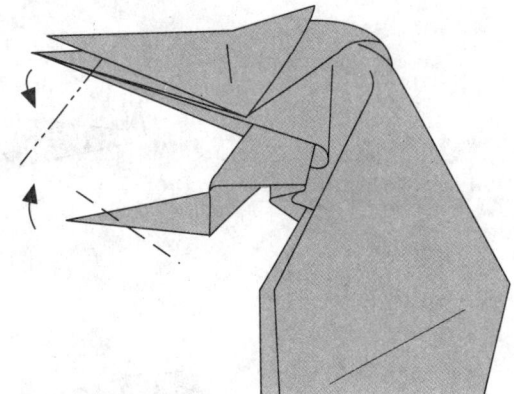

Reverse fold the lower jaw upwards.

Reverse fold the tips of the lower and upper jaws to form the teeth.

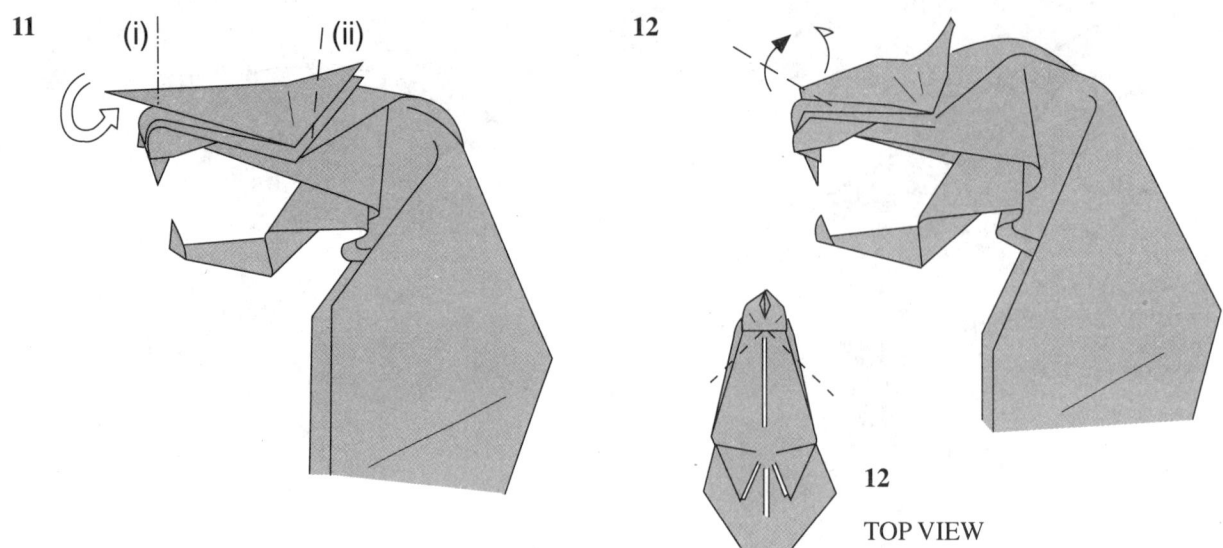

(i) Tuck in the tip of the flap at the nose area.
(ii) Fold the triangular flaps forward to form the horny ridges above the eyes.

Fold upwards to form the nostrils.

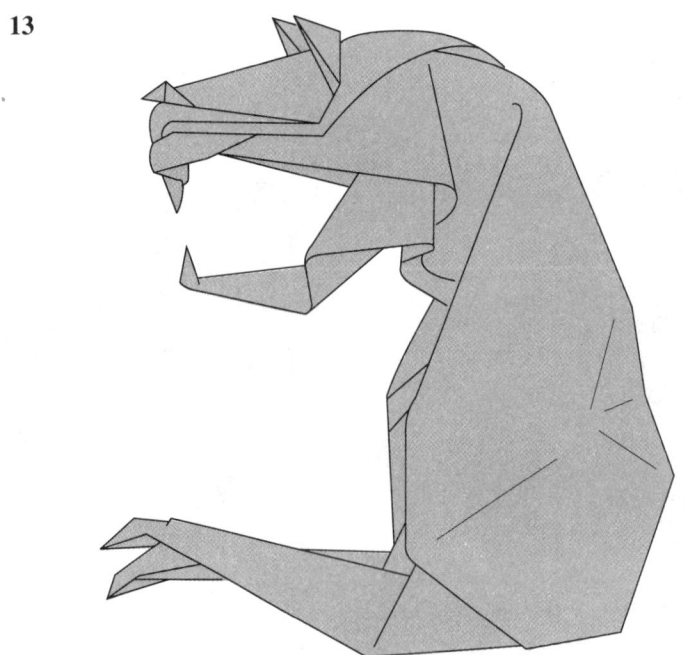

The completed *Allosaurus* head

Sink fold (see *Tyrannosaurus* model step 10(iii)) the area at the back of the head. This forms the shape for the neck and shoulders.

The *Allosaurus* body

14 **15**

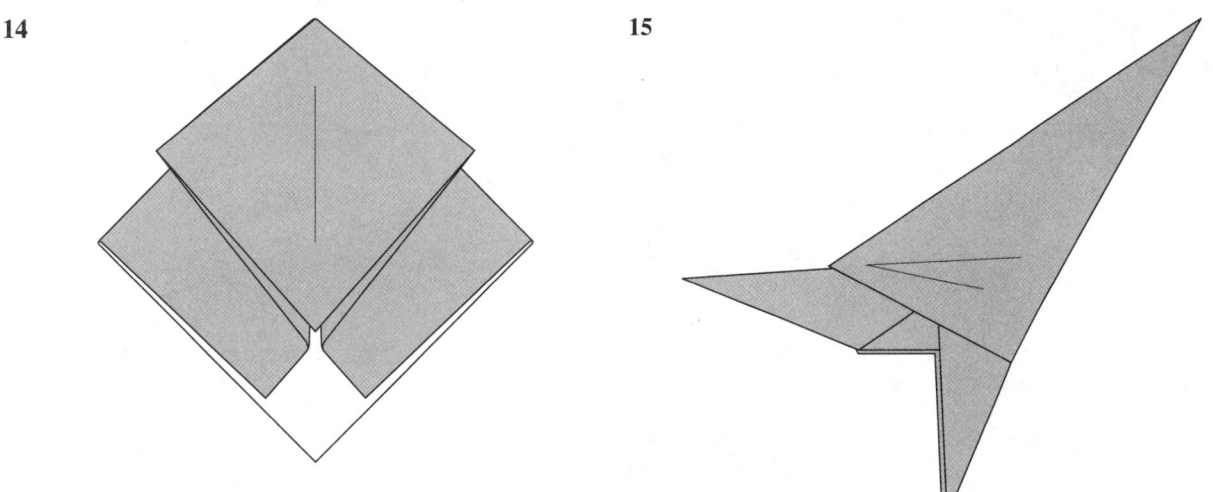

(i) Use a piece of 21 cm square paper.
(ii) Start by folding an offset preliminary base, offset 1.5 cm.
(iii) Proceed to fold a tail base A.

Follow steps 12(iv) to 17 of the *Tyrannosaurus* model.

16

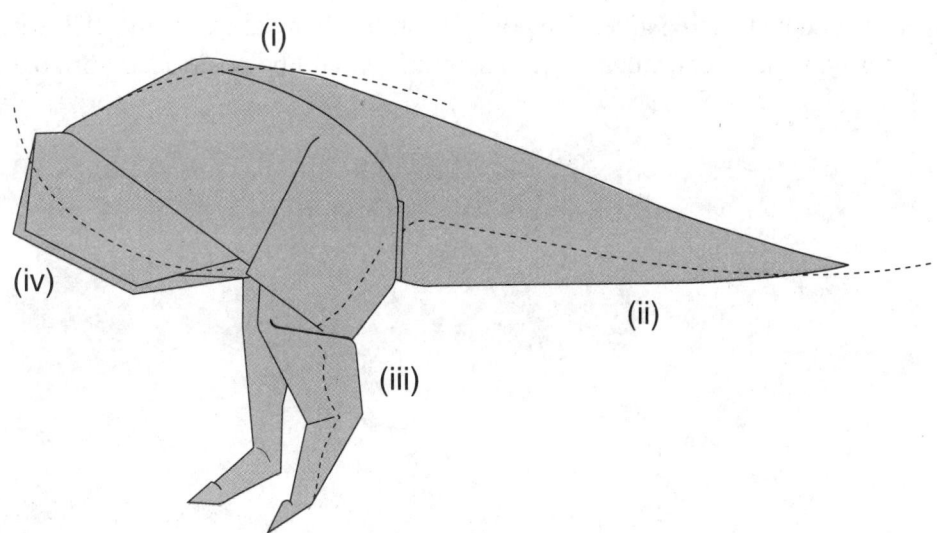

The completed *Allosaurus* body and tail

You can easily change the shape by folding in on the following areas :
(i) Back : Tuck in to make the back flatter or pull to make it more hunched.
(ii) Tail : Fold inwards to vary the thickness of the tail.
(iii) Legs : Fold inwards to vary the thickness of the leg.
        : Vary the positions of your leg folds to give them longer shins or longer thighs.
(iv) Belly : Tuck in and shape the underbelly to give it a fatter or thinner body.

17

The completed *Allosaurus* model

Join the head and body using glue. The postures of the big meat-eaters like *Allosaurus*, *Tyrannosaurus* and *Ceratosaurus* are very much alike. Their tails should be positioned horizontally.

Megalosaurus

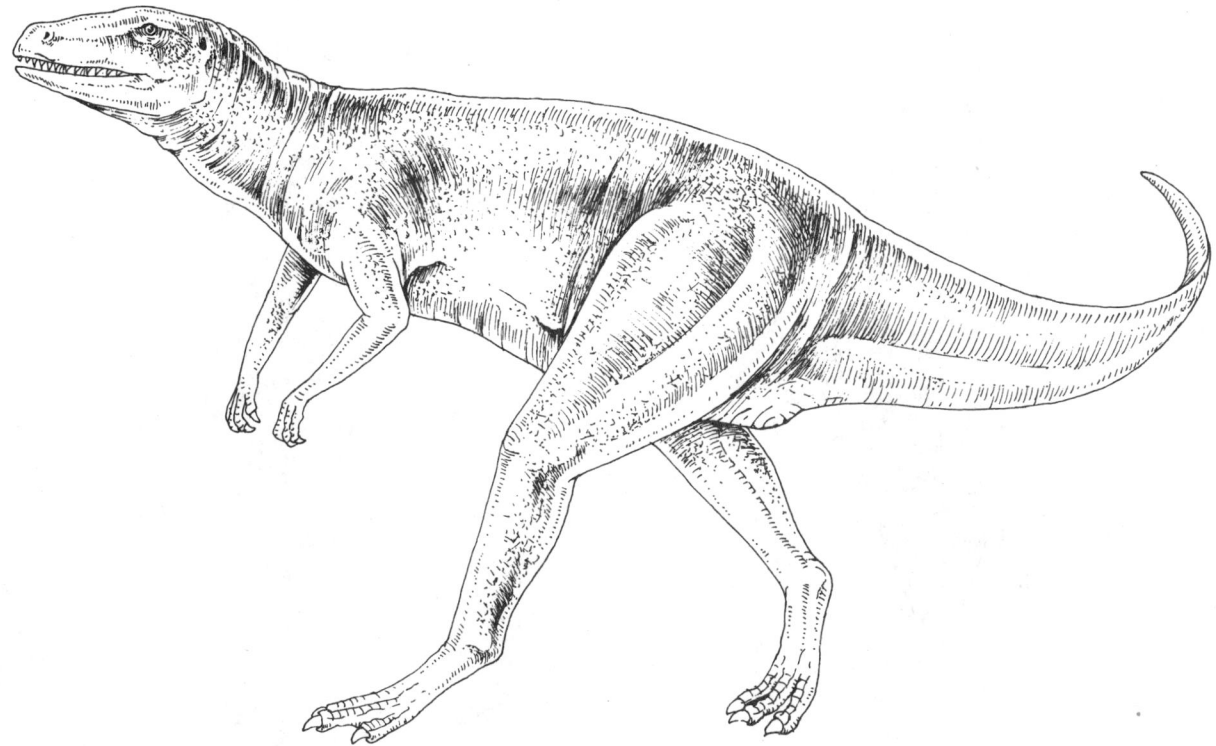

Megalosaurus (meaning "big reptile") was a large meat-eating theropod living during the Early Jurassic period. This fearsome hunter is about 30 ft (9 m) long, has a curved flexible neck, and powerful limbs. The head of this dinosaur is narrow and its jaws are lined with blade-like serrated teeth.

The *Megalosaurus* head

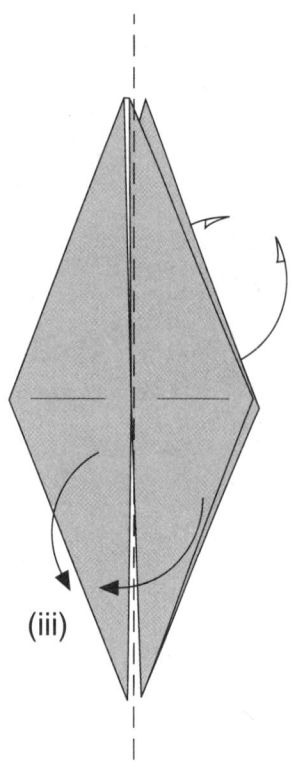

(i) Use a piece of 15 cm square paper.
(ii) Start by folding a bird base.
(iii) Fold the opposite sides together.

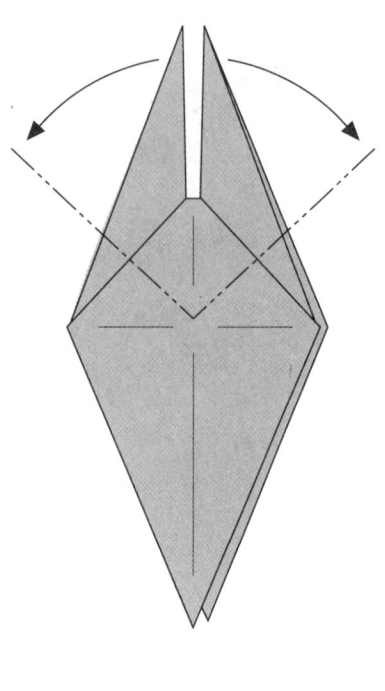

Reverse fold 90 degrees downwards to form the forelimbs.

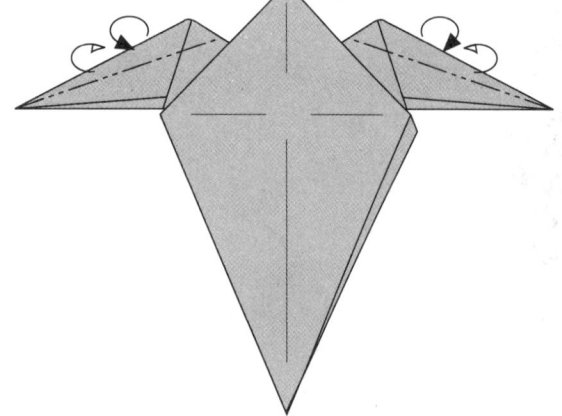

Fold inwards to make the forelimbs thinner. This fold will determine the thickness of the forelimbs.

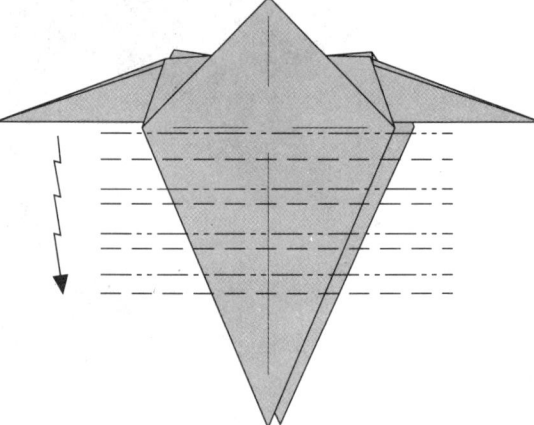

Do a series a "pleats" i.e. a mountain fold followed by a valley fold on the two bottom flaps. This forms the neck and gives it a "stretched" look.

5

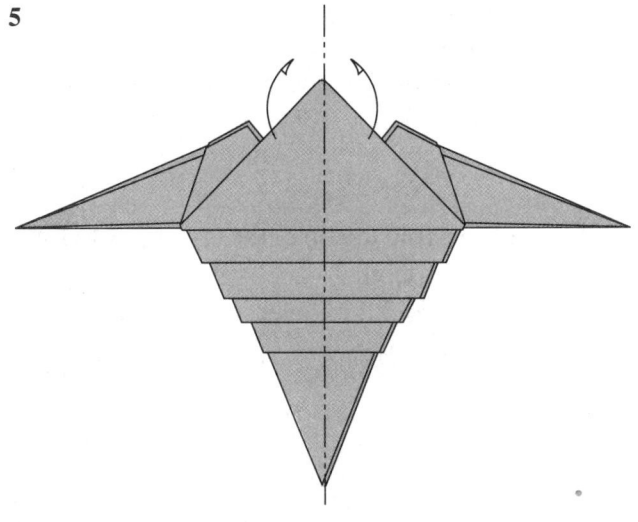

Fold the model in half.

6

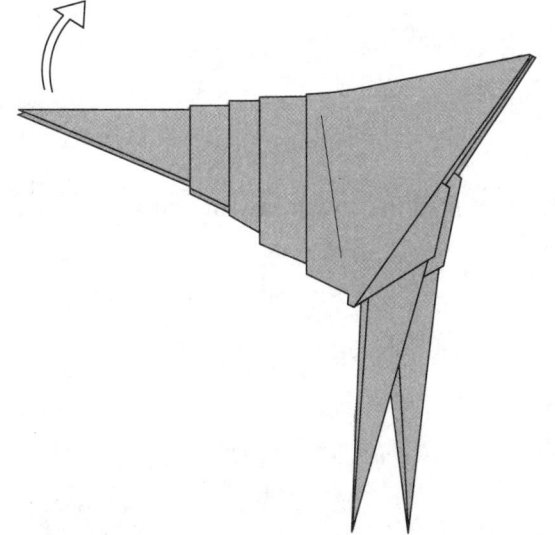

Arch the neck upwards.

7

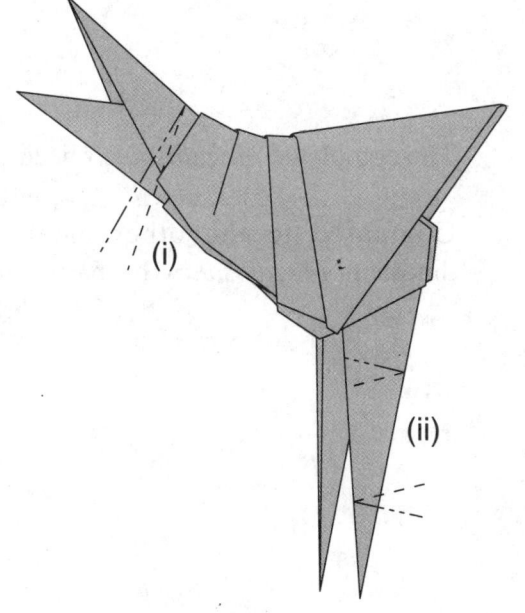

(i) Crimp fold both layers downwards to form the head with a lower jaw.
(ii) Crimp fold the forelimbs to form the elbows and hands (refer to the *Allosaurus* or *Ceratosaurus* models).

8

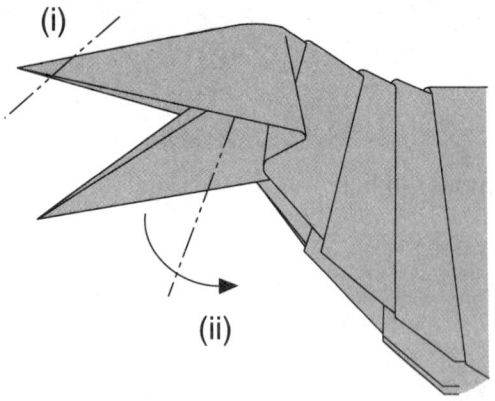

(i) Reverse fold the tip of the upper jaw to form the upper teeth.
(ii) Reverse fold the lower jaw downwards.

9

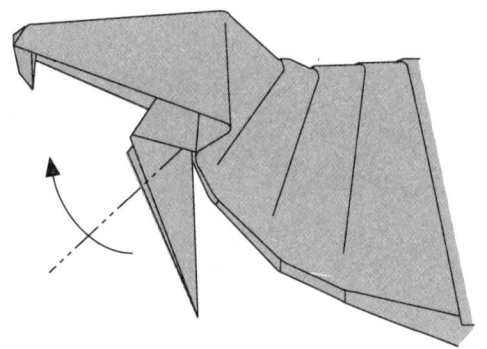

Reverse fold the lower jaw upwards.

10

The completed *Megalosaurus* head

Compared to the other meat-eating dinosaurs, *Megalosaurus* has narrower jaws.

The *Megalosaurus* body

11

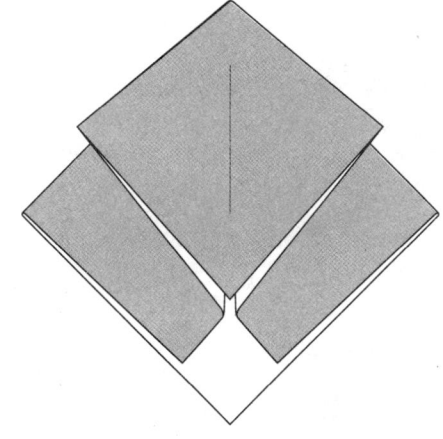

12

(i) Use a 21 cm square piece of paper.
(ii) Start by folding an offset preliminary base, offset 2 cm.
(iii) Proceed to fold a tail base A.

Follow steps 12(iv) to 17 of the *Tyrannosaurus* model. The body shape of *Megalosaurus* should be very similar to *Ceratosaurus*.

13

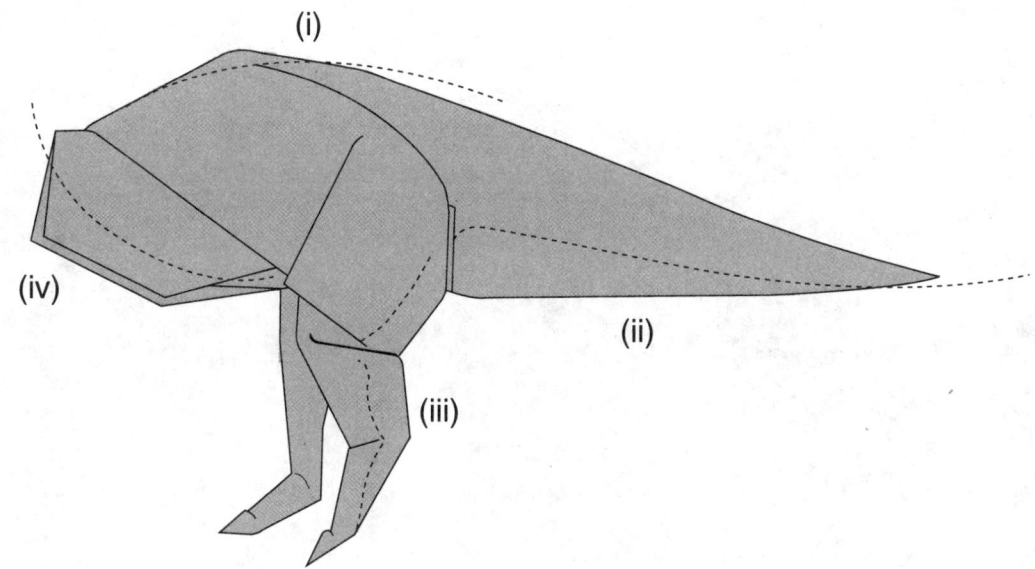

The completed *Megalosaurus* body and tail

You can easily change the shape by folding in on the following areas :
  (i) Back: Tuck in to make the back flatter or pull to make it more hunched.
 (ii) Tail : Fold inwards to vary the thickness of the tail.
(iii) Legs : Fold inwards to vary the thickness of the leg.
      : Vary the positions of the leg folds to give them longer shins or longer thighs.
(iv) Belly : Tuck in and shape the underbelly to give it a fatter or thinner body.

14

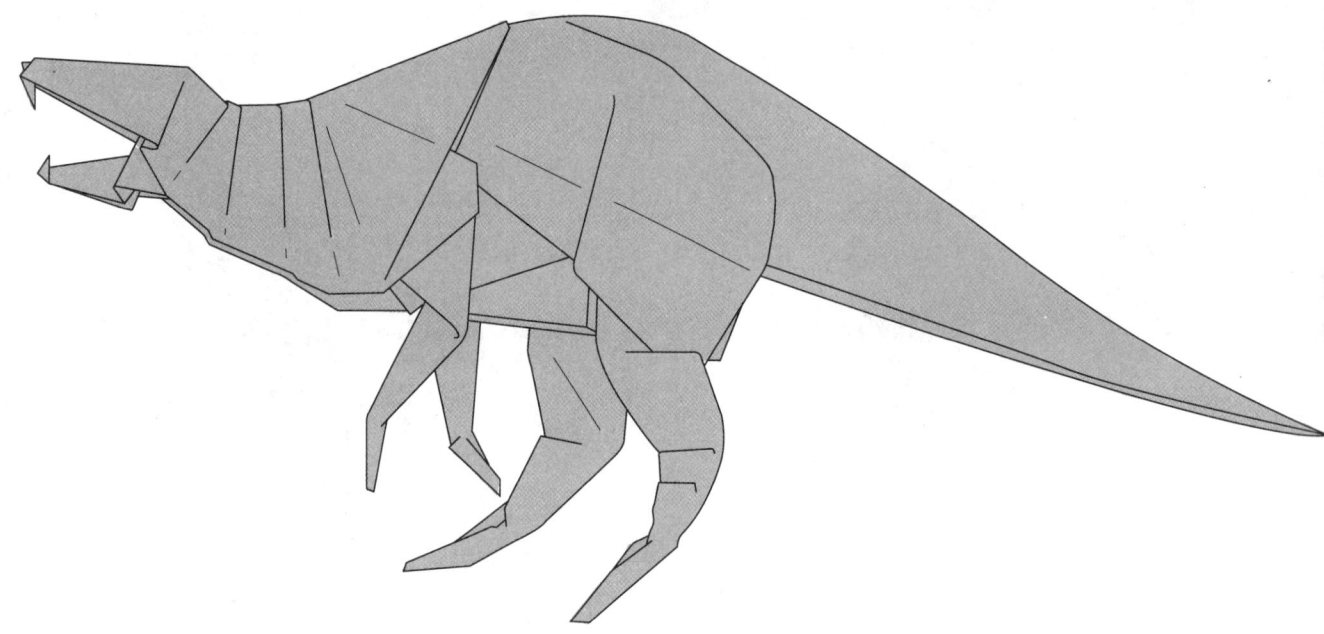

The completed *Megalosaurus* model

Join the head and body using glue. The *Megalosaurus* here has been given a crouching posture with its neck arched upwards.

Deinonychus

Deinonychus, nicknamed "Terrible Claw", is a swift, medium-sized theropod (13 ft /4 m). However, it is much larger than its relatives, *Velociraptor* and *Dromaeosaurus*. On the second toe of each foot is a massive sickle-shaped claw that has earned *Deinonychus* its nickname. This massive claw is used as its primary weapon in attacking prey. Its strong tail aids in balancing when *Deinonychus* uses its legs as a weapon.

The *Deinonychus* head

1

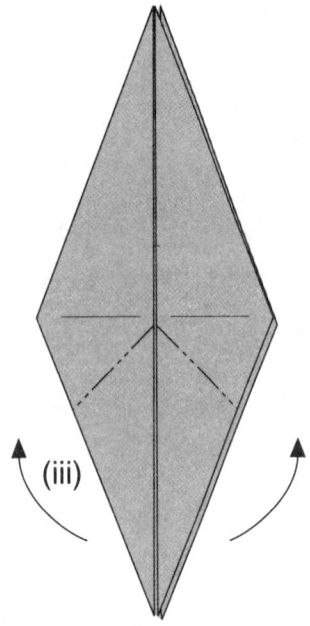

(i) Use a piece of 14 cm square paper.
(ii) Start folding a bird base.
(iii) Reverse fold the two forelimbs upwards.

2

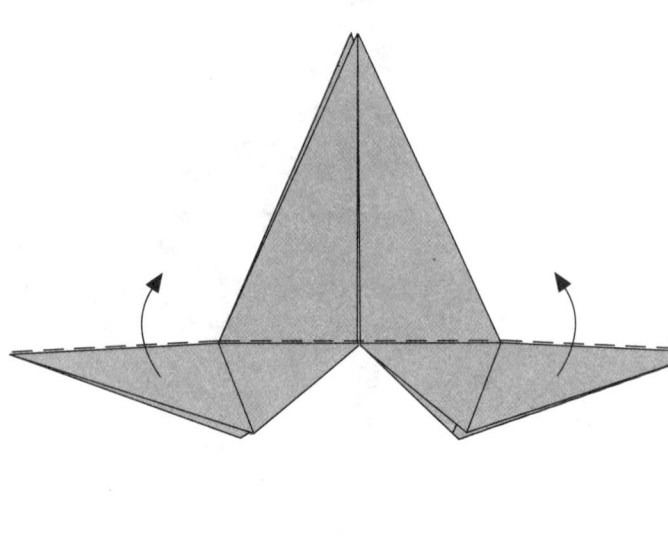

Open up the two flaps.

3

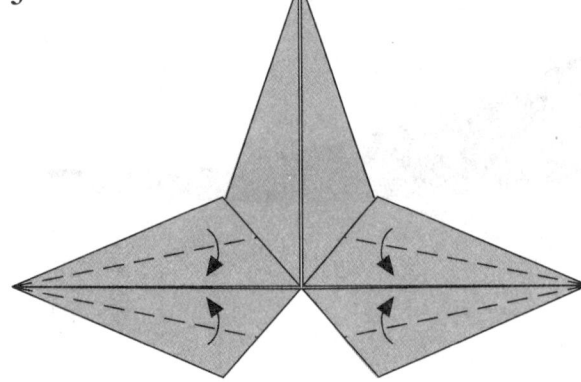

Fold inwards to make the forelimbs thinner.

4

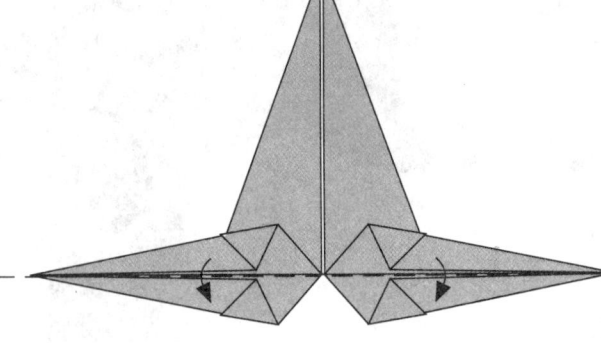

Fold downwards.

86

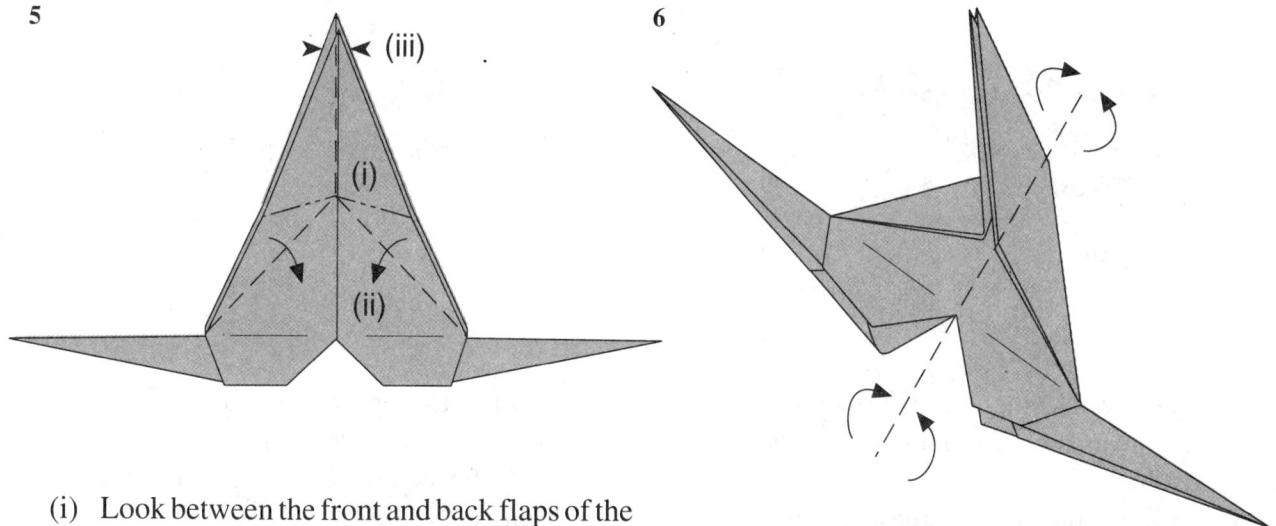

(i) Look between the front and back flaps of the top portion. You will see a triangular section. The tip of the triangular section is where you want your creases to meet.
(ii) Valley fold to the right and left to make the left and right creases. Make sure these creases meet at the position in (i).
(iii) Fold the right and left edges (both layers) inwards along the creases made in (ii). The upper portion will automatically lift (see step 6).

Fold the model in half.

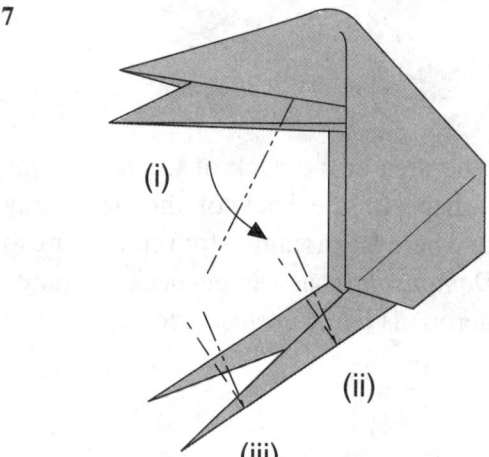

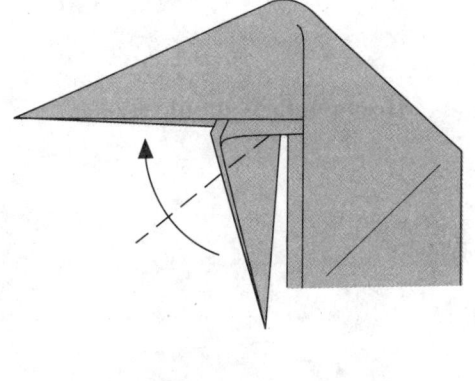

(i) Reverse fold downwards the lower flap to form the lower jaw.
(ii) Crimp fold upwards to form the elbows.
(iii) Crimp fold upwards to form the hands. Curve the hands in a C-shape to form its sickle-shaped claws.

Reverse fold the lower jaw upwards.

9

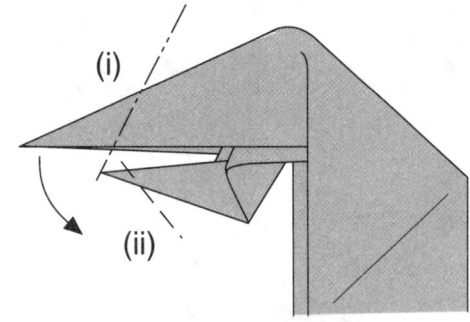

(i) Reverse fold the end of the upper portion downwards to form its snout and upper teeth.
(ii) Reverse fold the tip of the lower jaw to form the lower teeth.

10

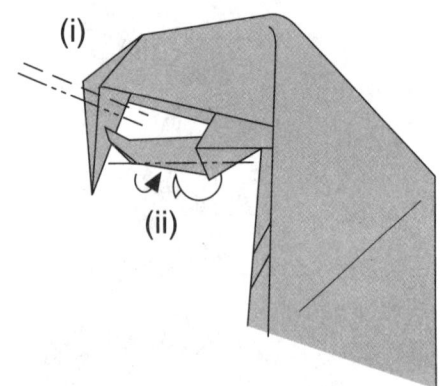

(i) Shorten the upper teeth by folding them upwards and downwards again.
(ii) At the lower jaw, fold inwards to make them thinner.

11

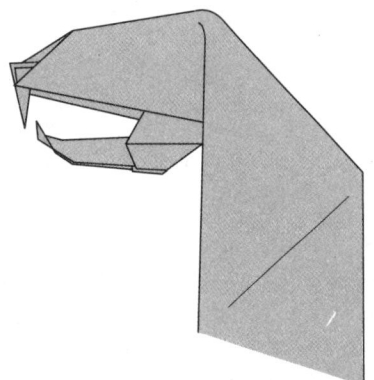

How the face should look

12

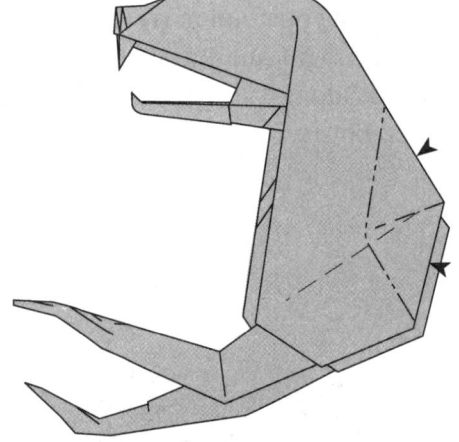

Sink fold the area at the back of the head. This gives the shape of the back of the head. Pay attention to where the mountain fold creases are to be made. *Deinonychus* has a longer neck compared to other theropods like *Ceratosaurus*.

13

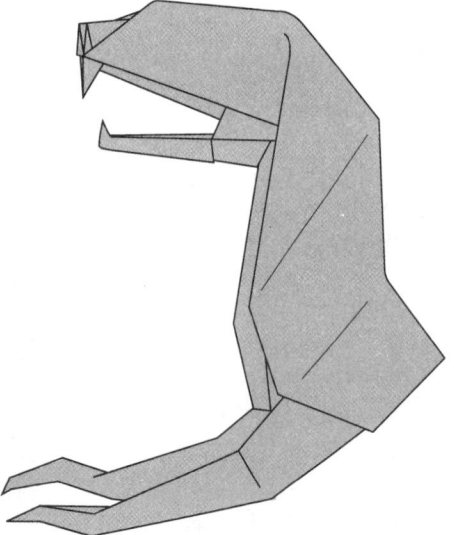

The completed *Deinonychus* head

The *Deinonychus* body

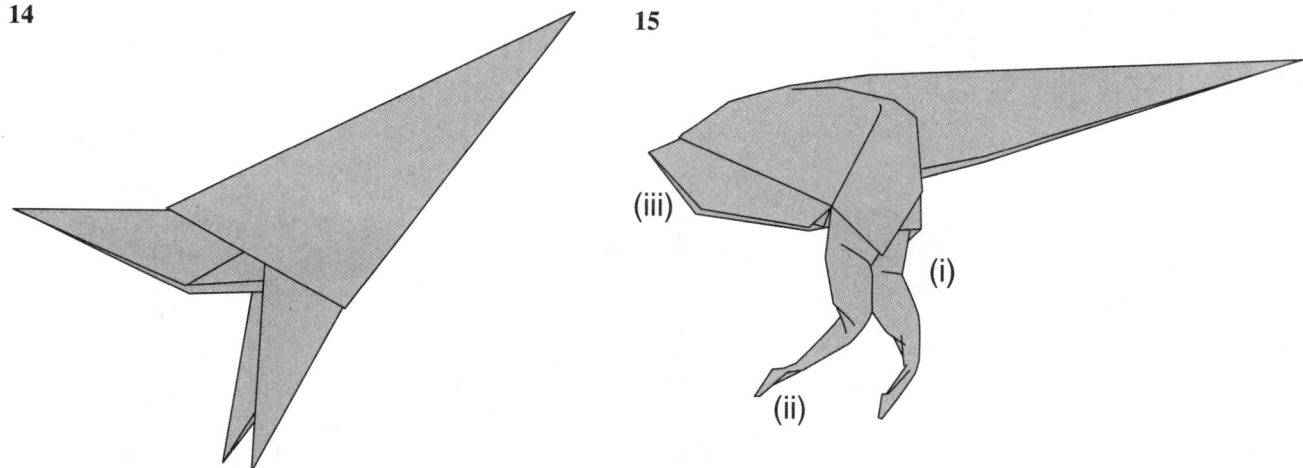

(i) Use a 21 cm square piece of paper.
(ii) Fold an offset preliminary base, offset 3 cm.
(iii) Fold a tail base A.
(iv) Follow steps 16(iv) to 26 of the *Compsognathus* model. Note that *Deinonychus* should have a thicker tail and legs than *Compsognathus*.
(v) Do step 27(ii) of the *Compsognathus* model.

(i) Crimp fold to form the ankles and feet (see any dinosaur model). You will want to make the feet slightly longer.
(ii) Curve the feet in a C-shape to form the sickle-shaped claws..
(iii) Tuck in the rest of the body as shown. (You can fold any way you like, just keep the folds hidden.)

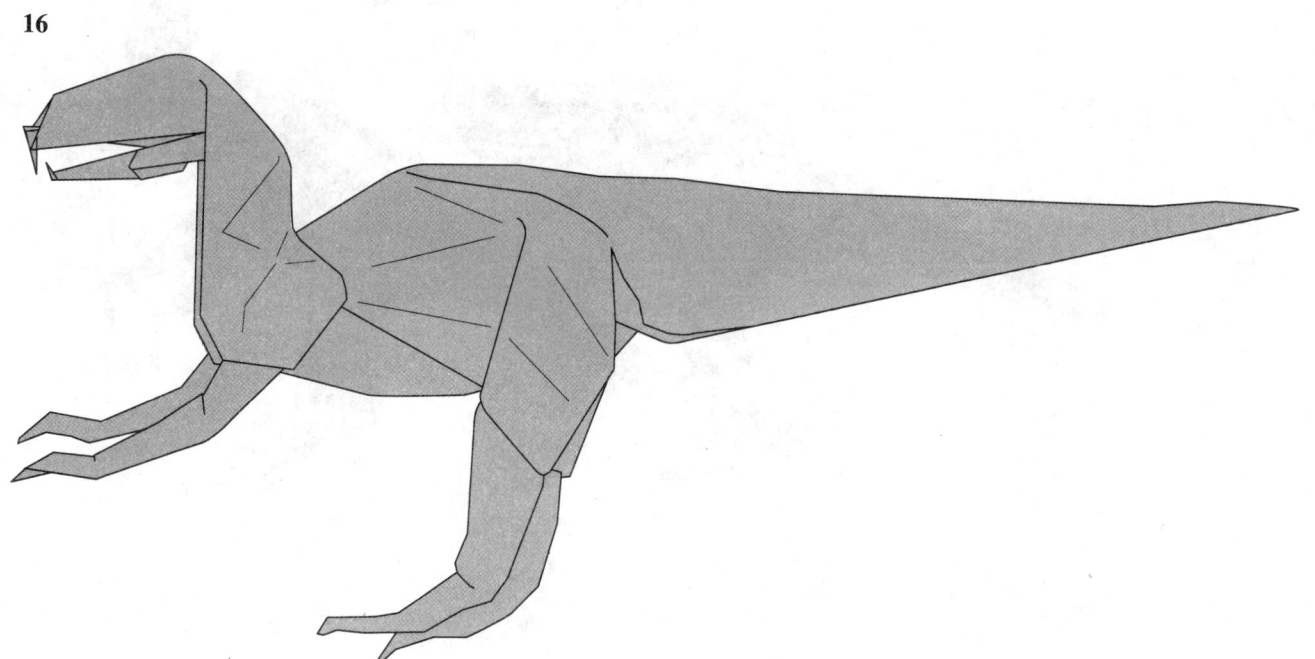

The completed *Deinonychus* model

Join the head and body together using glue. *Deinonychus* is a very agile hunter, using its claws to slash at its prey. The posture that you adopt for it should not be "docile".

Coelophysis

Coelophysis (meaning "hollow form") was a small (10 ft /3 m long) meat-eating theropod which lived during the Late Triassic to Early Jurassic periods. It has a long neck, a longish and flattish head, long forelimbs, a slim body and a long tail. It is a very fleet-footed dinosaur.

The *Coelophysis* head

1

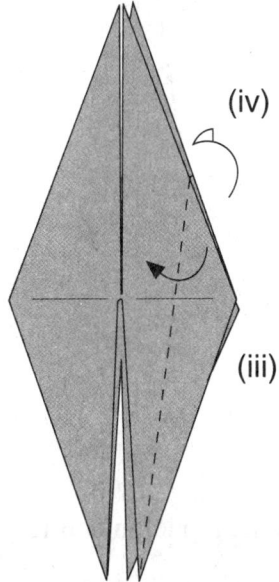

(i) Use a thin piece of 15 cm square paper.
(ii) Start from a bird base.
(iii) Fold the right edge towards the middle.
(iv) Repeat for the reverse side of the model.

2

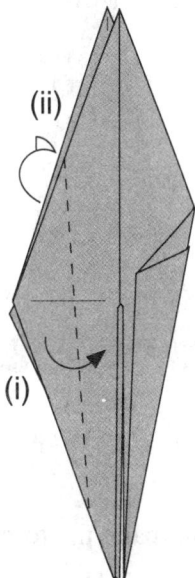

(i) Fold the left edge towards the middle. Note that the crease does not meet at the bottom point.
(ii) Repeat for the reverse side.

3

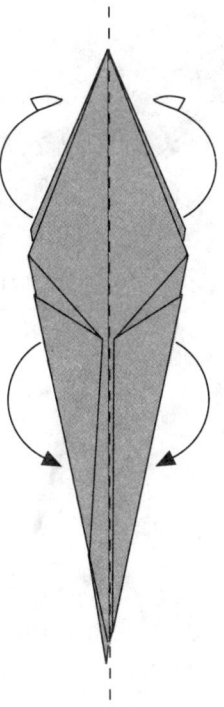

Fold the opposite sides together and then turn the model upside down 180 degrees to get to step 4. Note that the front flap has the pointed tip.

4

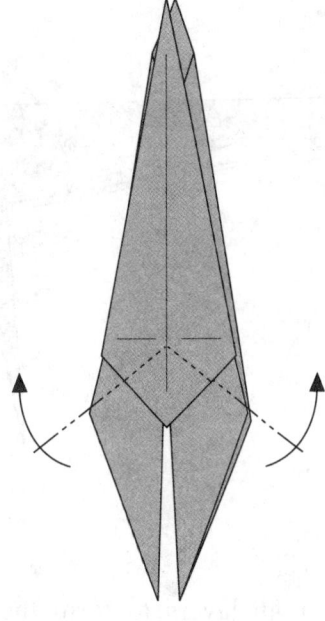

Reverse fold both flaps upwards to form the forelimbs.

5 6

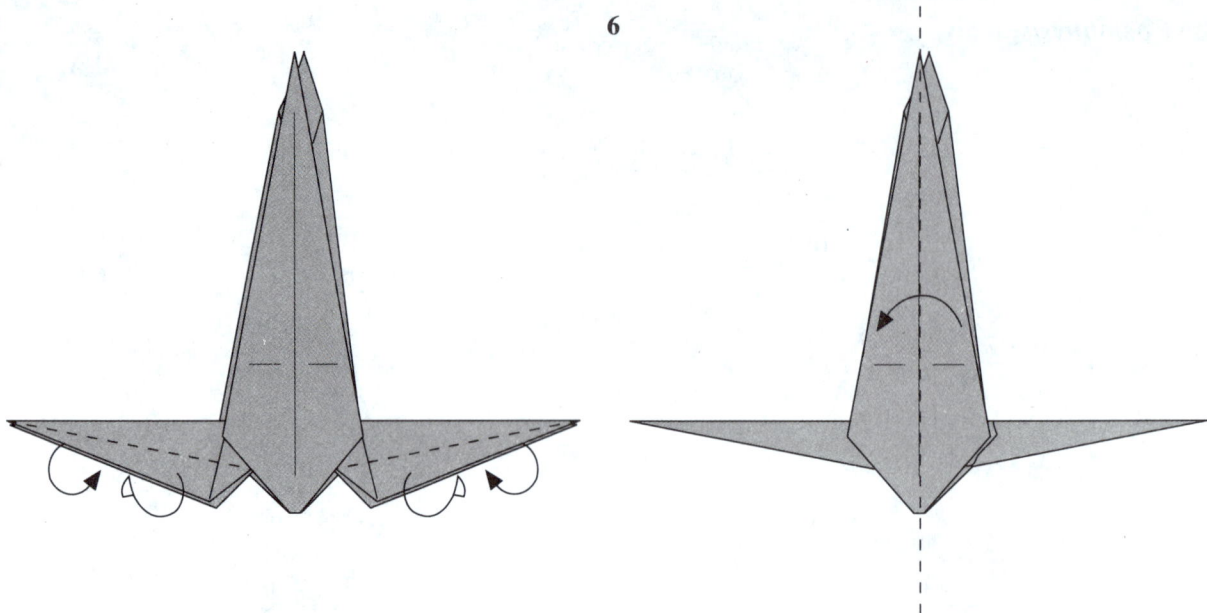

Fold inwards to make the forelimbs thinner.

Fold the model in half (forward).

7 8

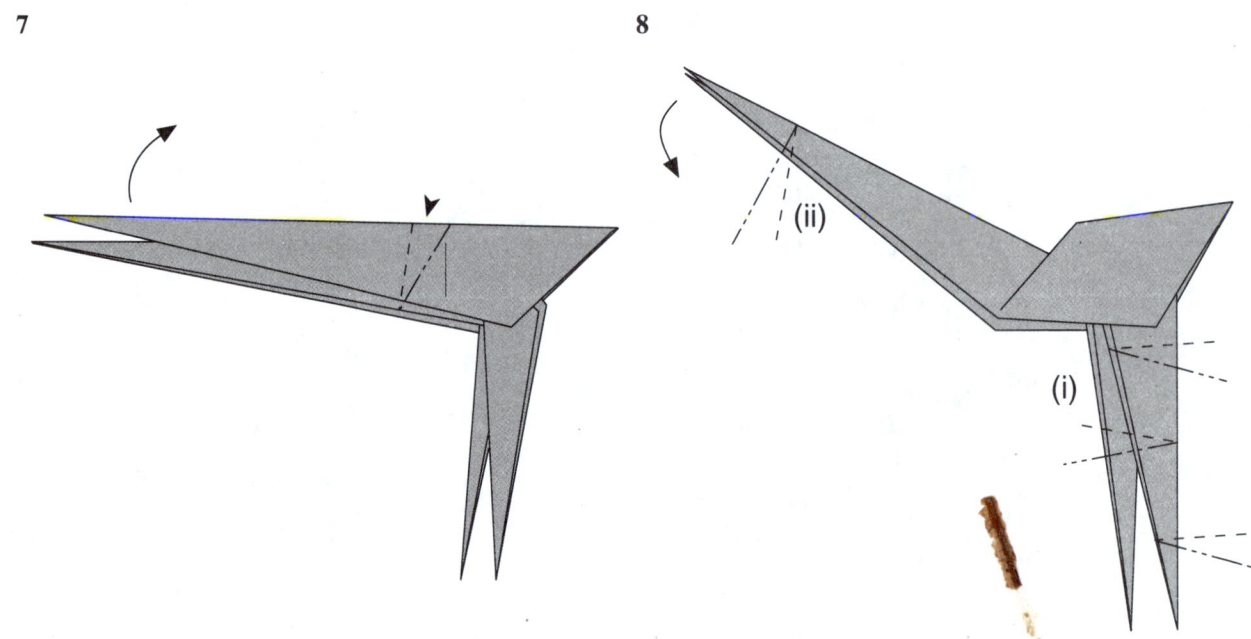

Crimp fold both layers to form the neck and shoulders. (To execute this fold, do a reverse fold downwards along the mountain fold crease and then reverse fold upwards along the valley fold crease.)

(i) Crimp fold the forelimbs to form the shoulder, elbow and hands as shown in step 9.
(ii) Crimp fold the neck downwards to form the head.

9

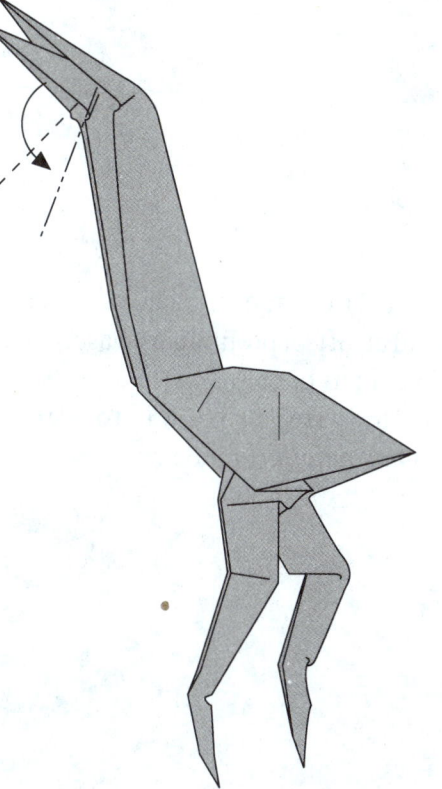

Pull down the lower flap and reverse fold downwards to form the lower jaw.

10

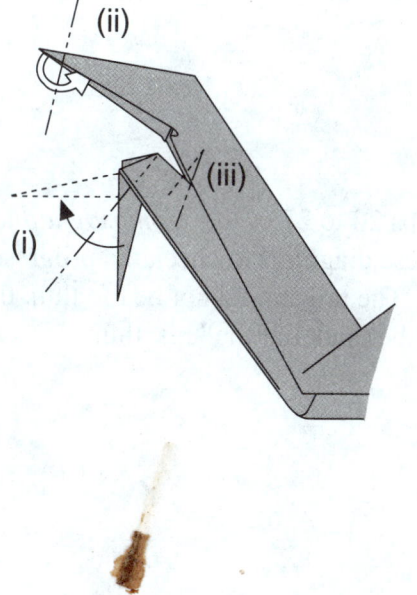

11

(i) Reverse fold the lower jaw upwards.
(ii) Tuck in the tip of the upper jaw. Make sure that the lengths of the lower jaw and the upper jaw are the same.
(iii) Crimp fold the neck near the base of the head to angle the head downwards.

The completed *Coelophysis* head

The *Coelophysis* body

12

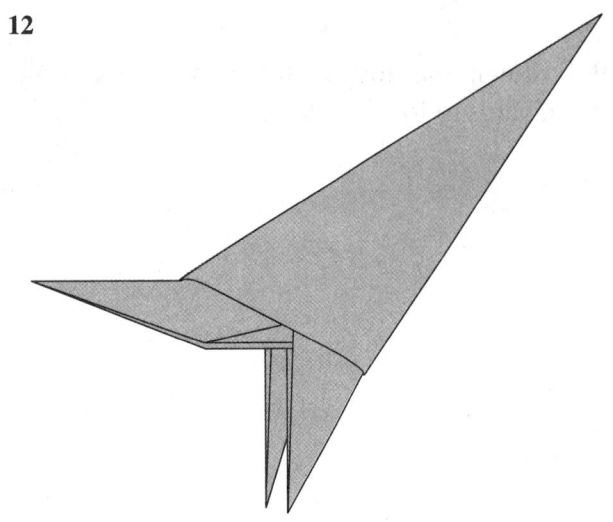

(i) Use a 21 cm square piece of paper.
(ii) Fold an offset preliminary base, offset 3 cm.
(iii) Fold a tail base A.
(iv) Follow steps 16(iv) to 19 of the *Compsognathus* model.

13

Do steps 20 to 27 of the *Compsognathus* model. Use these diagrams to check the progress of your model. The tail should not be too thin, the thighs should be thick but the legs thin.

14

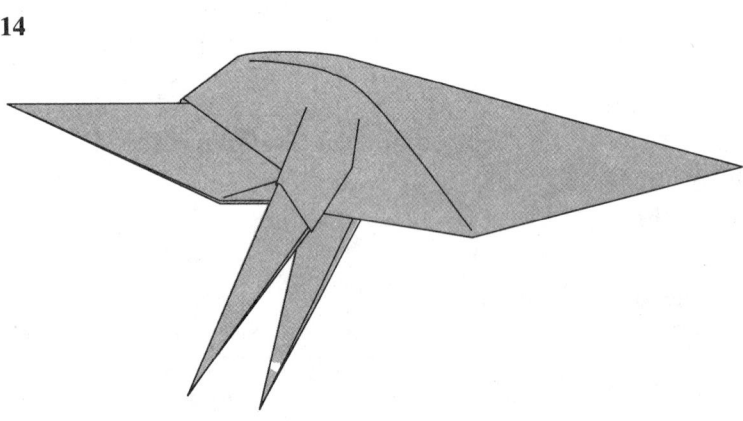

15

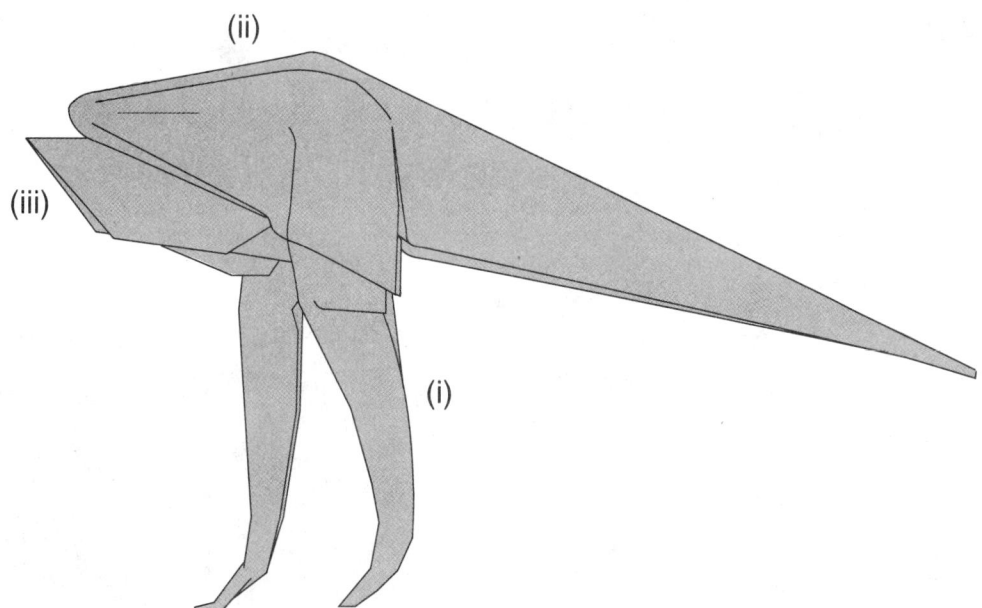

(i) Crimp fold to form the ankles and feet (see any dinosaur model). Give your model a longer shin to give it a more bird-like leg.
(ii) Flatten the back by folding in more paper at the back crease.
(ii) Tuck in the body to give it a narrow tapering profile. The *Coelophysis* has a long, flattish and narrow body profile.

16

The completed *Coelophysis* model

Join the head and body with glue. The *Coelophysis* model is in an upright position.

Velociraptor

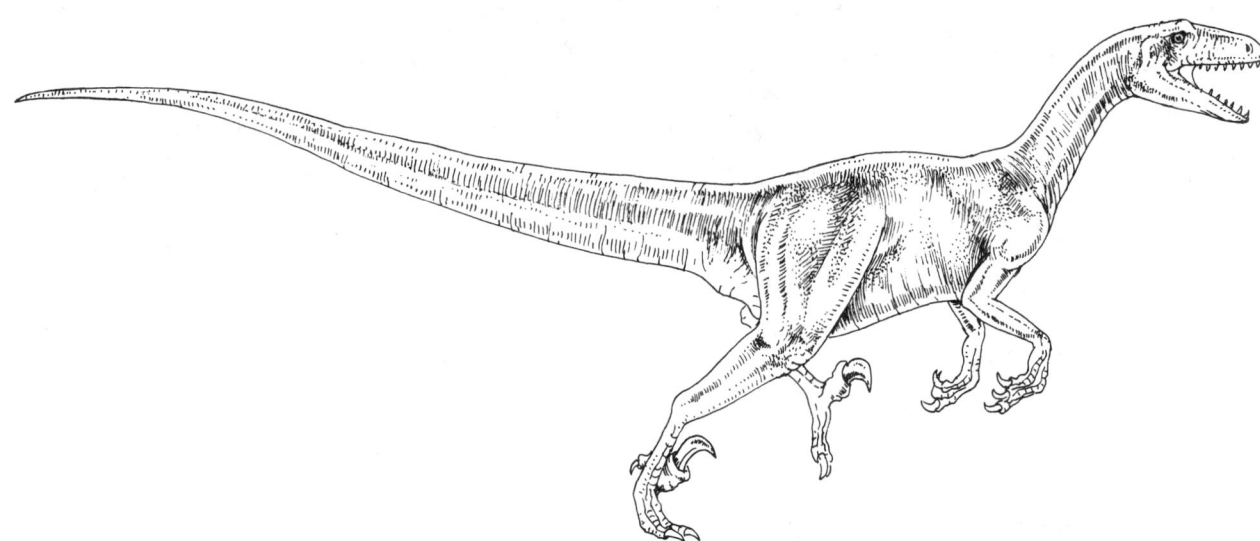

Velociraptor (meaning "swift robber") was a medium-sized meat-eating theropod (6 ft /1.8 m) which lived during the Late Cretaceous period. It is lightly built with long arms and slender legs that allow it to move swiftly and with agility. On its hands and legs are scythe-like claws that it uses for slashing its prey.

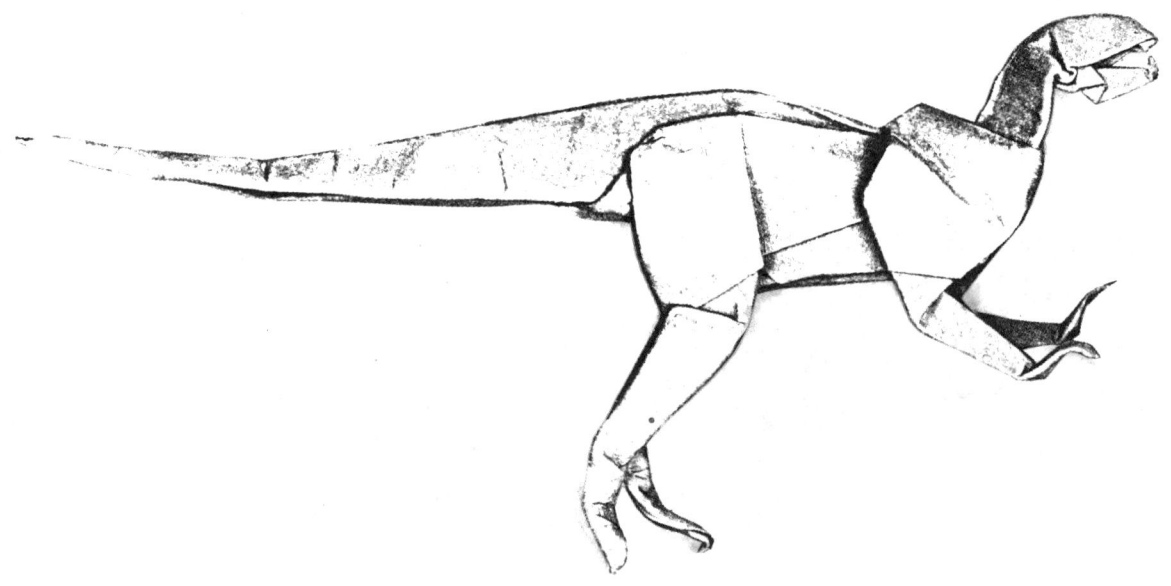

The *Velociraptor* head

1

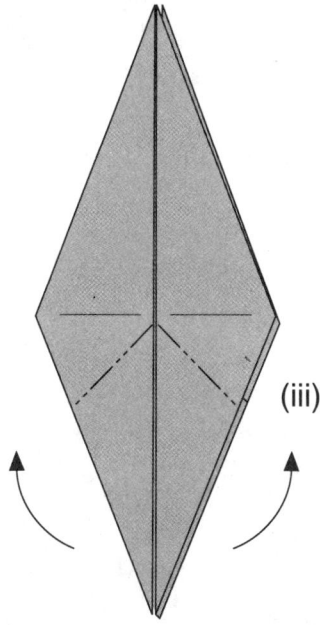

(i) Use a 15 cm square piece of paper.
(ii) Start from a bird base.
(iii) Reverse fold the two forelimbs upwards.

2

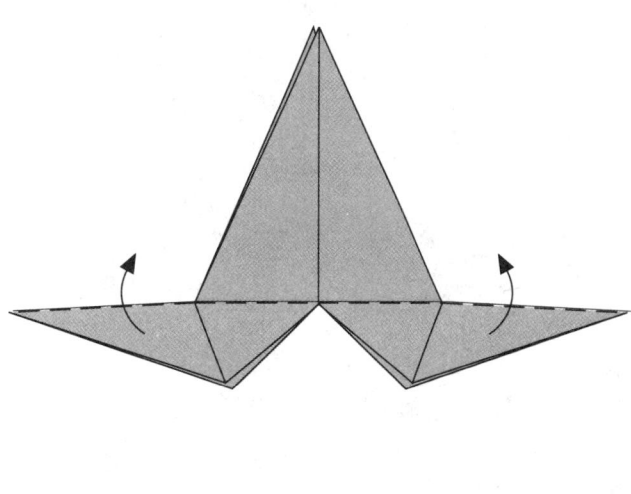

Open up the two flaps.

3

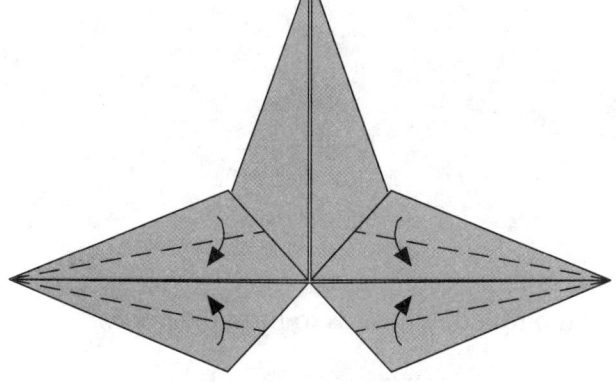

Fold inwards to make the forelimbs thinner.

4

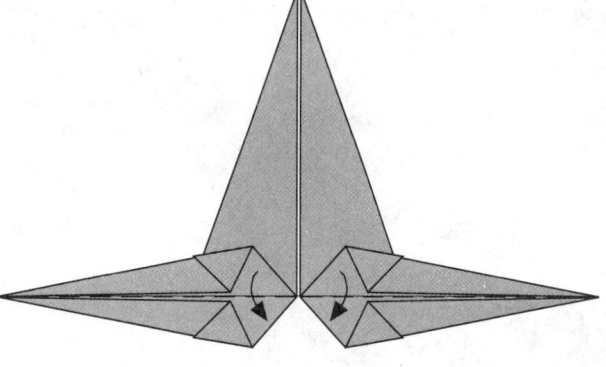

Fold down.

97

5

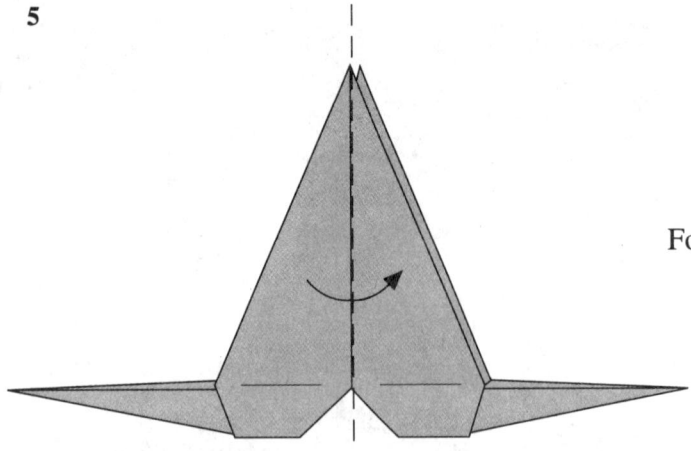

Fold the model in half.

6

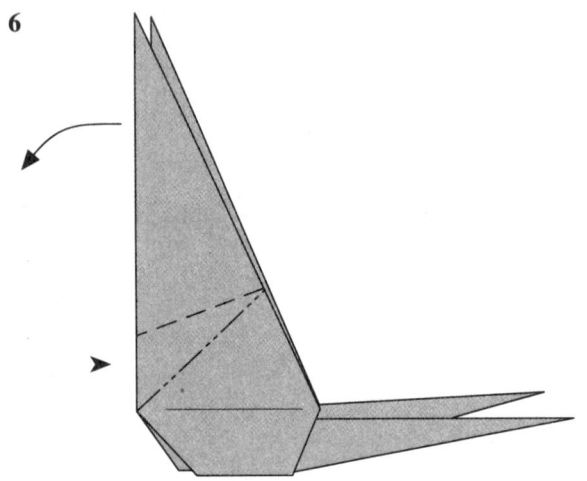

Crimp fold to form the neck and shoulders. (To execute this fold, reverse fold to the right along the mountain fold crease and then reverse fold upwards to the left along the valley fold crease.)

7

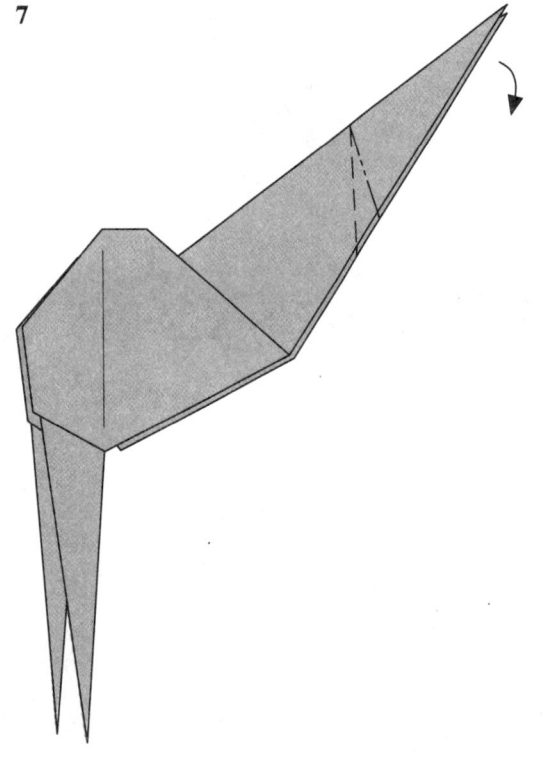

Crimp fold downwards to form the head.

8

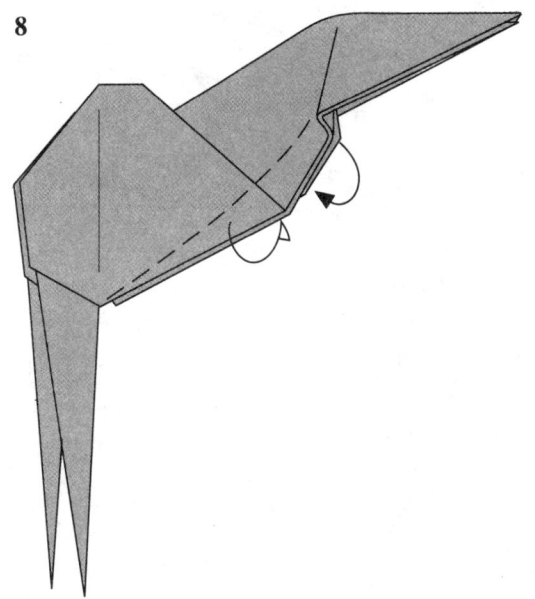

Tuck in the lower edge of the neck to make it thinner. The neck should be thinnest at the base of the head.

9

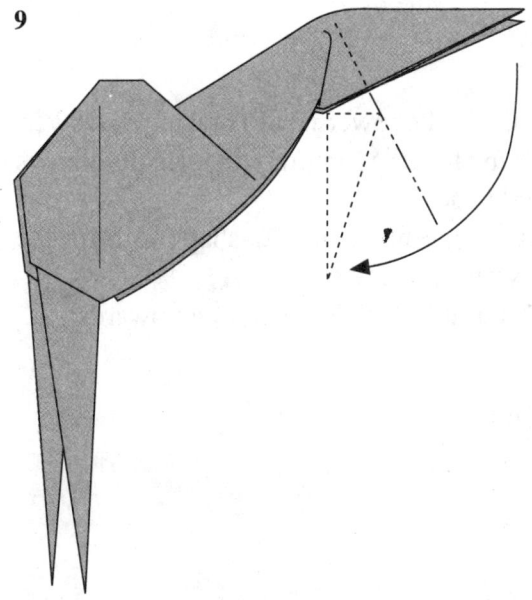

Reverse fold the lower flap downwards to form the lower jaw.

10

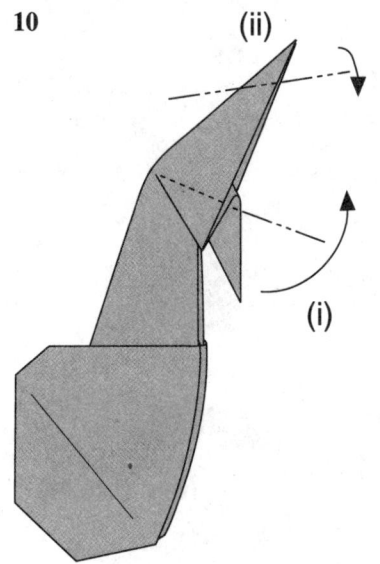

(i) Reverse fold the lower flap upwards to shape the lower jaw.
(ii) Reverse fold the upper jaw downwards to form the snout. Pay attention to the angle of this fold. The head of *Velociraptor* is narrow and tapering at the mouth. The lengths of the upper and lower jaw should be about the same.

11

Tuck in the tip of the upper jaw upwards.

12

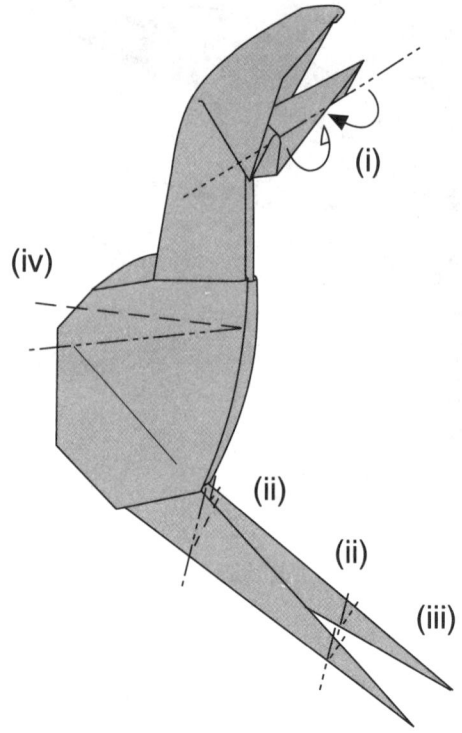

(i) Tuck in the lower jaw to make it narrower.
(ii) Crimp fold the forelimbs to form the elbows and hands.
(iii) Curve the hands in a C-shape to form the scythe-like claws.
(iv) Crimp fold the shoulder area upwards.

13

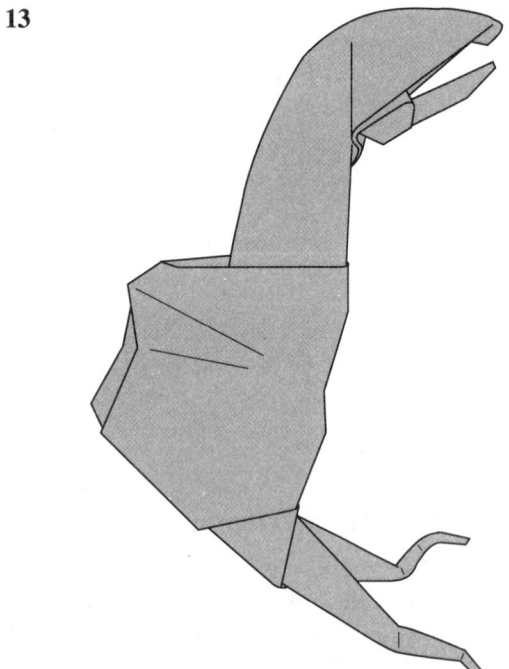

The completed *Velociraptor* head

The *Velociraptor* body

14

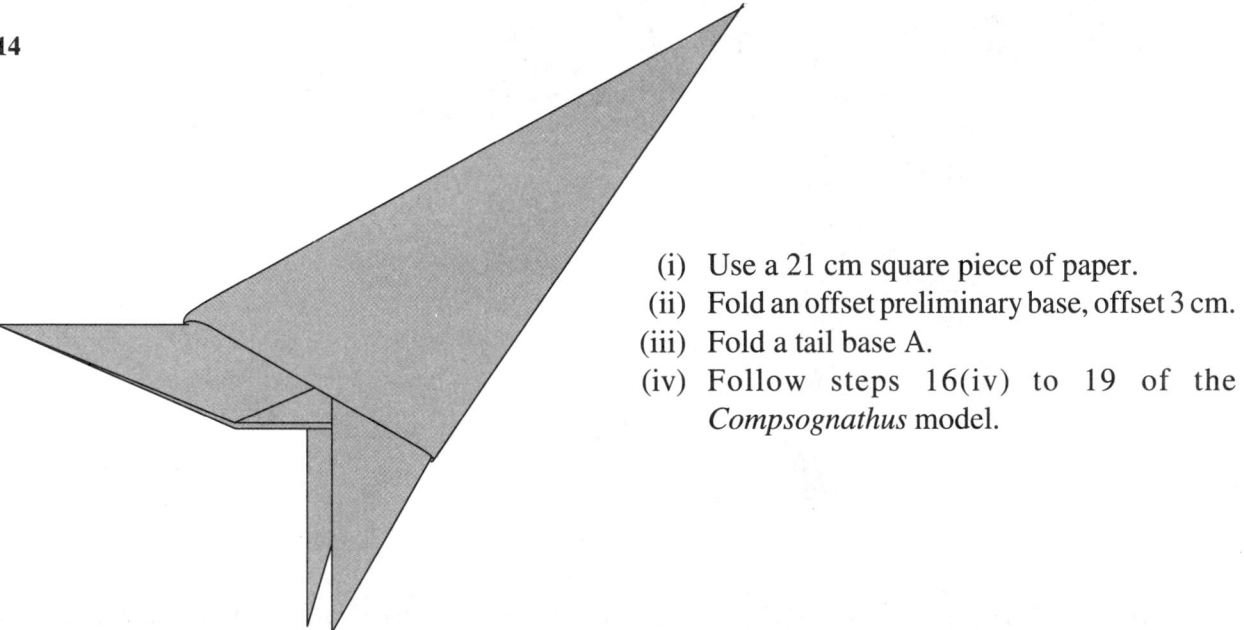

(i) Use a 21 cm square piece of paper.
(ii) Fold an offset preliminary base, offset 3 cm.
(iii) Fold a tail base A.
(iv) Follow steps 16(iv) to 19 of the *Compsognathus* model.

15

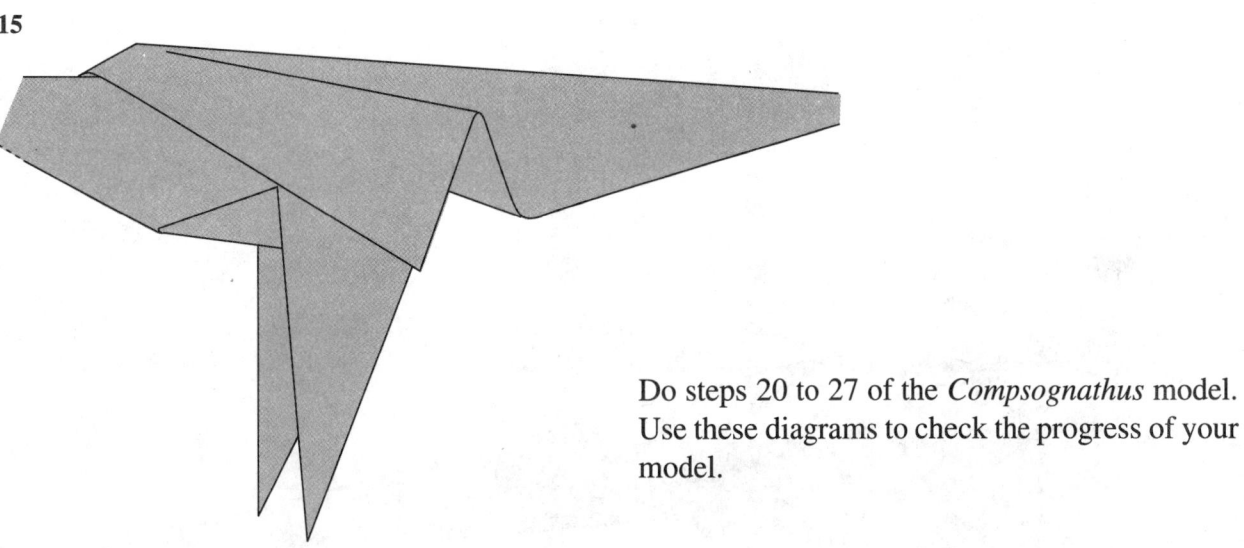

Do steps 20 to 27 of the *Compsognathus* model. Use these diagrams to check the progress of your model.

16

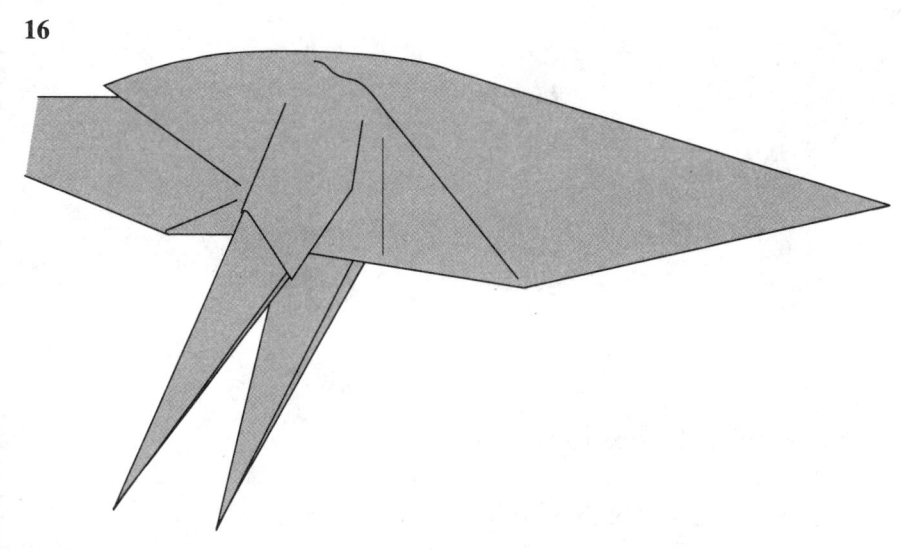

17

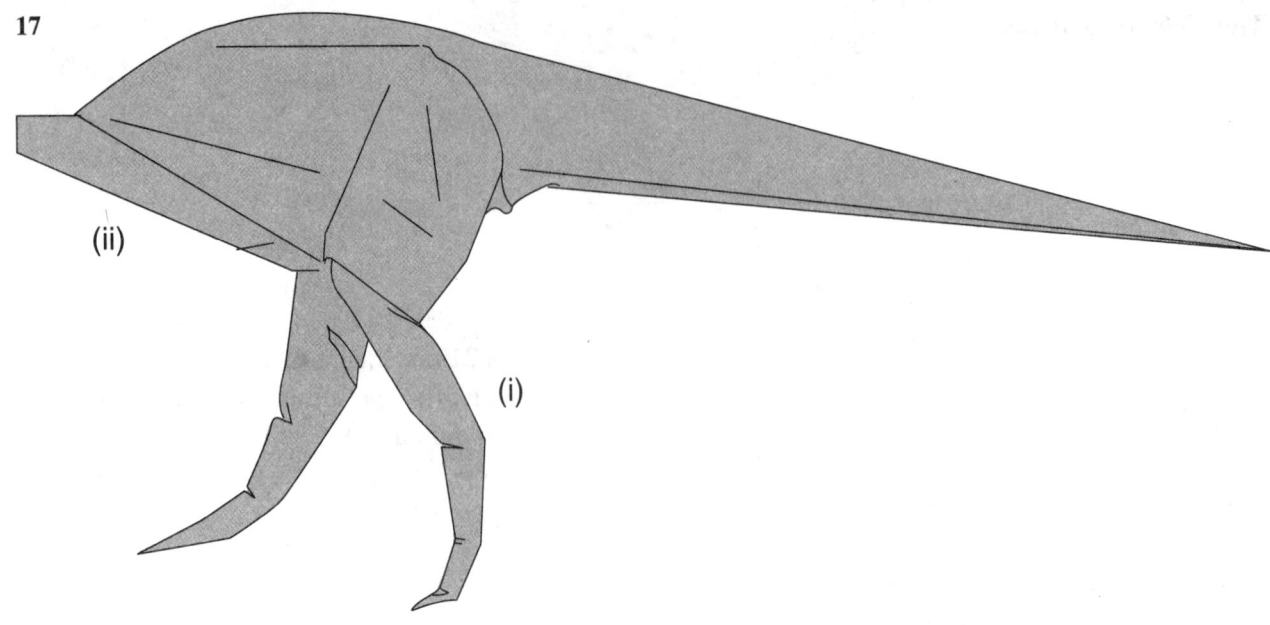

(i) Crimp fold to form the ankles and feet (see any dinosaur model). Give your model a longer shin to give it the bird-like legs.

(ii) Tuck in the body to give it a narrow tapering profile.

18

The completed *Velociraptor* model

Join the head and body with glue.

Brachiosaurus

Brachiosaurus is the tallest sauropod, measuring 75 ft (23 m) long and standing 40 ft (12 m) high (equivalent to a four-storey building). Because it has such a long neck, it does not need to rise on its hind legs to reach its food source. It has powerful forelimbs, short hind legs and a downward sloping back which ends in a short tail. The head of *Brachiosaurus* is crest-shaped and its teeth are spoon-shaped with sharp edges that are ideal for cutting and cropping leaves.

The *Brachiosaurus* head

1

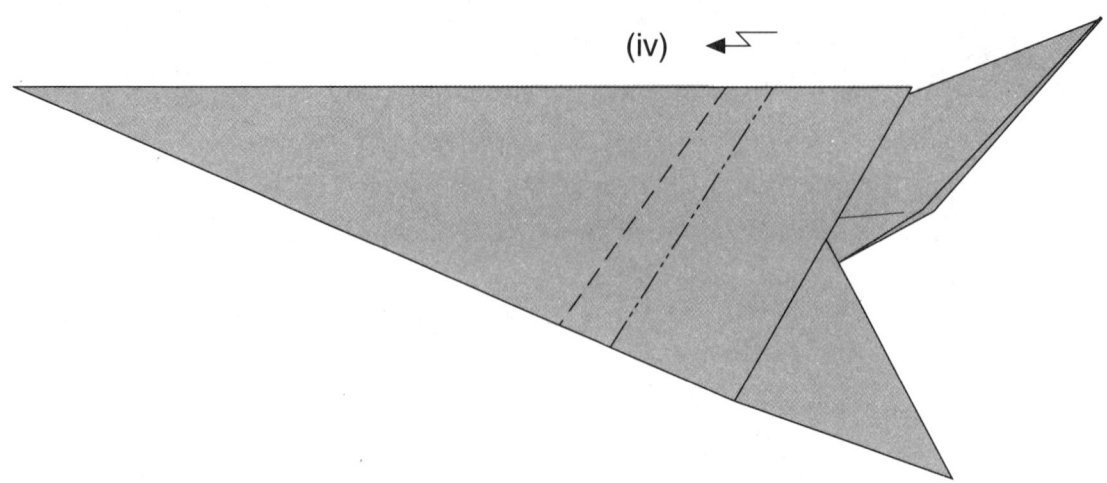

(i) Use a piece of 25 cm square paper.
(ii) Fold an offset preliminary base, offset 7 cm.
(iii) Fold a tail base B.
(iv) Crimp fold to form the shoulders and neck. (Do a reverse fold downwards along the mountain fold crease, then a reverse fold upwards along the valley fold crease.) Note the position of these folds which define the neck and shoulders. The longer the forelimbs, the shorter will be the length of the neck.

2

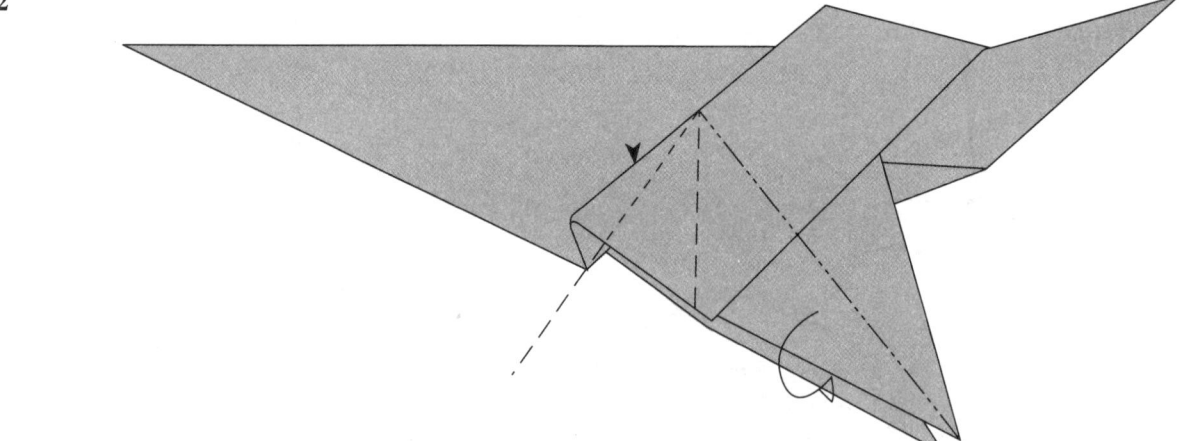

Halve the thickness of the forelimbs by folding the outer edge inwards. Lift the legs up and backwards (to the right) to help you execute this fold. Repeat for the other side.

3

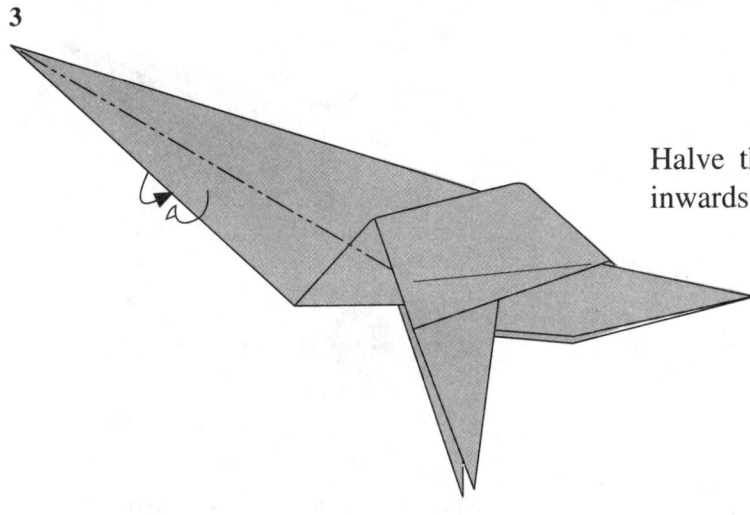

Halve the thickness of the neck by folding it inwards.

4

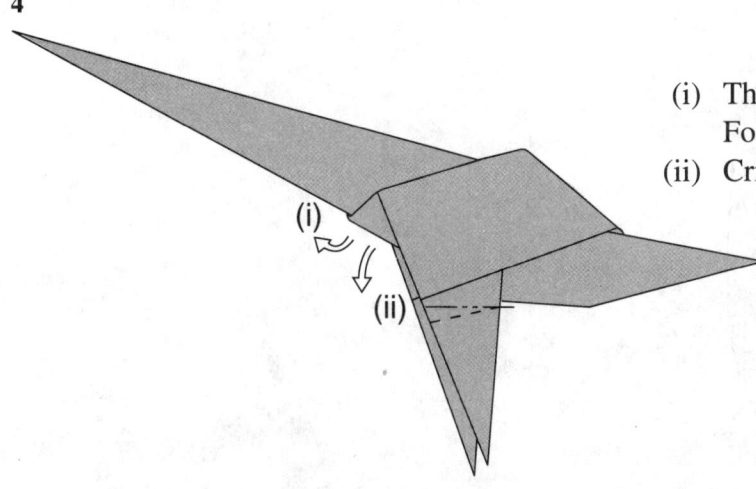

(i) The base of the neck must be properly folded. Follow step 5 of the *Diplodocus* model.
(ii) Crimp fold to bend the forelimbs forward.

5

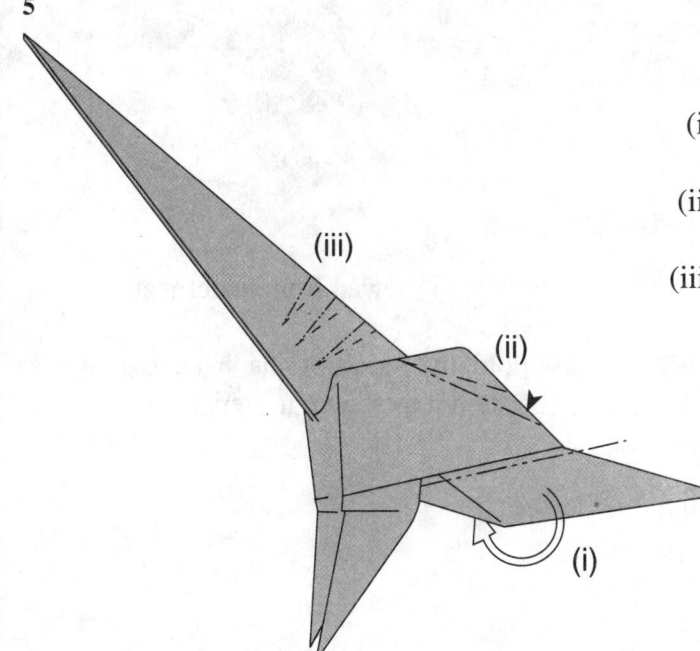

(i) Tuck in the rest of the body. Fold any way you like, so long as you hide it from view.
(ii) (Optional) Crimp fold the back so that the muscular back muscles are shaped.
(iii) Bend the neck to an upright position by making a series of crimp folds along the back of the neck. (The easiest way is to open up the neck and make a series of mountain and valley folds.)

105

6

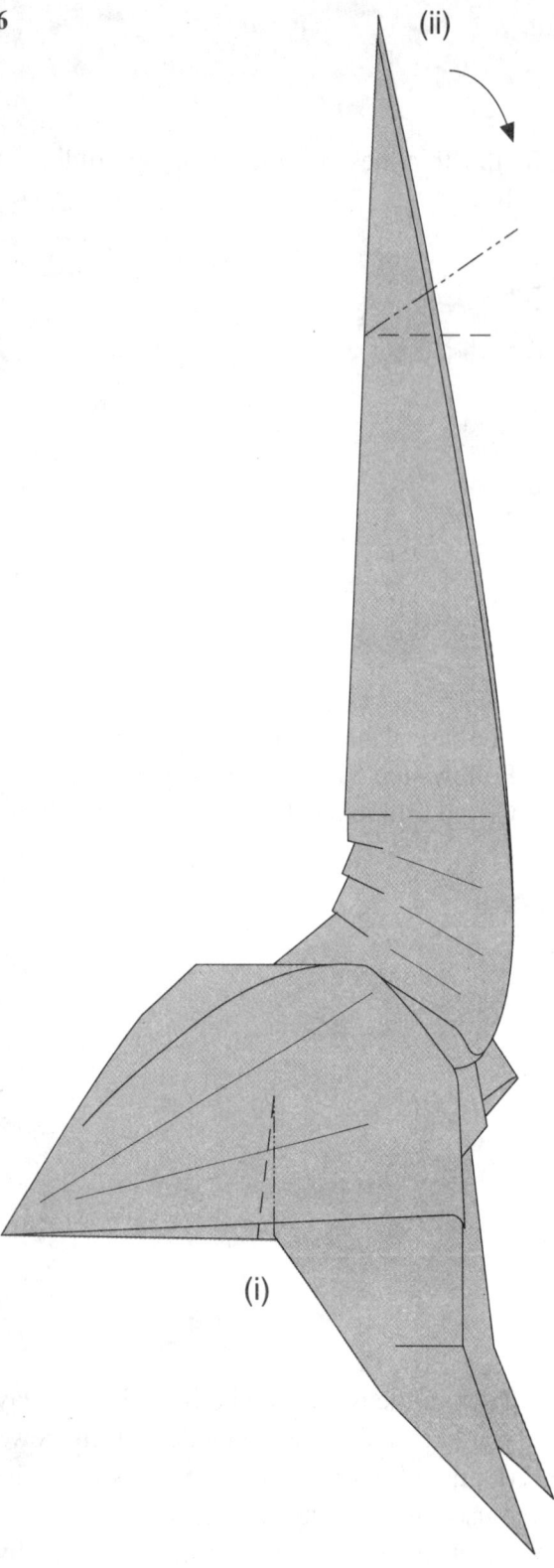

7

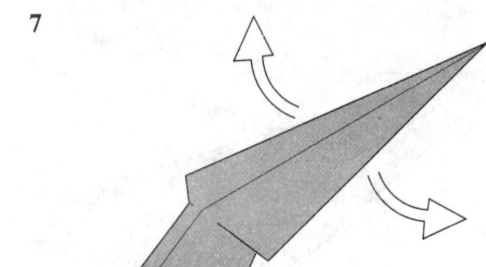

Pull out the previous folds from underneath the head, making sure that you unfold past the head crease made in the previous step.

8

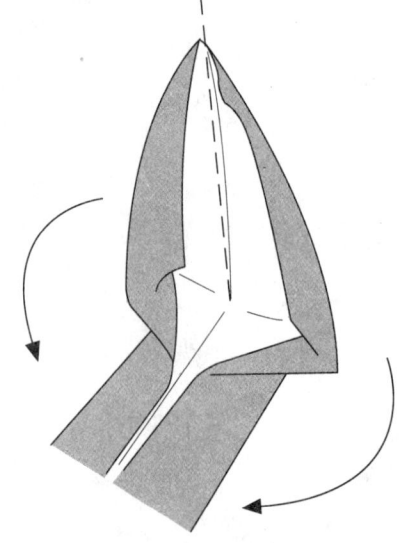

(Viewed from underneath)

(i) (Optional) Crimp fold to form the shape for the forelimbs. Push the body forward and the legs backwards to help you execute this fold.

(ii) Crimp fold the neck downwards to form the head. Unfold it.

Fold the sides of the head together to flatten it as shown in step 9.

9

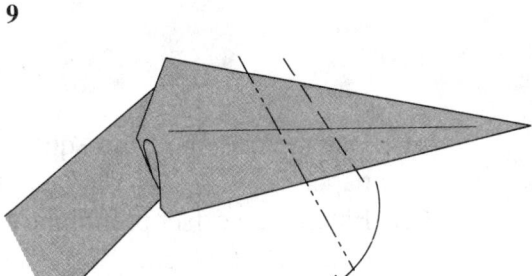

Reverse fold downwards along the mountain fold crease and then reverse fold upwards along the valley fold crease.

10

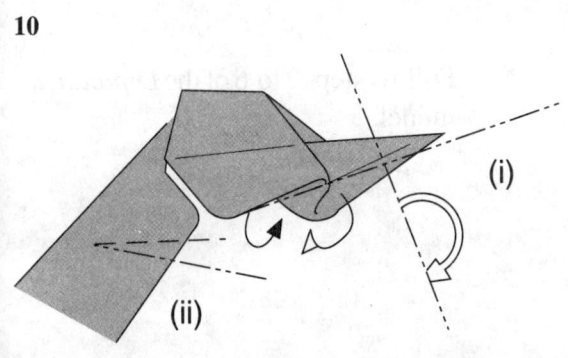

(i) Shape the head by tucking in the tip of the nose and making it narrower.
(ii) Crimp fold the neck near the base of the head to angle the head downwards.

11

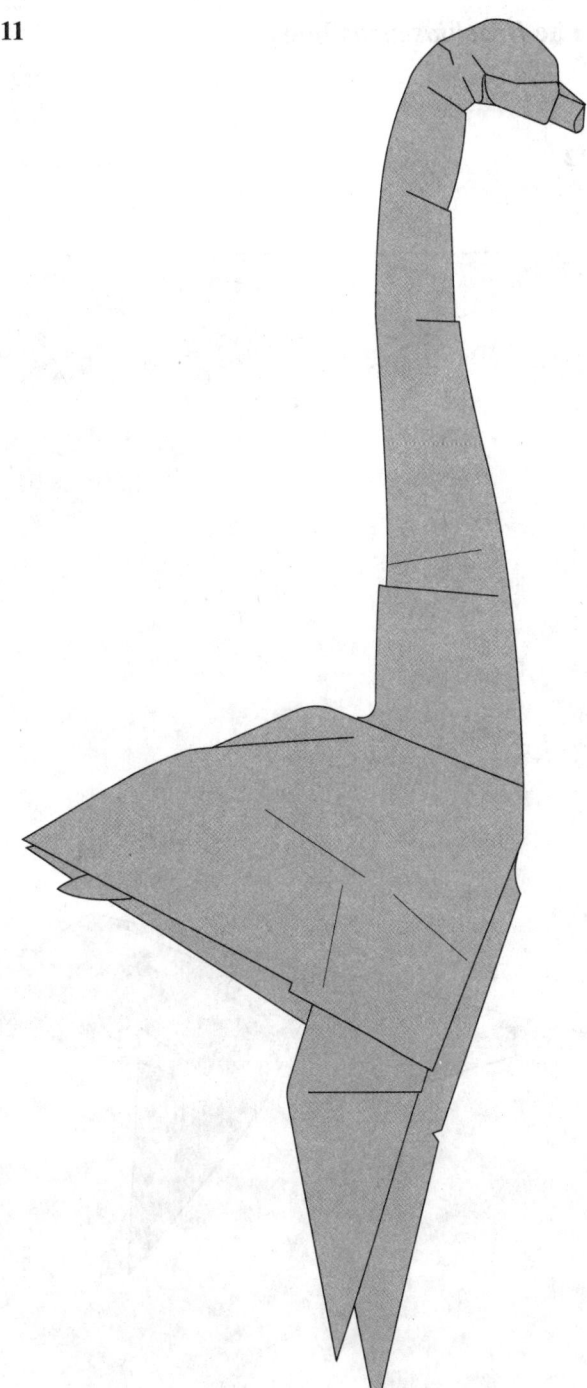

The completed *Brachiosaurus* head

You can tuck in the tips of the forelimbs to flatten them. Fold the neck inwards if the neck appears too thick. Add more crimp folds to curve it if the neck appears too straight.

The *Brachiosaurus* body

12

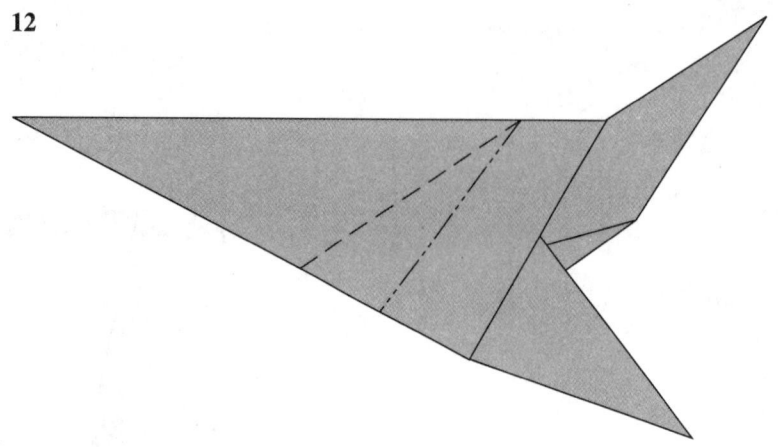

(i) Use a piece of 21 cm square paper.
(ii) Folding an offset preliminary base, offset 4.2 cm.
(iii) Proceed to fold a tail base B.
(iv) Crimp fold to form the back and hump of this sauropod. The position for this fold is fairly low down as *Brachiosaurus*' hindlimbs are shorter than its forelimbs.

13

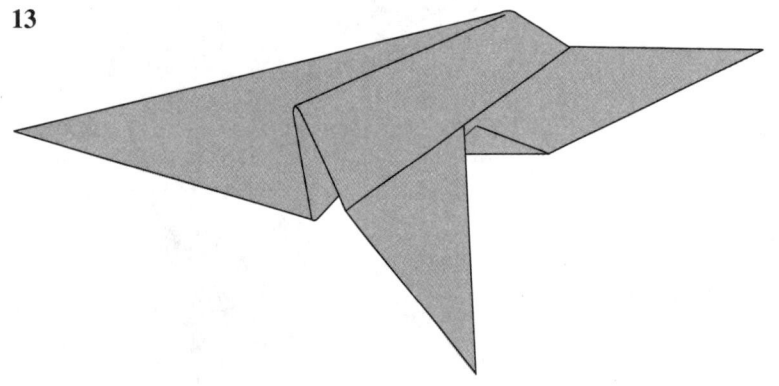

Follow steps 2 to 6 of the *Diplodocus* model.

14

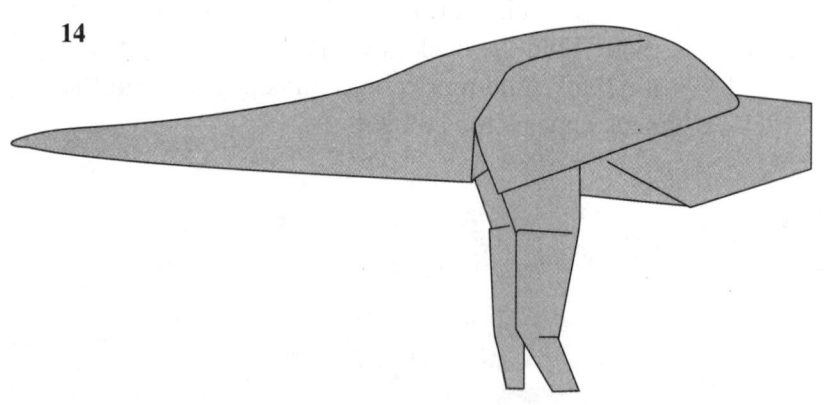

The complete *Brachiosaurus* body

Use this diagram as a guide as to how your model should look.

15

The completed *Brachiosaurus* model

Join the head to the body by placing the body underneath the head. Adjust the lengths of the legs so that the model is standing upright with a distinct downward sloping back.

Camarasaurus

Camarasaurus (meaning "chambered lizard") was a small (60 ft/18m) but heavily built sauropod living during the Late Jurassic period. It has a thick short neck and tail and a very compact body. The shape of its head is box-like and it has long nasal openings at the top of its head.

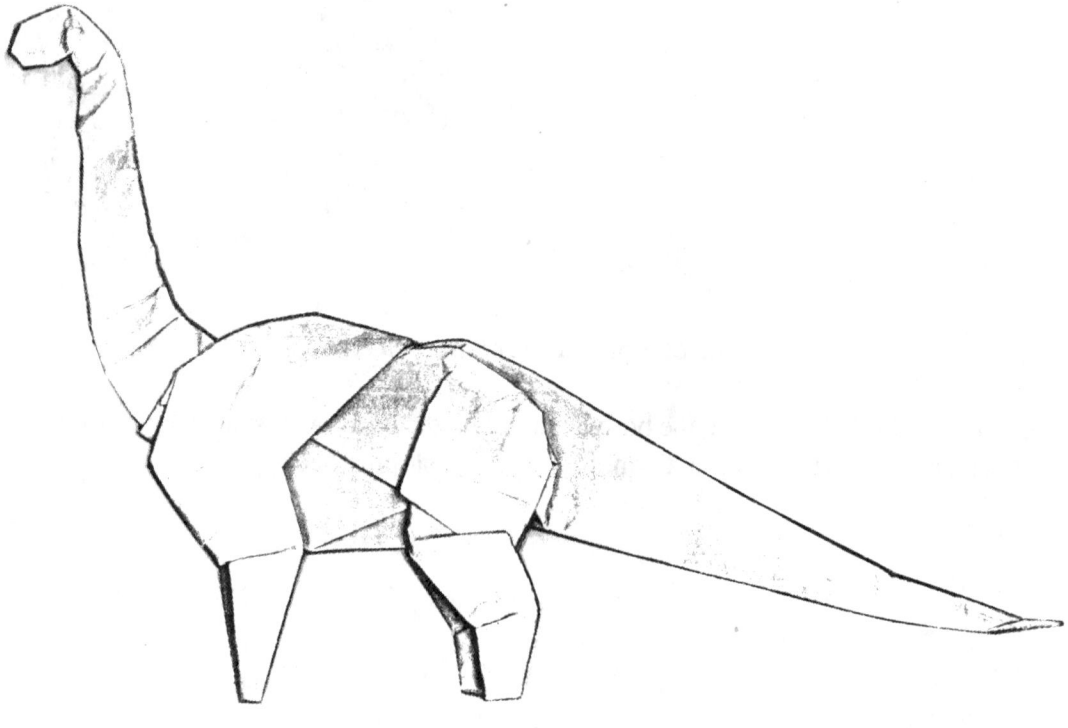

The *Camarasaurus* head

1

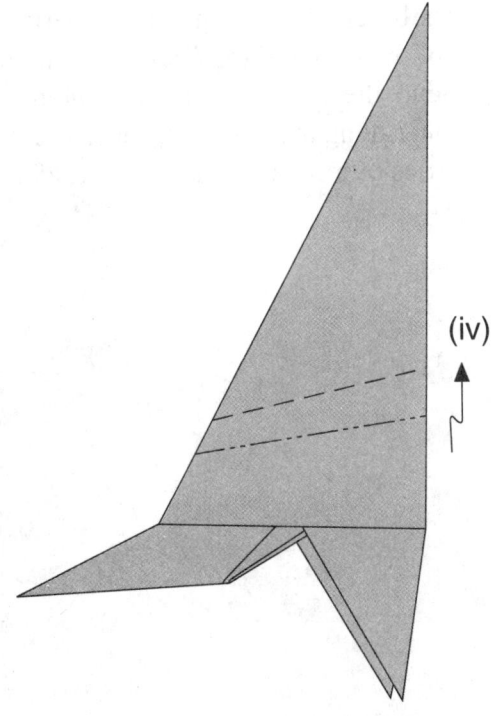

(i) Use a piece of 21 cm square paper.
(ii) Fold an offset preliminary base, offset 4.2 cm.
(iii) Then fold a tail base B.
(iv) Crimp fold to form the shoulders and neck. (Do a reverse fold downwards along the mountain fold crease, then a reverse fold upwards along the valley fold crease.) The position of this fold defines the neck and shoulders. (Remember: the longer the forelimbs, the shorter the length of the neck.)

2

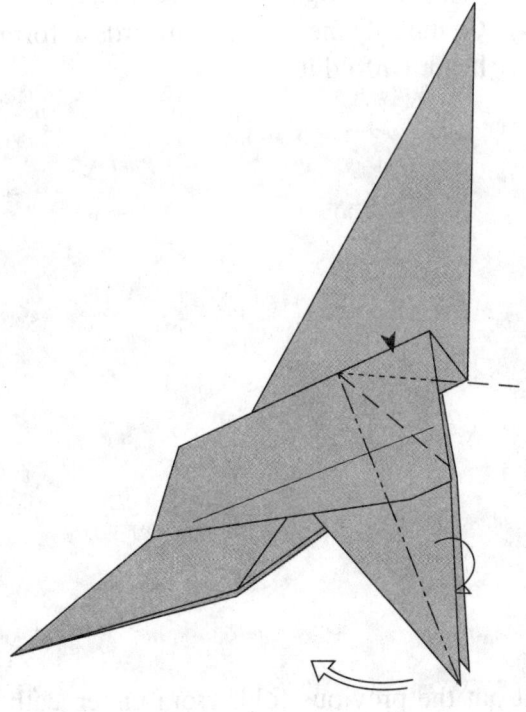

3

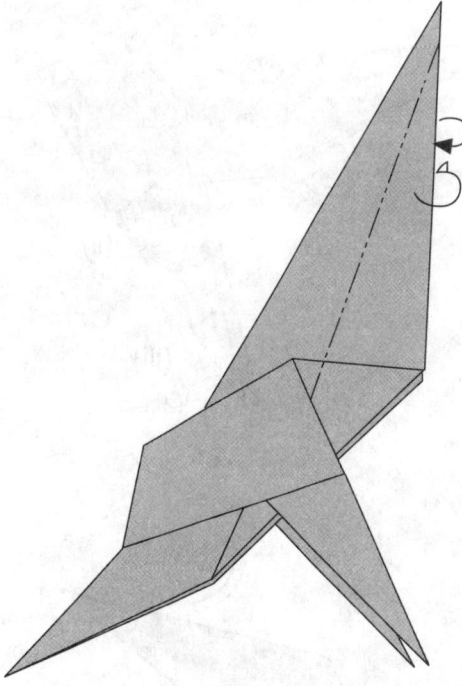

Halve the thickness of the forelimbs by folding the outer edge inwards. Lift the legs up and backwards (to the right) to help you execute this fold. Repeat for the other side.

Halve the thickness of the neck by folding it inwards.

111

4

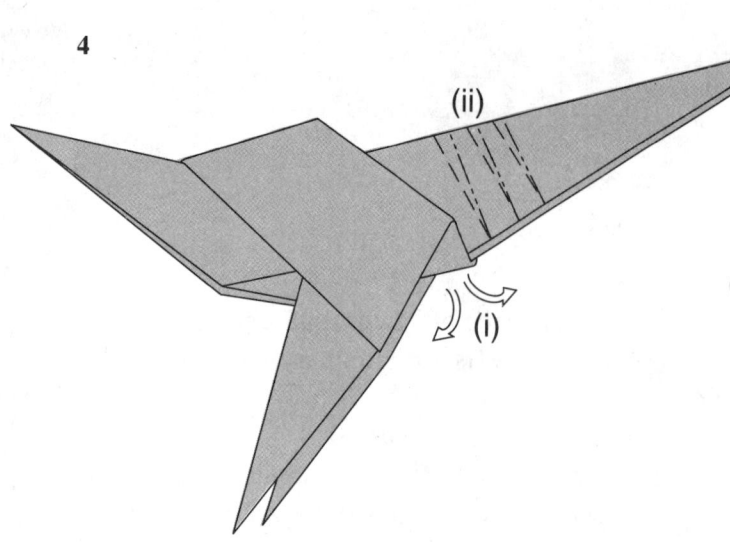

(i) The base of the neck must be properly folded. Follow step 5 of the *Diplodocus* model.
(ii) Bend the neck upright by making crimp folds along the back of its neck (i.e. make a series of mountain and valley folds).

5

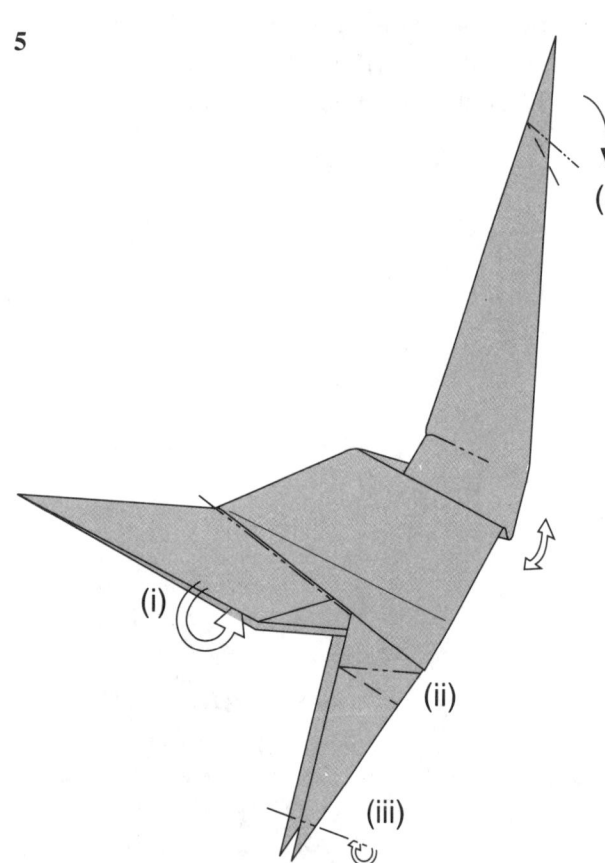

(i) Tuck in the rest of the body. Fold any way you like, so long as you hide it from view.
(ii) Crimp fold to bring the forelimbs forward.
(iii) Tuck in the tips of the forelimbs.
(iv) Crimp fold the neck downwards to form the head. Unfold it.

6

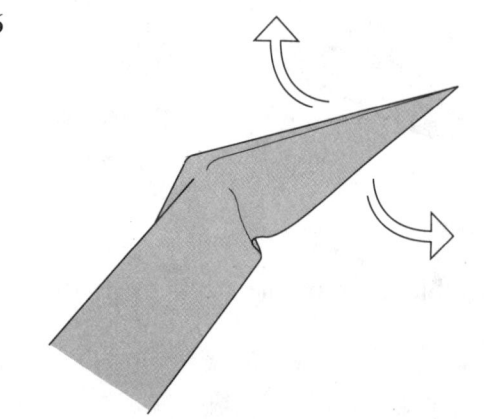

Pull out the previous folds from underneath the head, making sure that you unfold past the head crease made in the previous step.

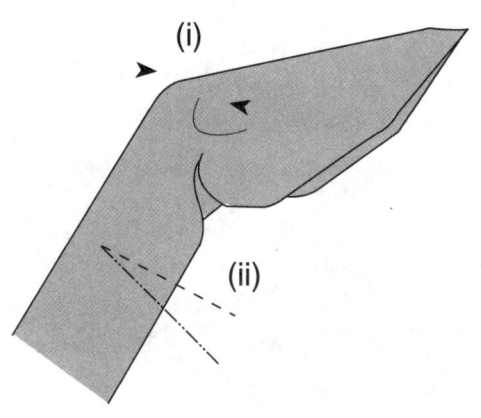 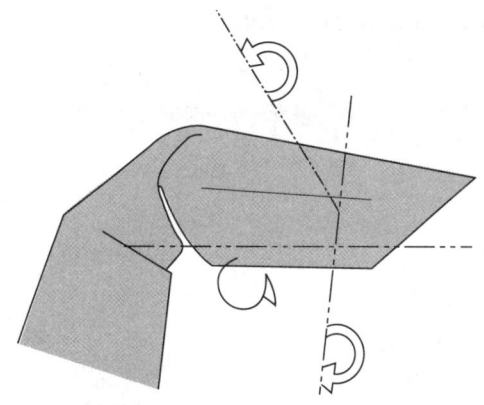

(i) Pinch the back of the head and then flatten the head.
(ii) Crimp fold the neck near the head to angle the head downwards.

Camarasaurus has a box-shaped head. Tuck inwards along the crease lines shown to get the box shape.

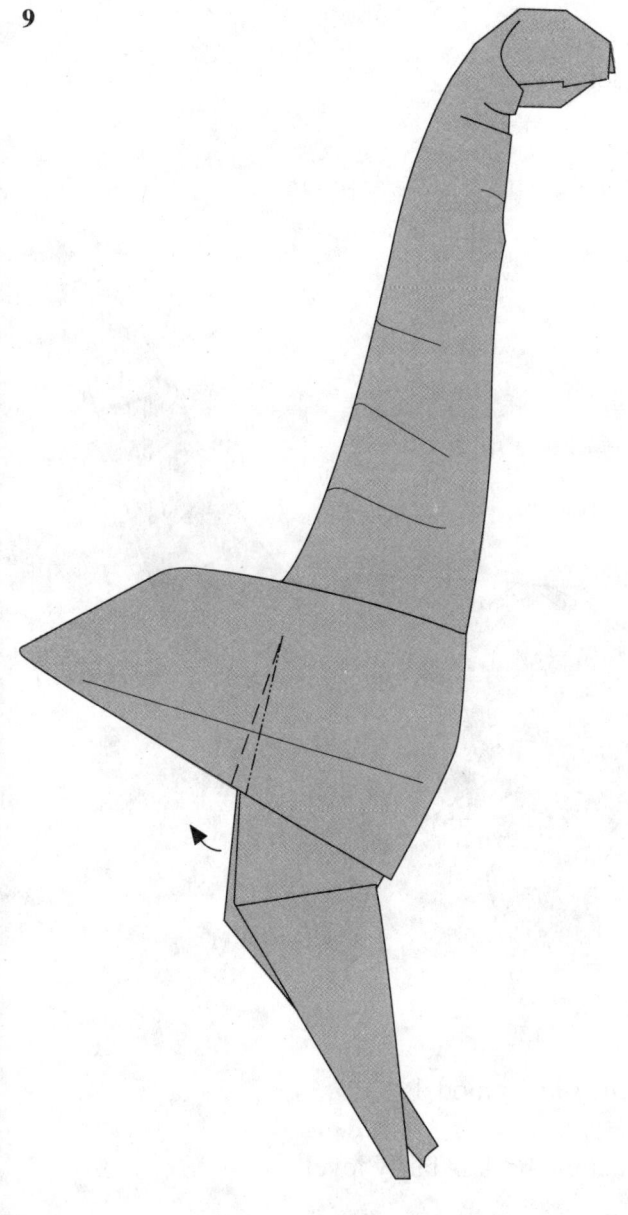

Crimp fold to form the shape for the forelimbs. Push the body forward and pull the legs backwards to help you execute this fold. The *Camarasaurus* head is now completed.

113

The *Camarasaurus* body

10

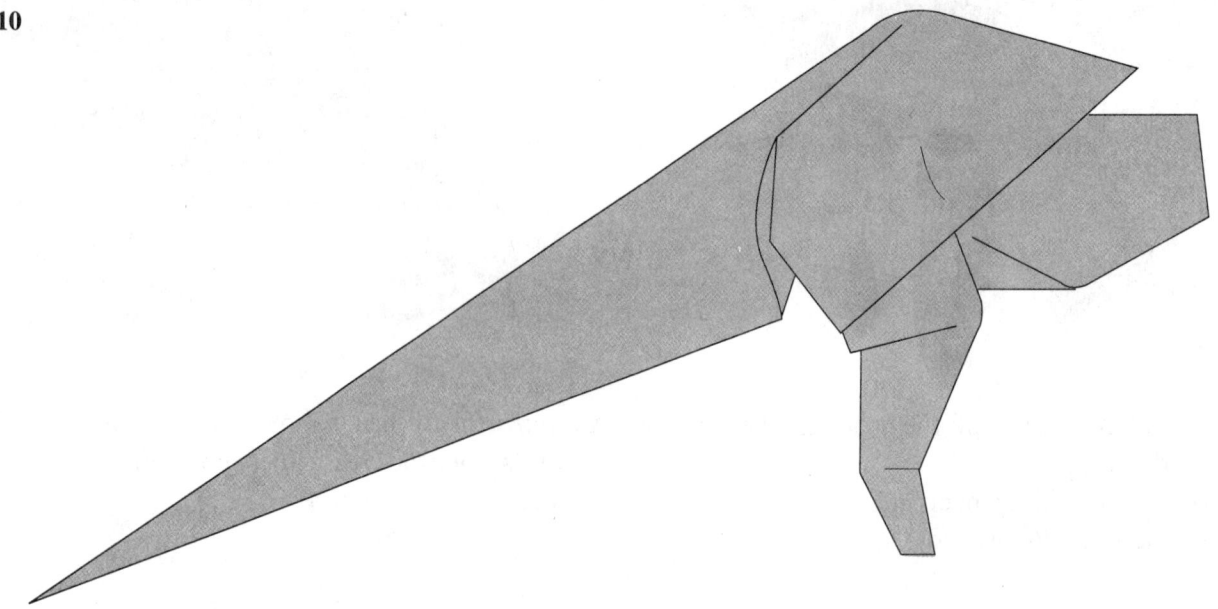

(i) Use a piece of 22.5 cm square paper.
(ii) Fold an offset preliminary base, offset 4.7 cm.
(iii) Proceed to fold a tail base B.
(iv) Follow steps 1(iv) to 6 of the Diplodocus model.

11

The completed *Camarasaurus* model

Join the head and body such that the back is fairly level.

Triceratops

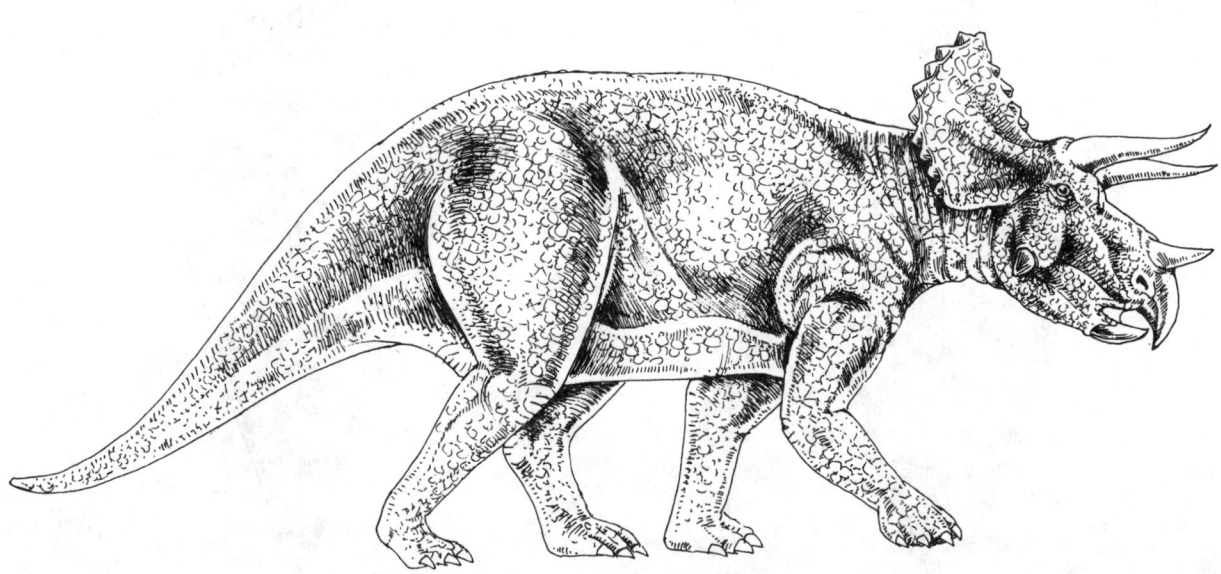

Triceratops (meaning "three-horned face") was a 30 ft (9 m) long ceratopsian living during the Late Cretaceous period. It is heavily built, very much like a tank, and has a magnificent head crest. *Triceratops* has a bony frill at the back of the skull which extends over the shoulders and neck, giving it some form of protection. Over its eyes are two formidable horns. A nasal horn is also found at the end of its beak-like mouth. This creature is vegetarian and supposedly gentle, living a lifestyle very much like that of the rhinoceros of today.

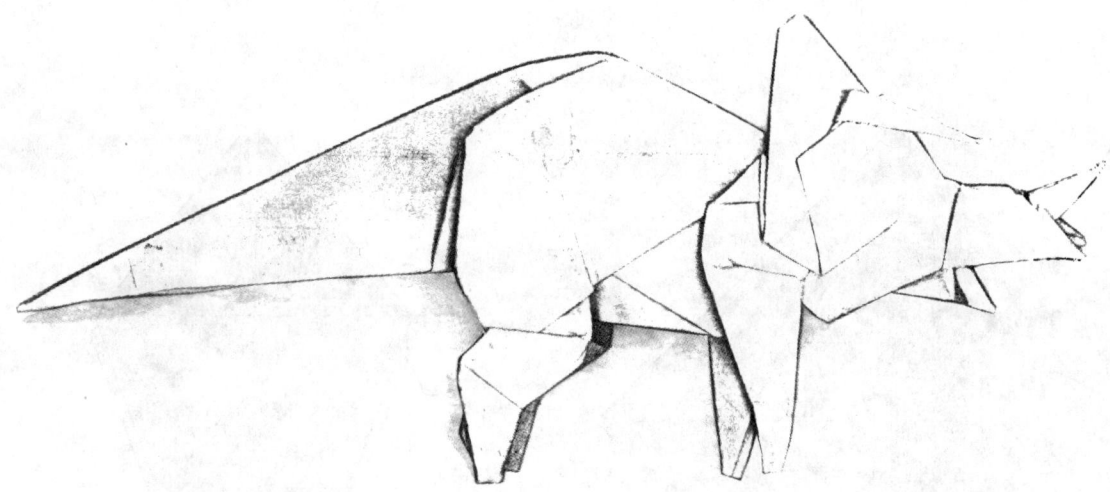

The *Triceratops* head

1

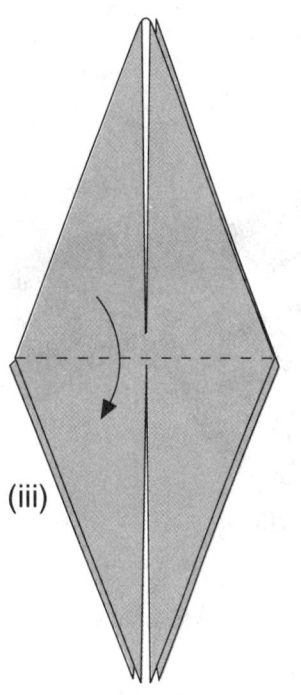

2a

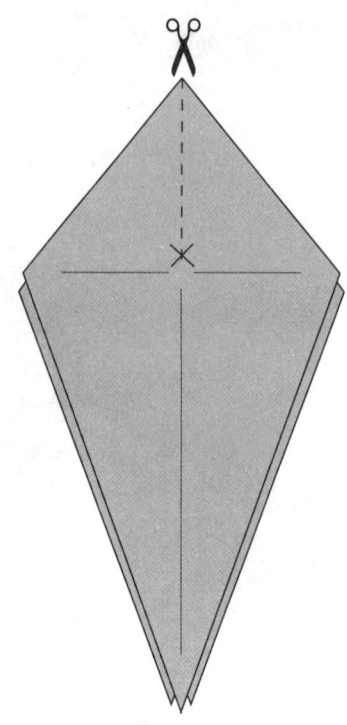

(i) Use a 16 cm square piece of paper.
(ii) Fold a bird base.
(iii) Fold the top portion downwards. Repeat for the other side.

Cut along the line. Take care that no other part of the model is cut except where shown in step 2b. (It may be easier to unfold the paper to step 2b, cut and then fold back to step 2a.)

2b

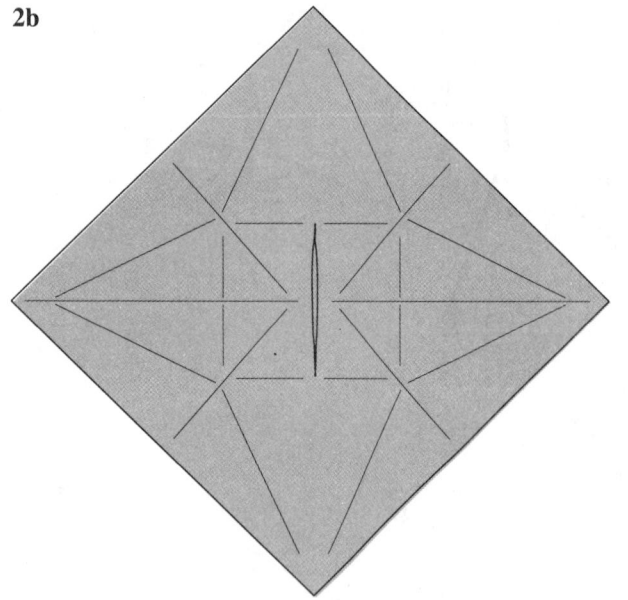

3

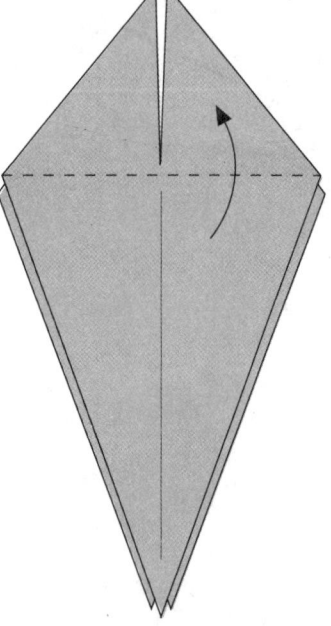

Fold the bottom flap upwards. Repeat for the other side.

4

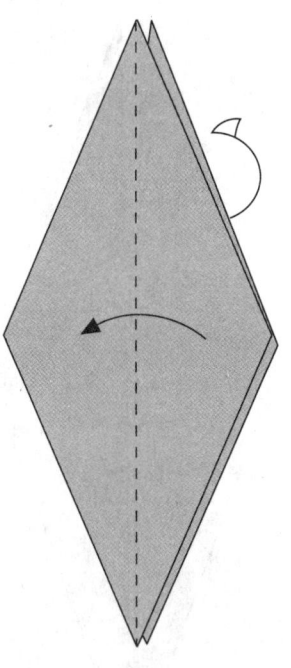

Fold the opposite sides together to get to step 5.

5

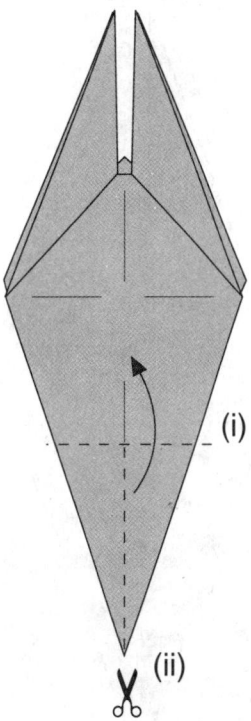

(i) Fold the first flap upwards.
(ii) Cut this flap as shown in step 6.

6

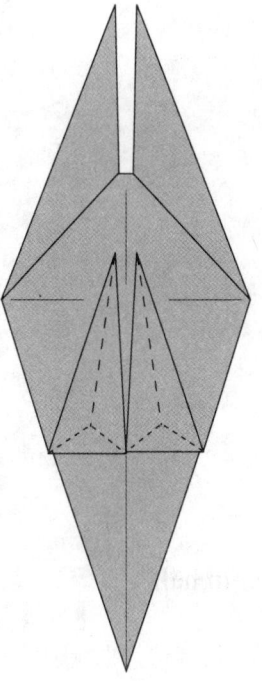

Rabbit-ear fold to get to step 7.

7

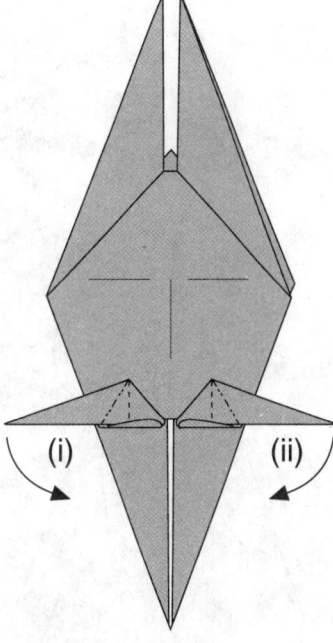

(i) Valley fold to the right and then fold downwards to get to the position in step 8.
(ii) Valley fold to the left and then fold downwards to get to the position in step 8.

8

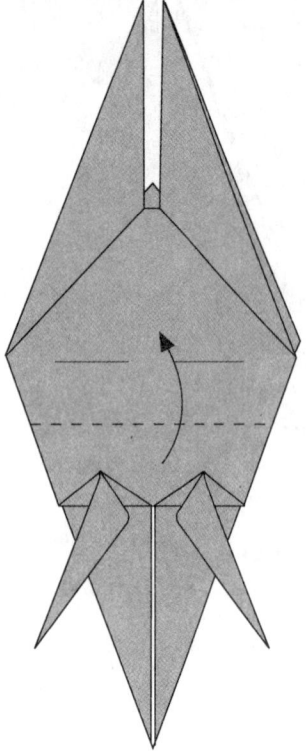

Fold upwards.

9

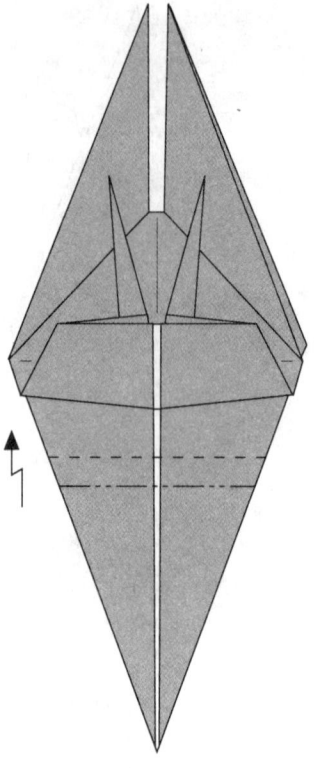

Fold upwards along the valley fold crease and then downwards again.

10

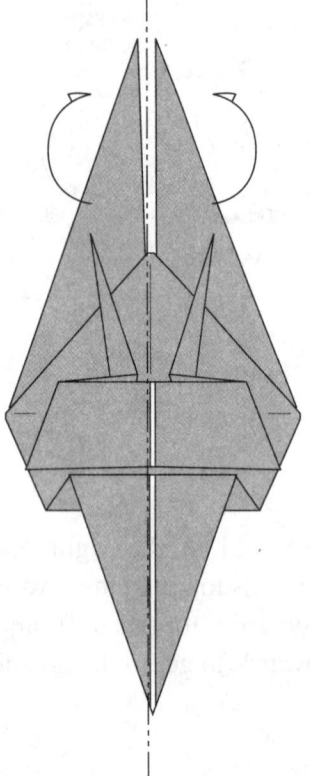

Fold the model in half.

11

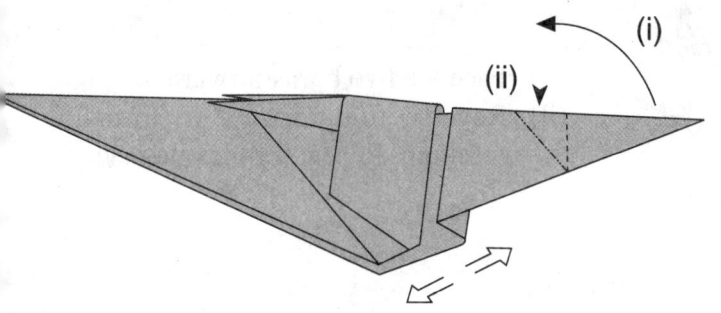

(i) Pull upwards and to the left to push out the bottom portion. Flatten the extended portion.
(ii) Crimp fold upwards to form the nose horn.

12

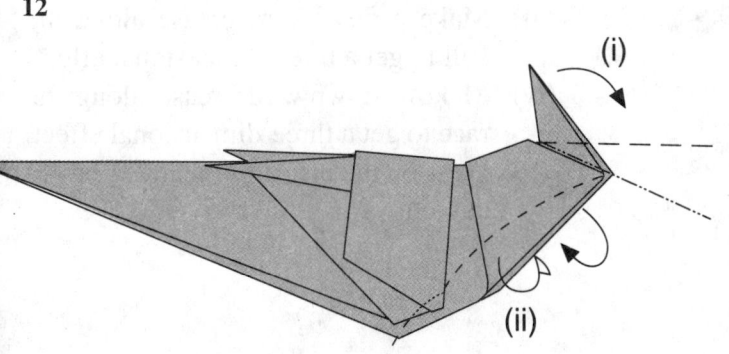

(i) Crimp fold the nose horn downwards as shown in step 13. Glue the tips of the snout together.
(ii) Tuck inwards in a curve to make the face thinner. Repeat for the other side.

13

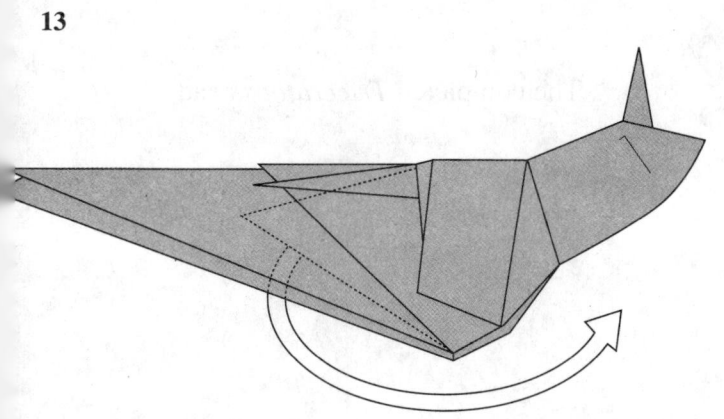

Fold the triangular flap (hidden beneath) over to the front to form the lower jaw. This lower jaw is short. But if it is ridiculously short compared to the face and snout, then you will have to shorten the face and snout by redoing step 9 or step 11(ii).

14

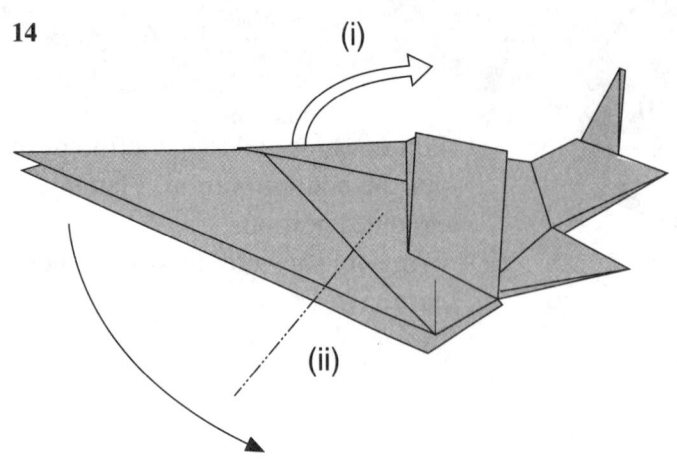

(i) Face the two horns forward.
(ii) Reverse fold forward to form the forelimb. Repeat for the other side.

15

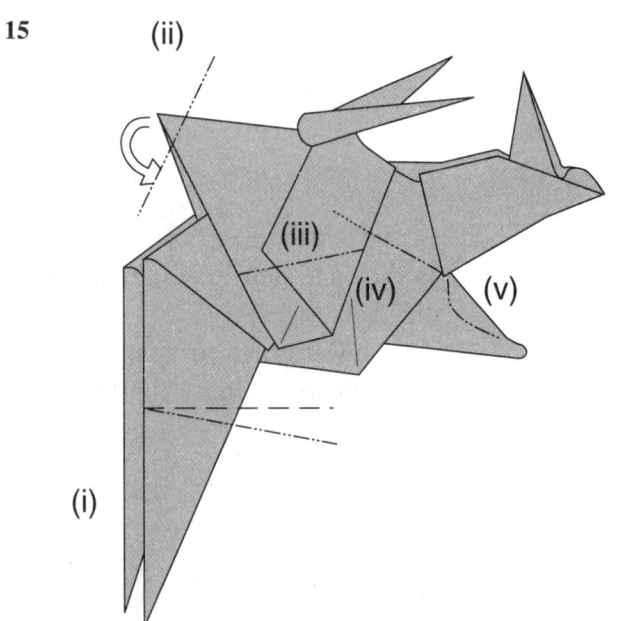

(i) Crimp fold the forelimbs forward.
(ii) Tuck in and flatten the tip.
(iii) Make a downward crease along the frill to get a three-dimensional effect.
(iv) Make a downward crease along the face to get a three-dimensional effect.
(v) Press on the inside of the lower jaw to curve it.

16

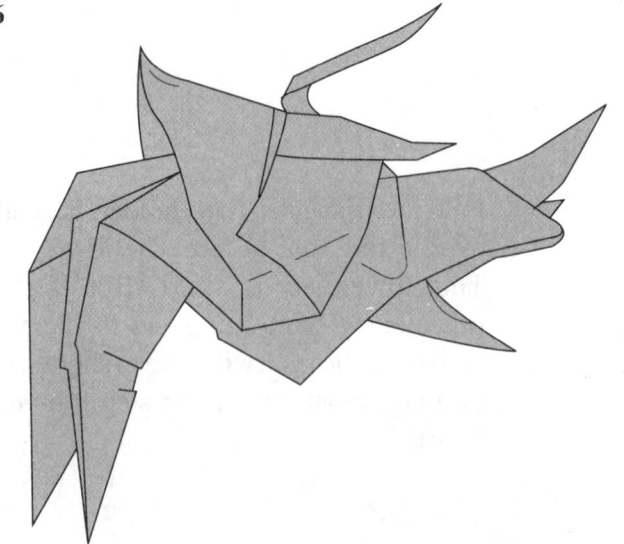

The completed *Triceratops* head

The *Triceratops* body

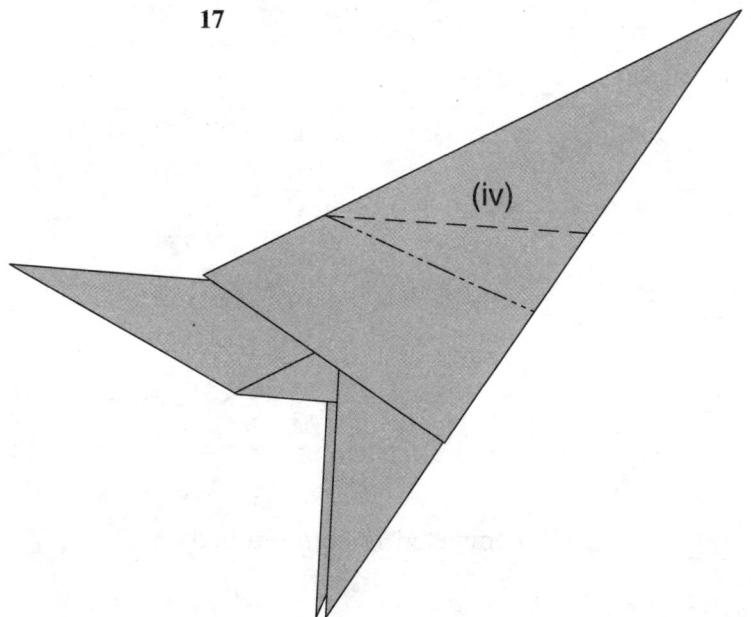

17

(i) Use a piece of 21 cm square paper.
(ii) Fold an offset preliminary base, offset 1.5 cm.
(iii) Fold a tail base A.
(iv) Crimp fold downwards to form the tail. (Make the fold fairly high up to give *Triceratops* a high humped back.)
(v) Follow steps 13 to 16 of the *Tyrannosaurus* model.

(Note: *Triceratops* has a high back, thick tail and sturdy legs. Bear this in mind when doing steps 13 to 16 of the *Tyrannosaurus* model. Step 15 of the *Tyrannosaurus* model may be skipped if the thickness of the legs is all right. In step 16, the tail needs to be thinned slightly only.)

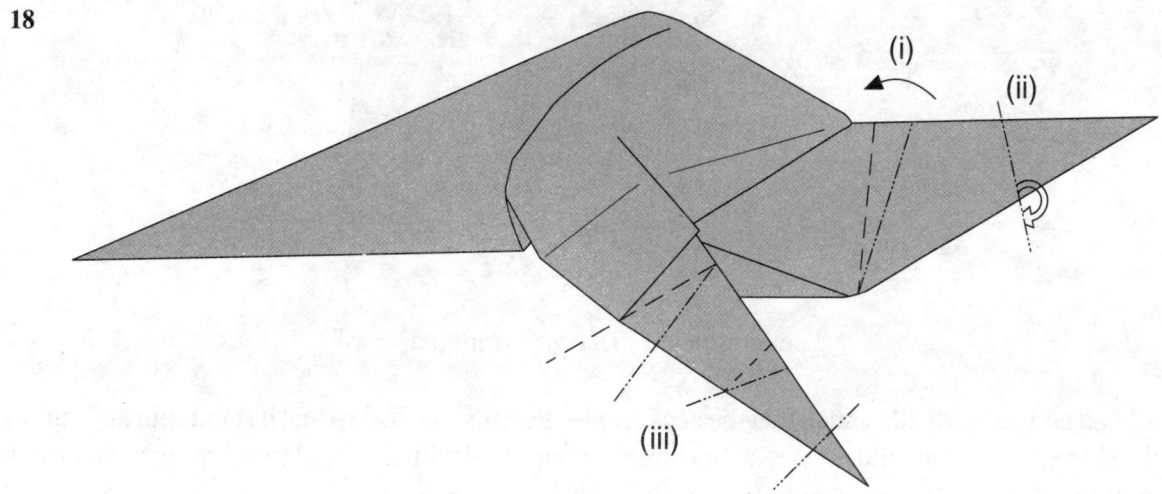

18

(i) Crimp fold to angle the back upwards.
(ii) Tuck in the end to hide it.
(iii) Crimp fold to form the knees and ankles. Tuck in the tips of the feet.

19

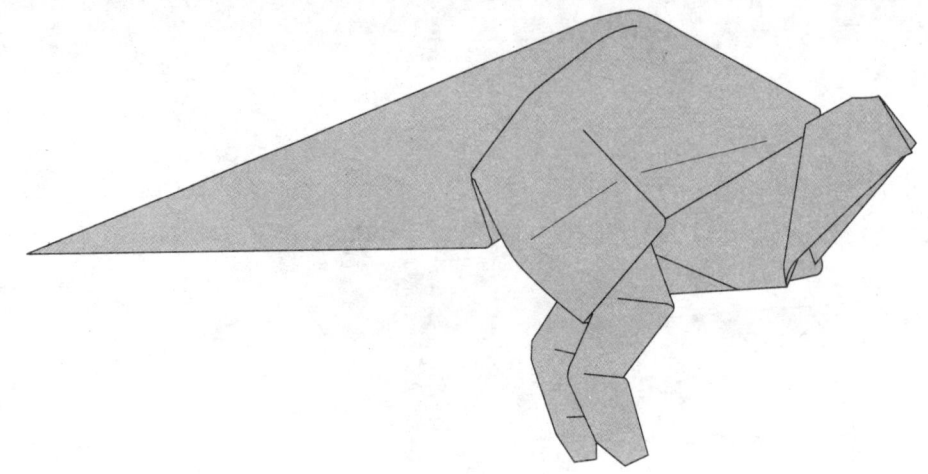

The completed *Triceratops* body

20

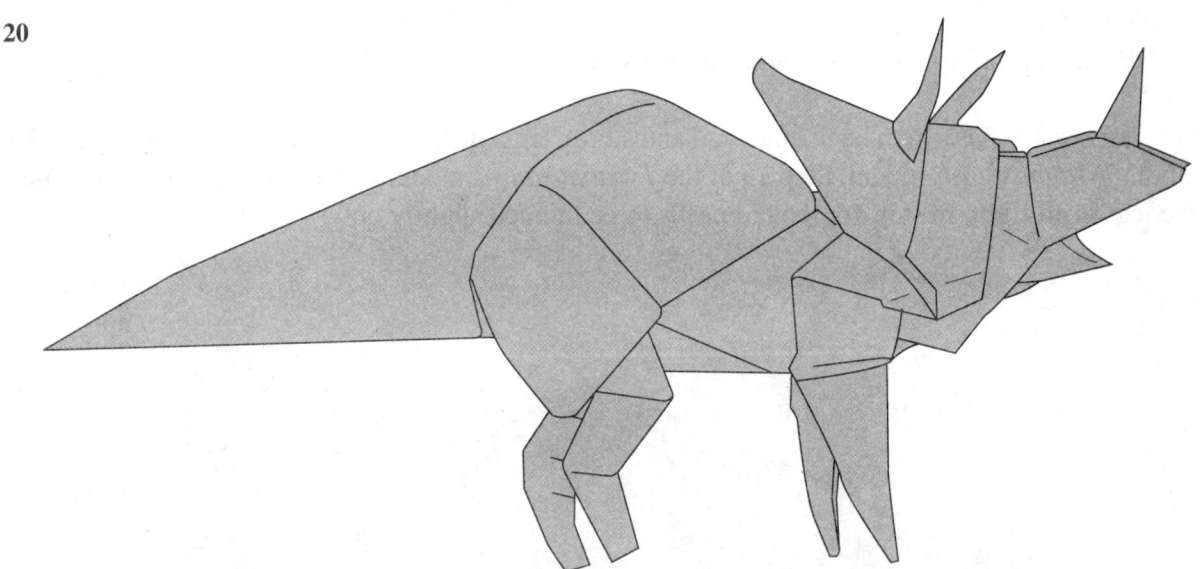

The completed *Triceratops* model

Join the head and body together such that the neck shows. Position the frill so that it stands out and curves down the sides. The face should not be flat but three-dimensional with the cheeks protuding out and then inwards at the bottom. The snout should be rounded out.

Stegosaurus

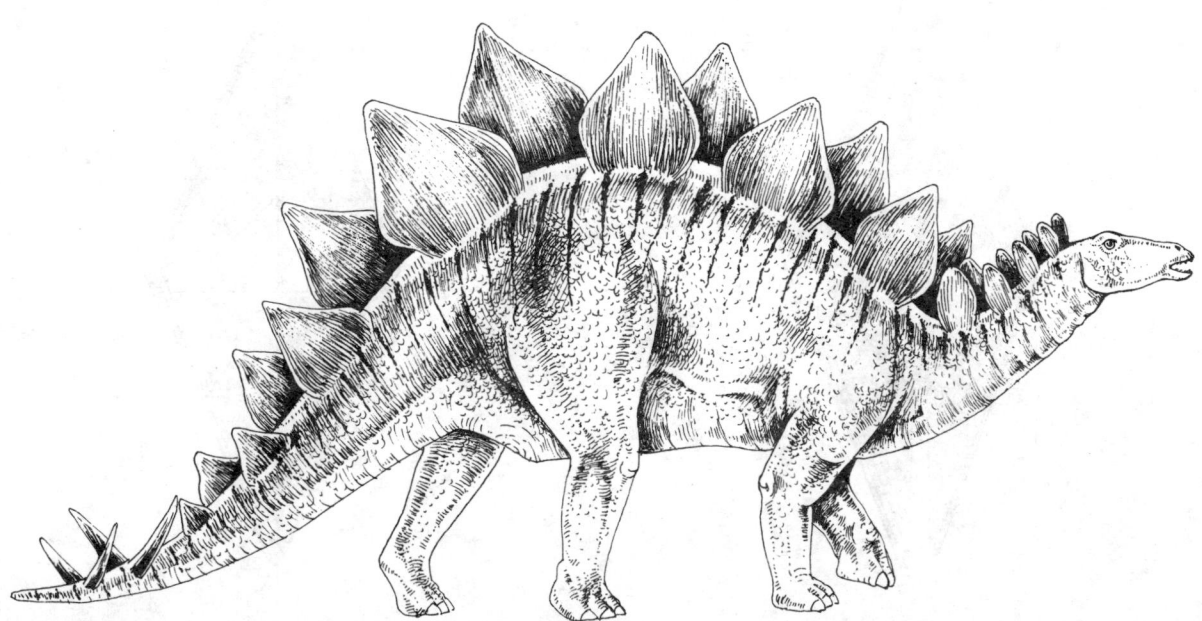

Stegosaurus was a giant plant-eating dinosaur 30 ft (9 m) long living during the Jurassic period. It is heavily armoured with an awesome array of bony plates along its back. These plates are capable of swivelling up or down to protect its back from any angle of attack. It is also thought that these plates may have helped to regulate its body temperature.

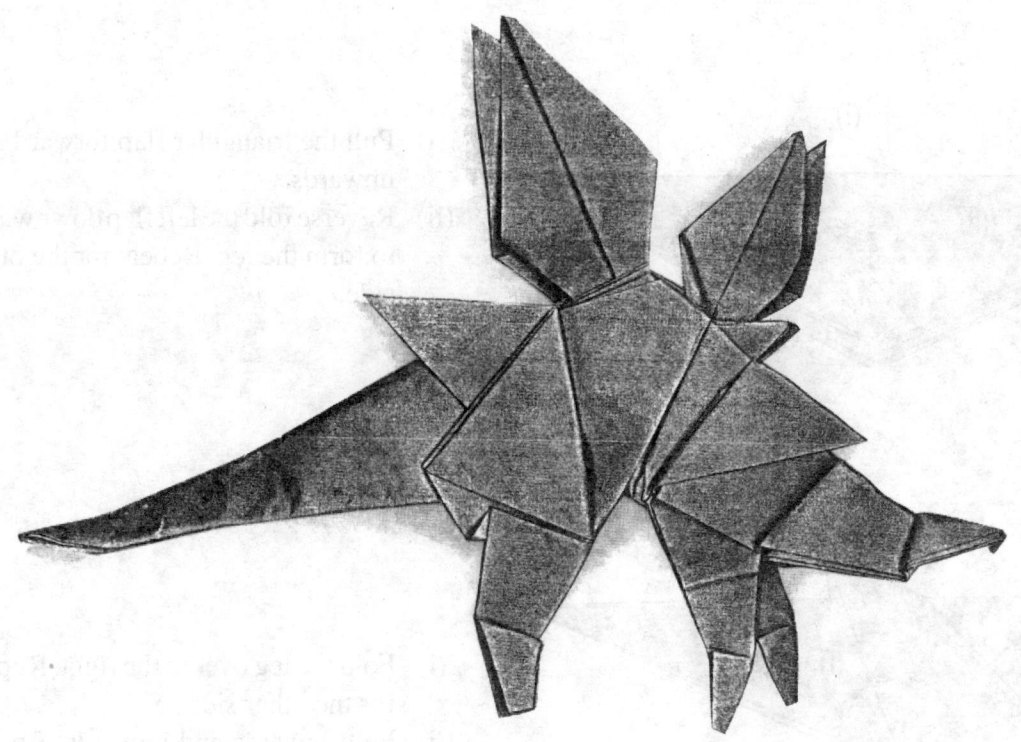

The *Stegosaurus* body

1

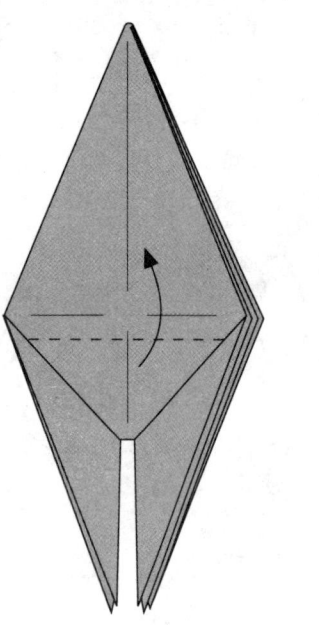

(i) Use a thin 29 cm square piece of paper.
(ii) Fold a frog base.
(iii) Fold the triangular flap upwards.

2

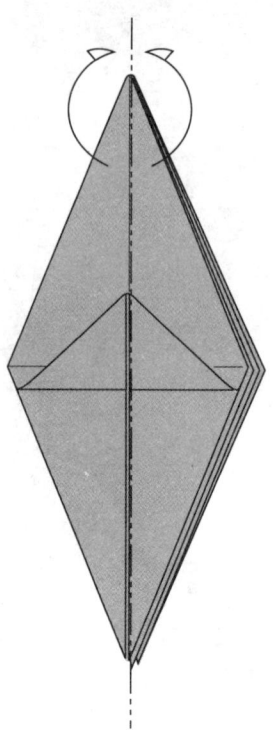

Fold the model in half.

3

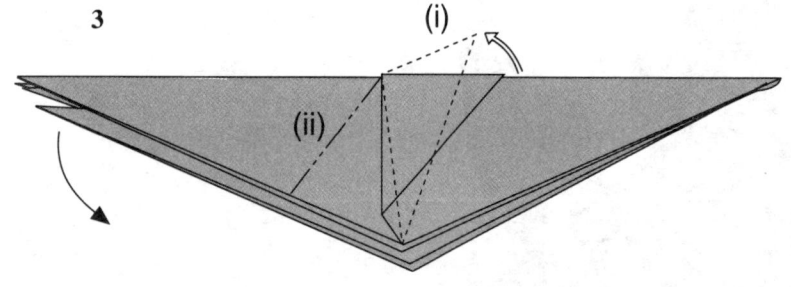

(i) Pull the triangular flap forward and upwards.
(ii) Reverse fold the left flap downwards to form the leg. Repeat for the other side.

4

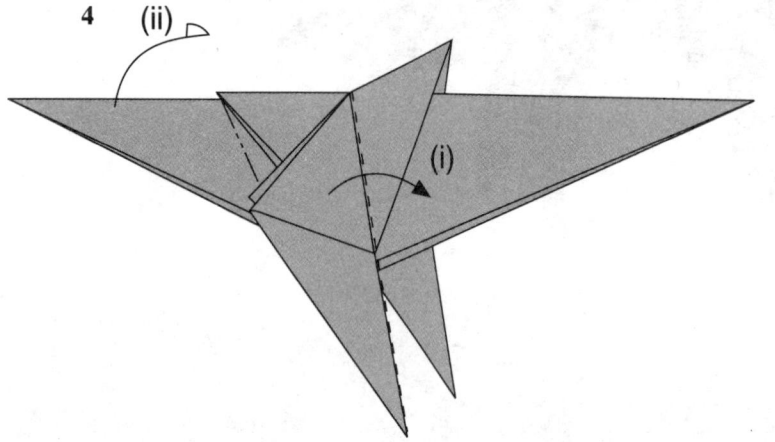

(i) Fold the leg over to the right. Repeat for the other side.
(ii) Fold inwards and upwards. Repeat for the other side.

124

5

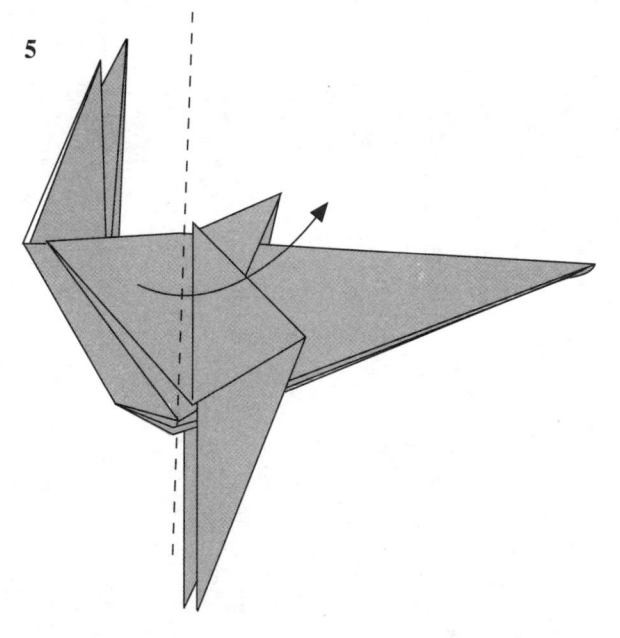

Fold to the right to reveal the inside.

6

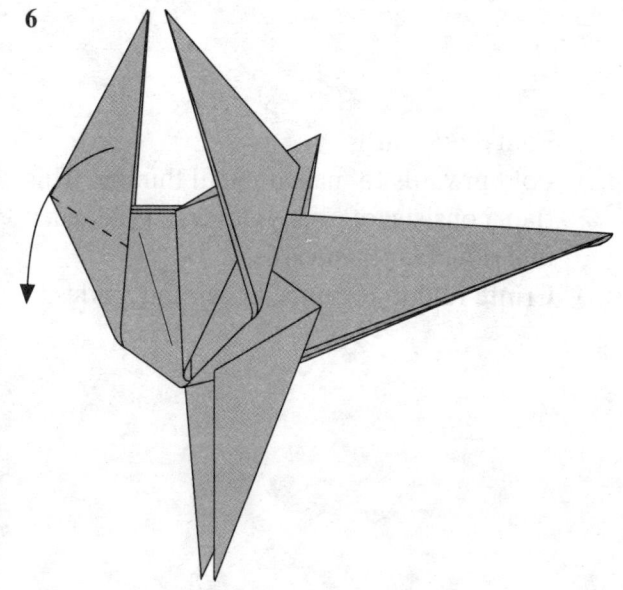

Fold downwards. Watch the angle of the fold.

7

Open up the flap and squash fold downwards. (One side of the squash fold will have two layers and the other side, 1 layer.)

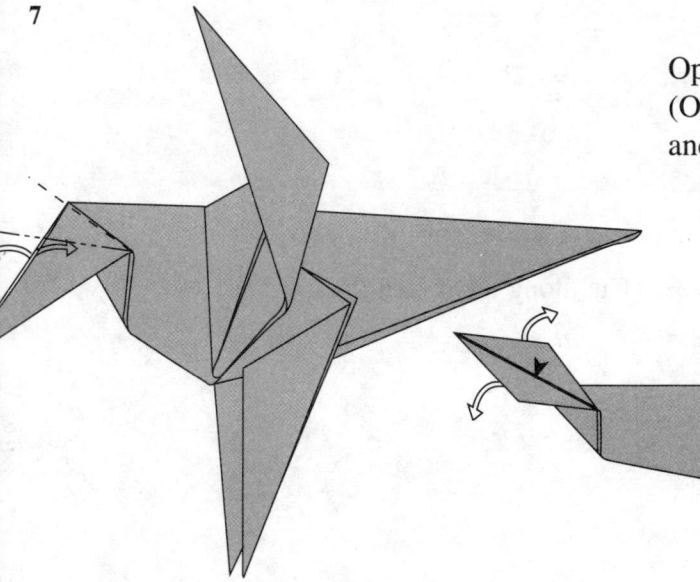

8

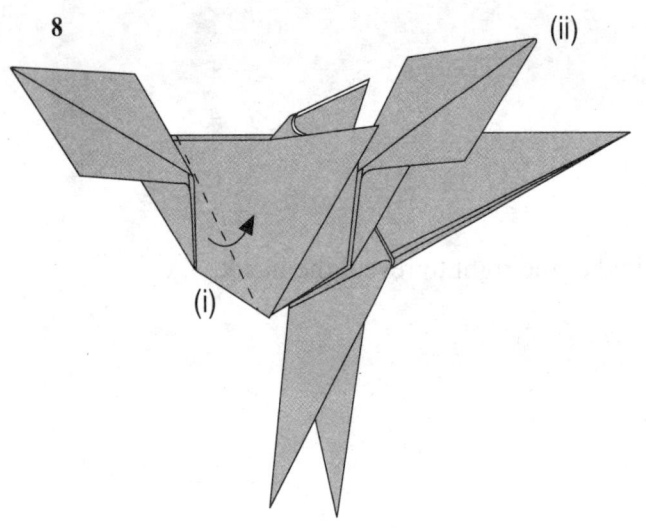

(i) Fold inwards.
(ii) Repeat steps 6 to 8 for the other side.

9

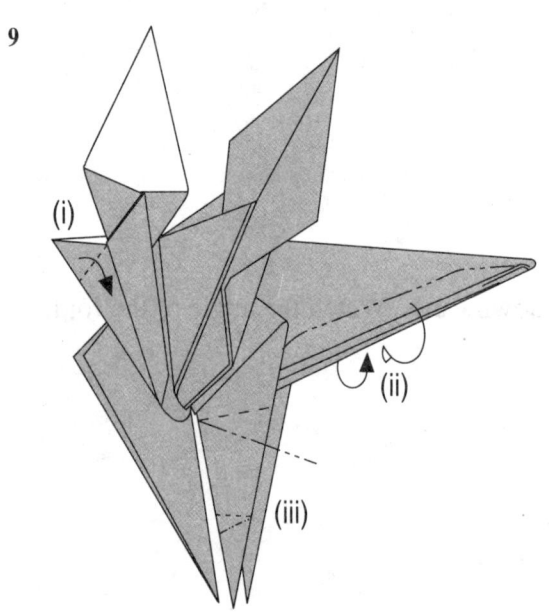

(i) Fold downwards.
(ii) Fold inwards to make the tail thinner. This flap consists of many layers. Fold each individual layer inwards.
(iii) Crimp fold to form the knees and ankles.

10

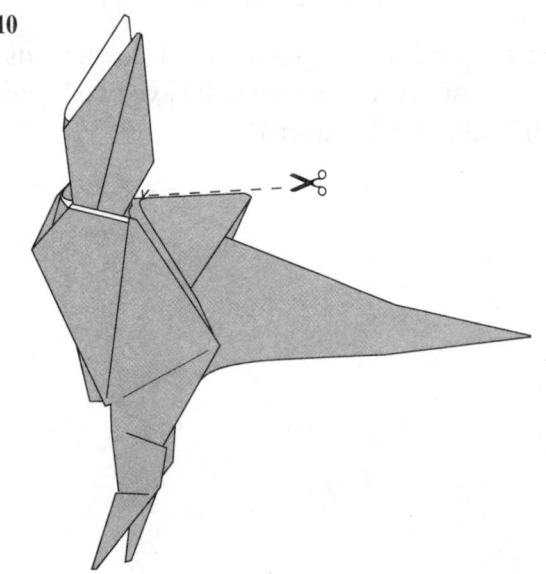

Cut along the dotted line.

The *Stegosaurus* head

11 **12**

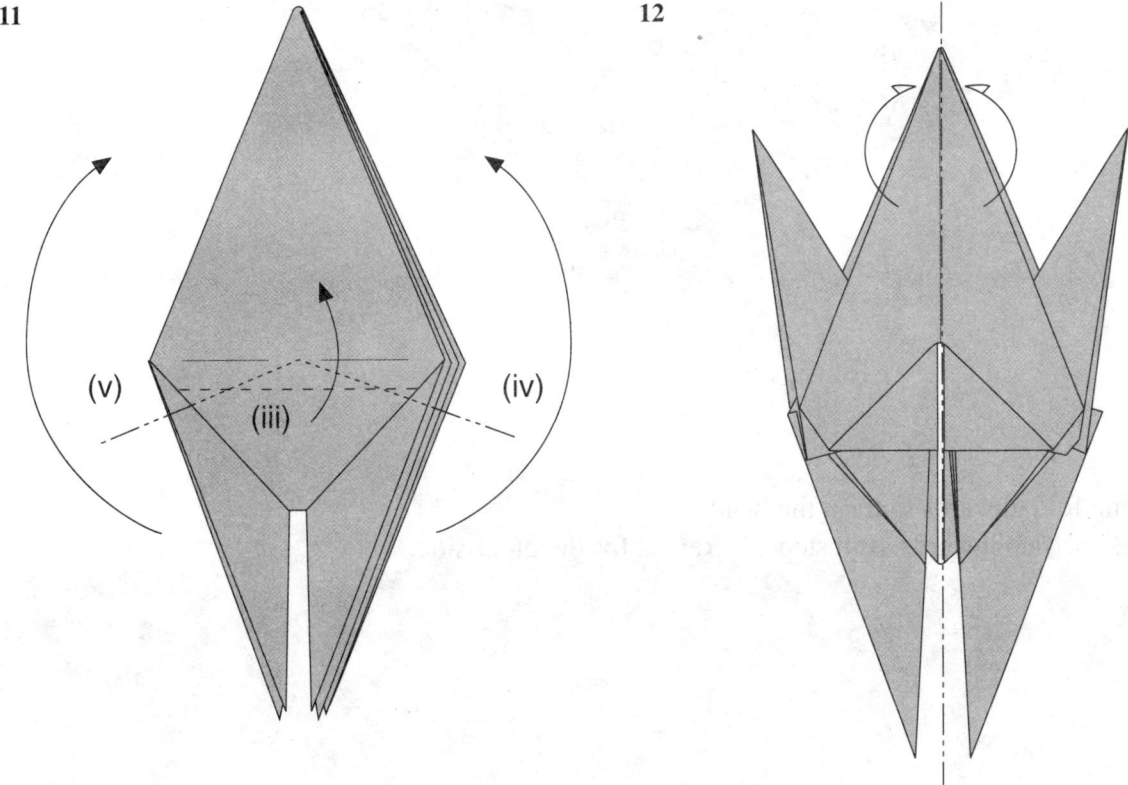

(i) Use a thin piece of 21 cm square paper.
(ii) Fold a frog base.
(iii) Fold triangular flap upwards.
(iv) Reverse fold the first right flap upwards (see step 12).
(v) Repeat (iv) for the left side.

Fold it in half.

13

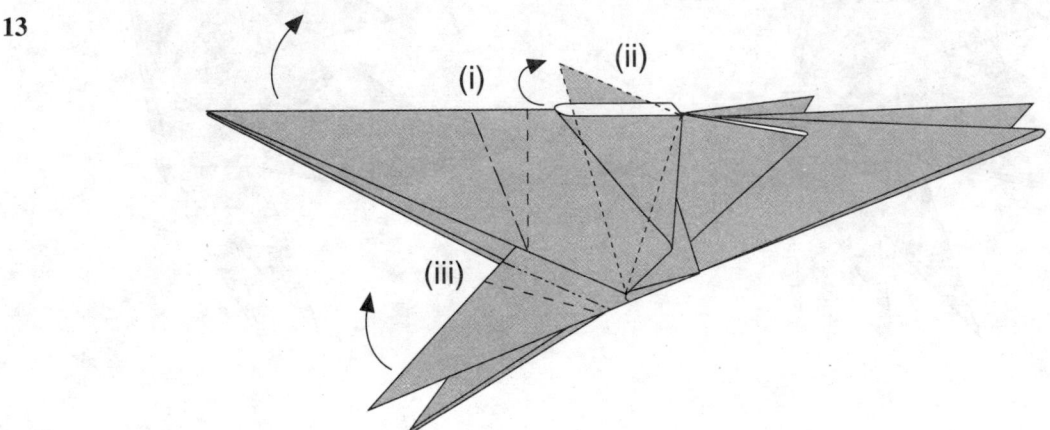

(i) Crimp fold upwards to form the neck and shoulders.
(ii) Pull the triangular flap upwards and towards the right.
(iii) Crimp fold the legs forward.

14

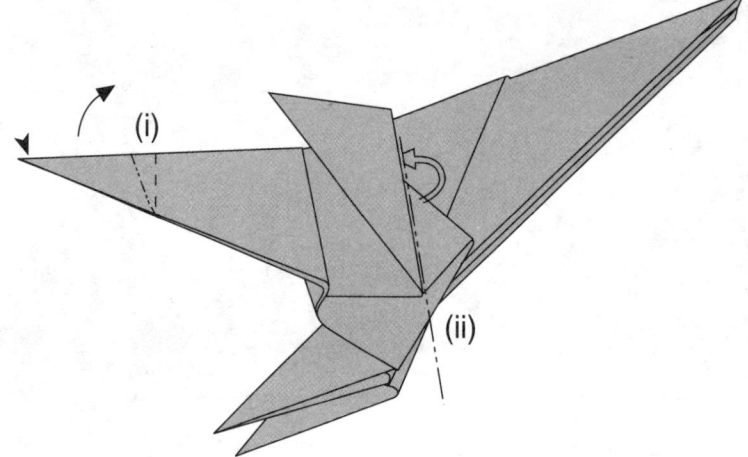

(i) Crimp fold upwards to form the head.
(ii) Tuck the flap inwards as in step 15. Repeat for the other side.

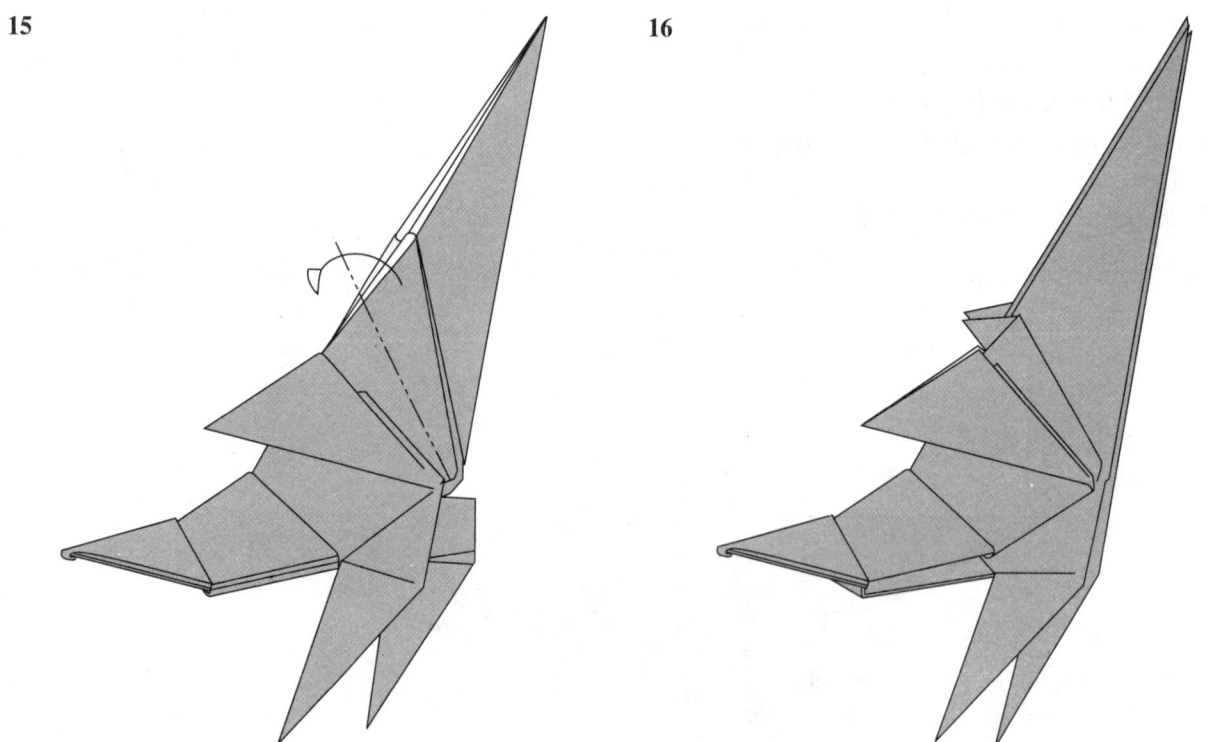

Fold inwards as shown in step 16. Repeat for the other side.

Turn the model over and open up the two top flaps apart to reveal the inside as shown in step 17.

17

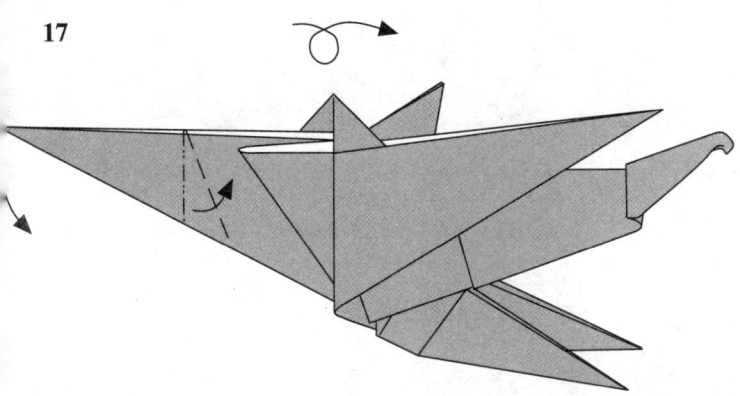

Valley fold and then mountain fold to get to step 18.

18

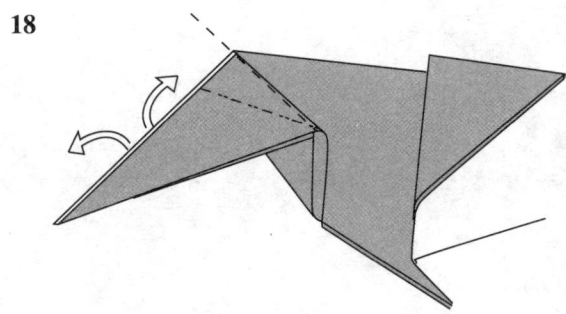

Open up the flap and squash fold downwards (same as step 7).

19

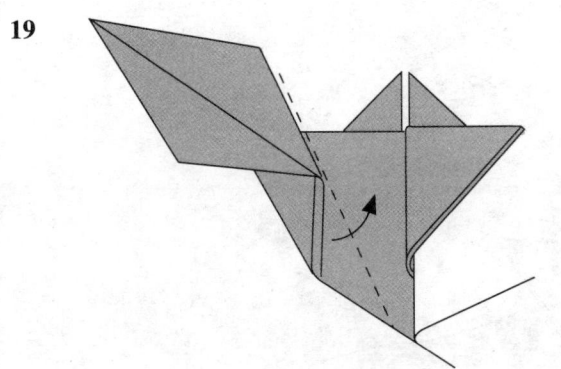

Fold over to the right.

20

Repeat steps 17 to 19 for the other side.

21

The completed *Stegosaurus* head

22

The completed *Stegosaurus* model

Join the head and body together using glue. Adjust the lengths of the legs accordingly.

Saurolophus

During the Cretaceous period, a group of dinosaurs flourished and were very successful. These dinosaurs are called hadrosaurs or duck-billed dinosaurs because of the shapes of their mouths. Many of them have spectacular crests on their heads. These dinosaurs are of similar size . They differ in the shapes of their crests. These crests are presumably used as recognition signals and for making sounds.

Hadrosaurs are vegetarians and thought to be swamp-dwelling. They have tightly packed grinding teeth for the type of diet found in the swamps.

Saurolophus has a large head and a pointed crest running upwards.

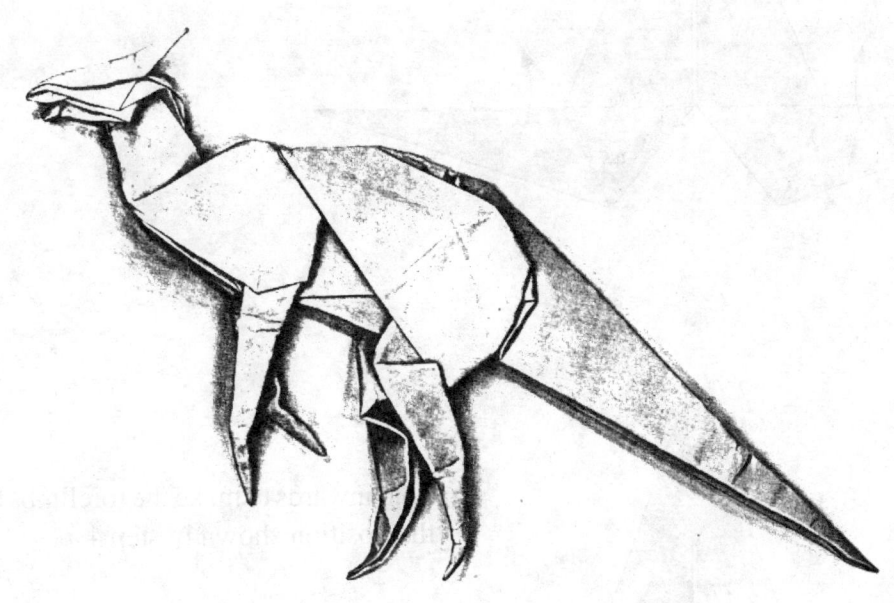

The *Saurolophus* head

1

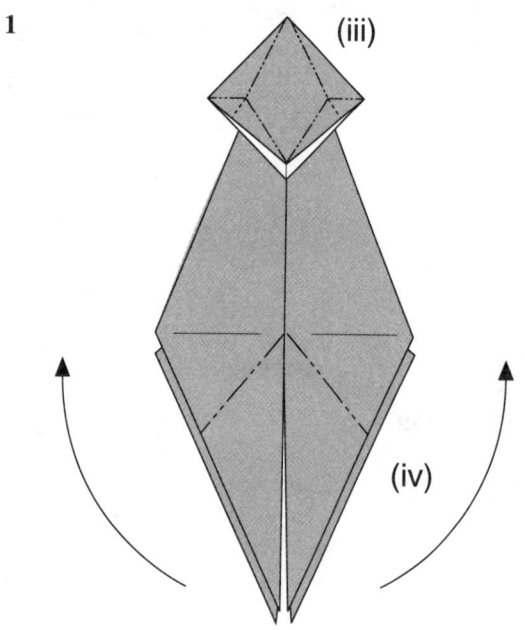

(i) Use a piece of 18 cm square paper.
(ii) Fold a hadrosaur base, offset 2.7 cm.
(iii) Frog fold the top square portion.
(iv) Reverse fold the two bottom flaps 90 degrees upwards to form the forelimbs.

2

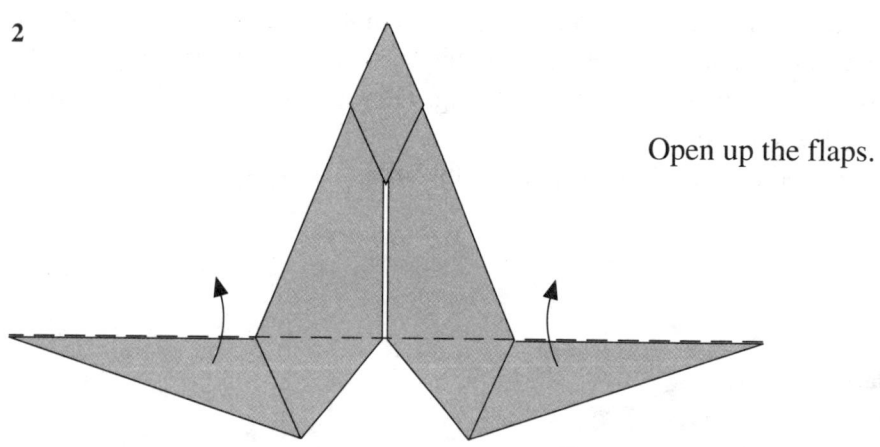

Open up the flaps.

3

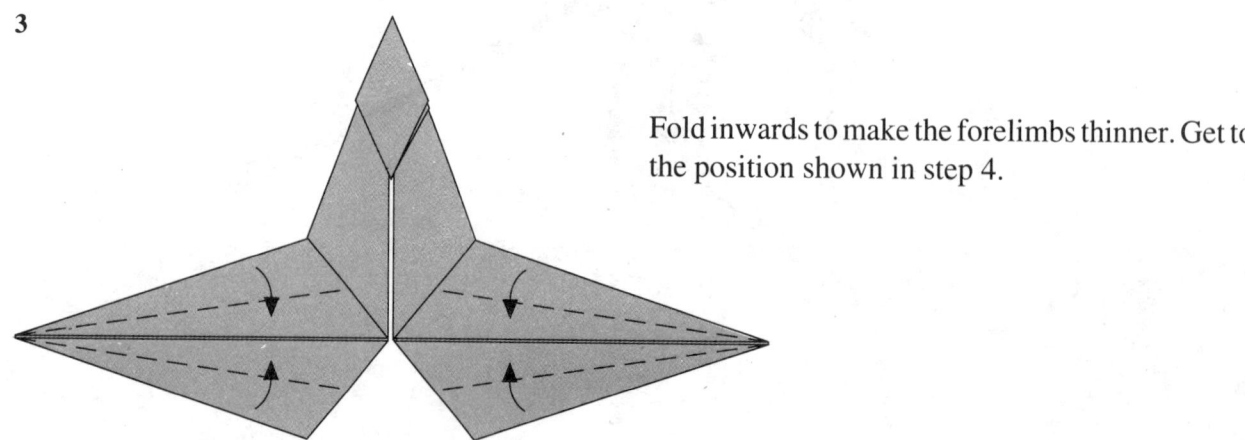

Fold inwards to make the forelimbs thinner. Get to the position shown in step 4.

132

4

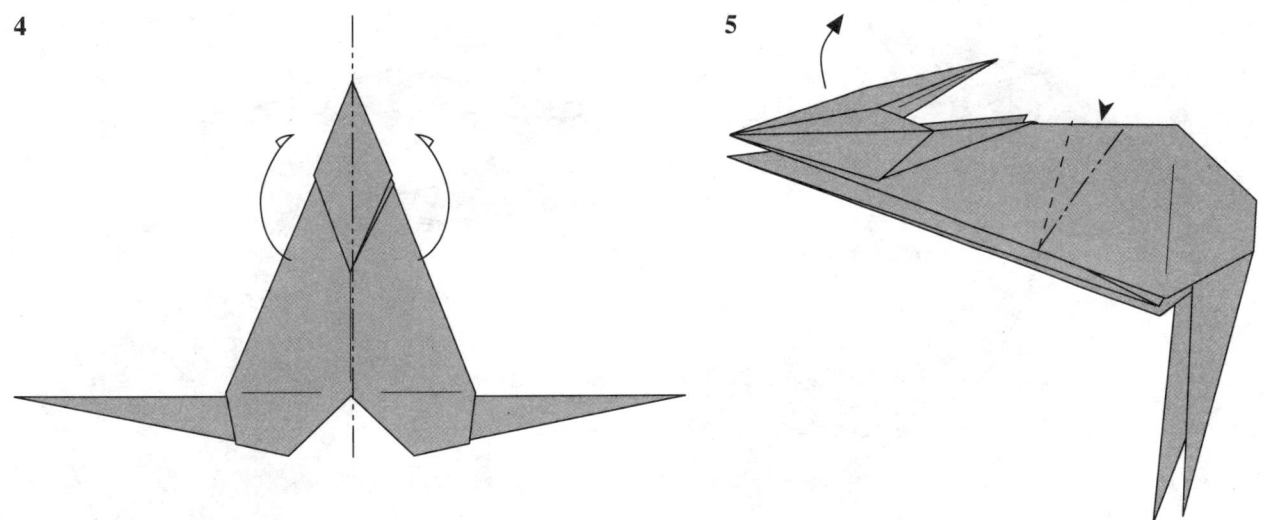

Fold the model in half.

5

Crimp fold to form the shoulders and neck.

6

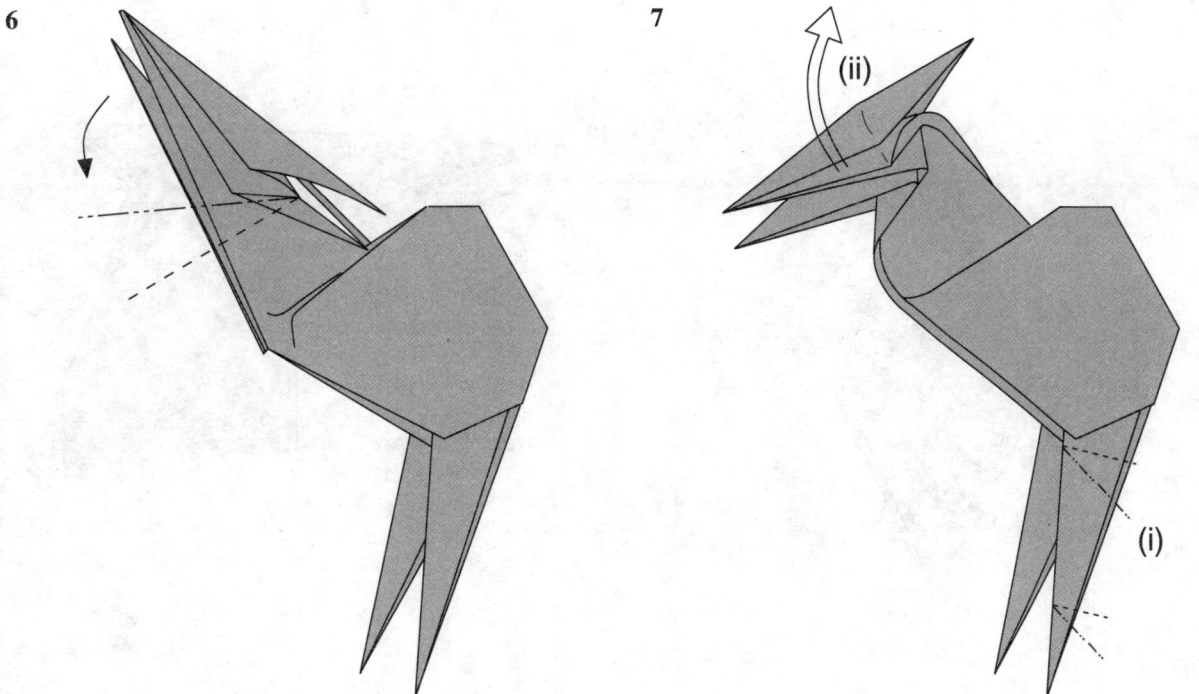

Crimp fold downwards to form the head.

7

(i) Crimp fold the forelimbs to form the elbows and hands.
(ii) Lift up the first two layers to reveal the hidden flap.

133

8

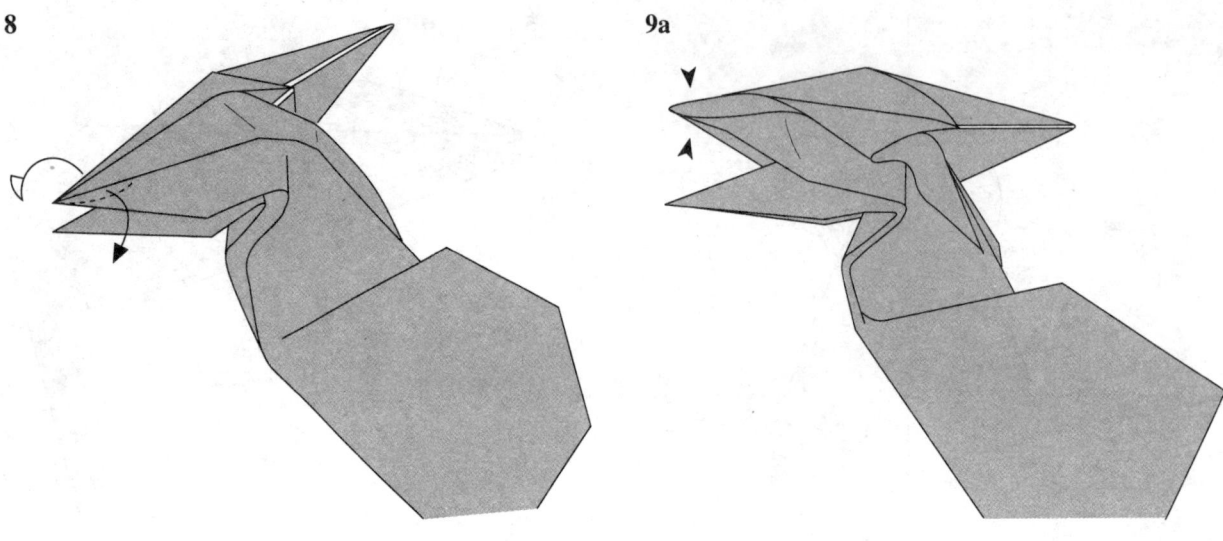

9a

Unfold the end part of the hidden flap inside-out. Repeat for the other side.

Pinch the tip and flatten the nose area with part of the hidden flap that has been turned inside-out. Repeat for the other side.

9b

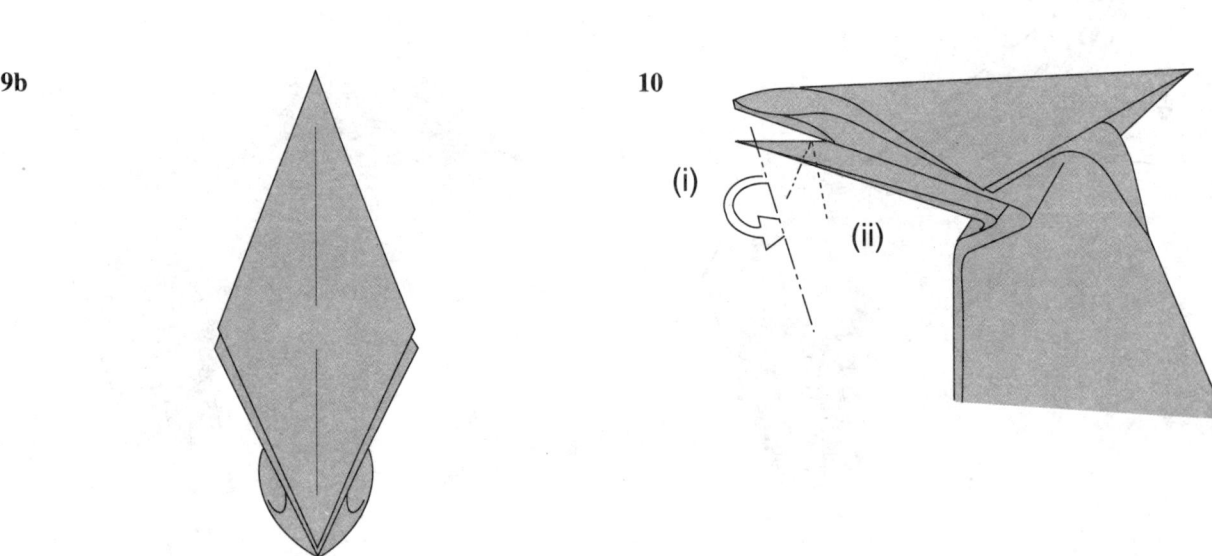

10

The diagram shows the head viewed from the top with the end part of the hidden flap turned inside-out.

(i) Tuck in the tip.
(ii) Crimp fold to form the mouth.

11

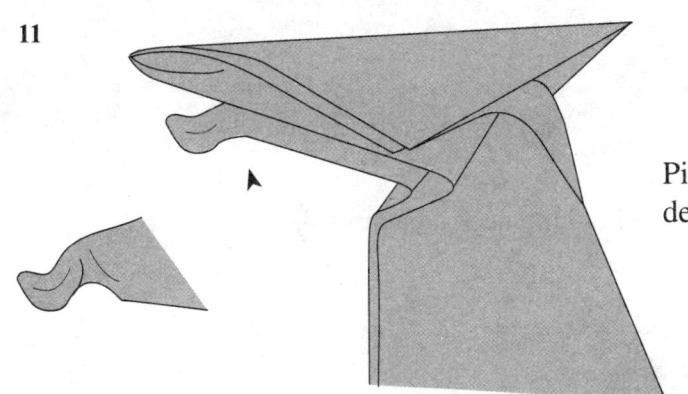

Pinch the area under the mouth to give it a small dent.

12

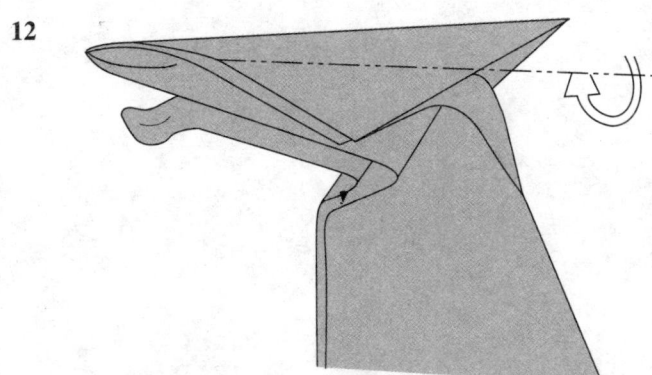

Tuck the flap inwards. Repeat for the other side.

13

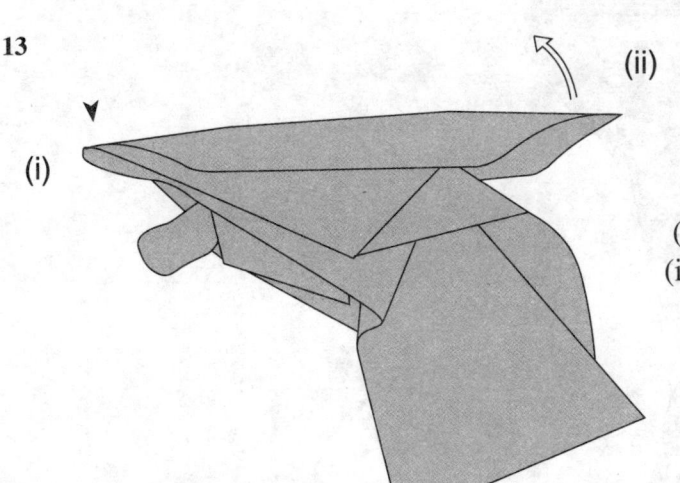

(i) Angle the nose area downwards.
(ii) Angle the tip of the crest upwards.

14

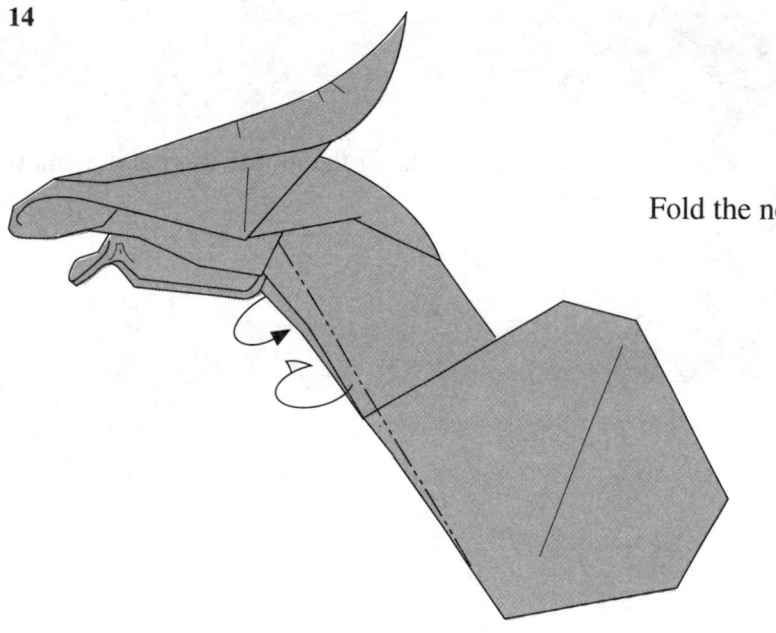

Fold the neck area inwards.

15

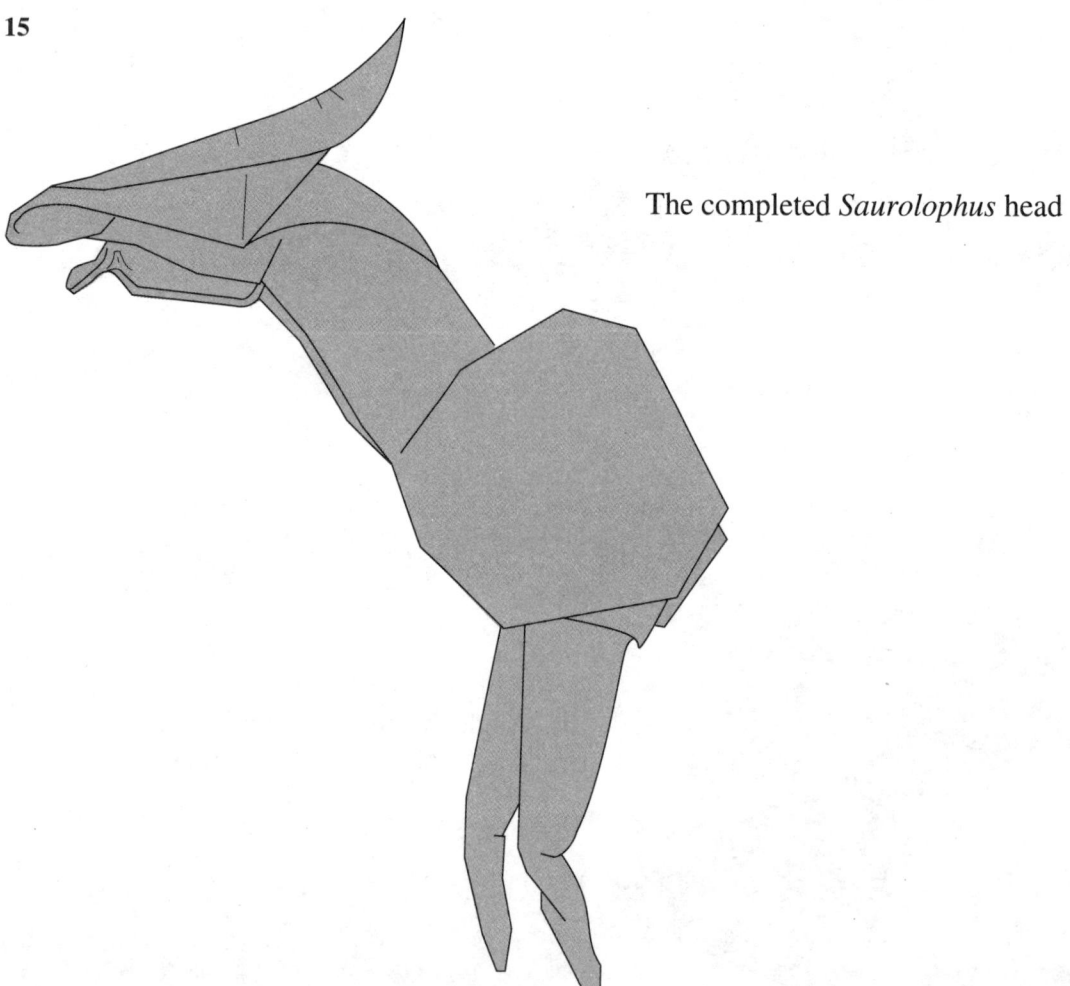

The completed *Saurolophus* head

The *Saurolophus* body

16

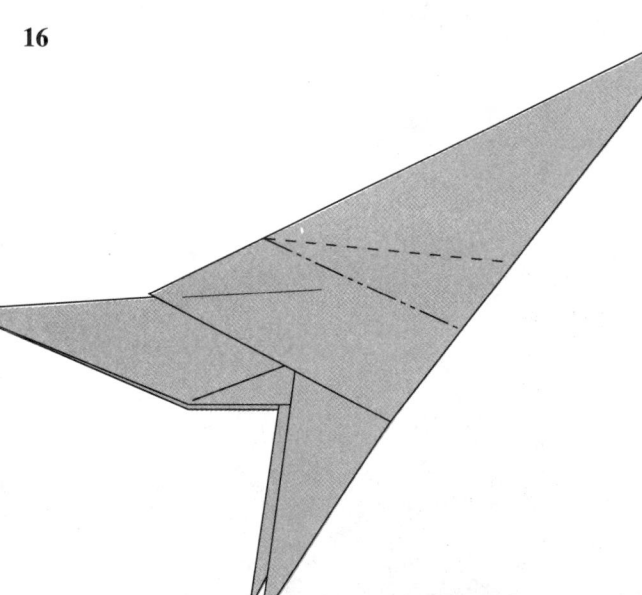

(i) Use a piece of 21 cm square paper.
(ii) Fold an offset preliminary base, offset 3 cm.
(iii) Fold a tail base A.
(iv) Crimp fold downwards to form the tail.
(v) Follow steps 13 to 18 of the *Tyrannosaurus* model.

(Remember: The *Saurolophus* has thinner legs, thinner thighs and a hunched back compared to *Tyrannosaurus*.)

17

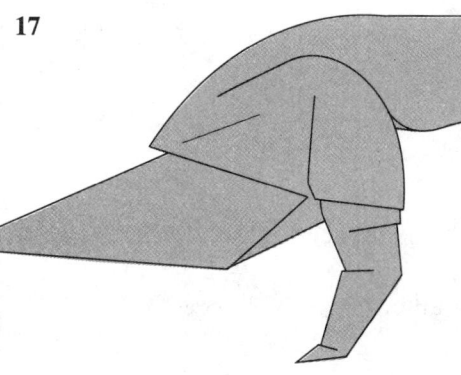

You can give the model a crouching posture by angling the legs forward and lifting the tail high up away from the feet.

18

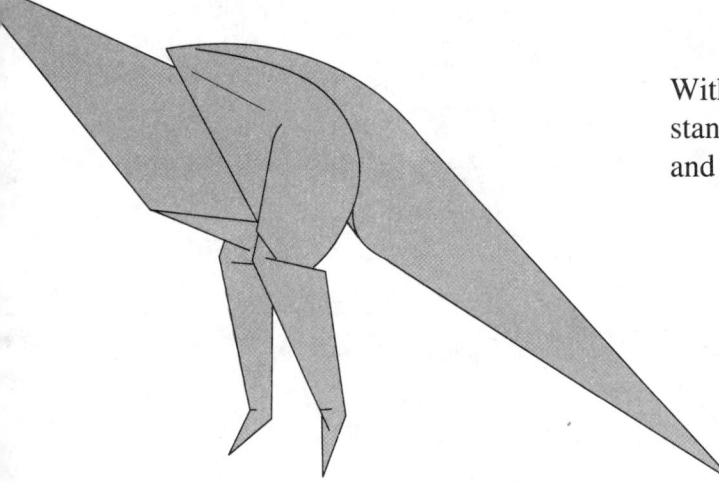

With the same model, you can change it to a standing position by angling the legs backwards and bringing the tail closer to its feet.

137

19

The completed *Saurolophus* model

Join the head and body together with glue.

Parasaurolophus

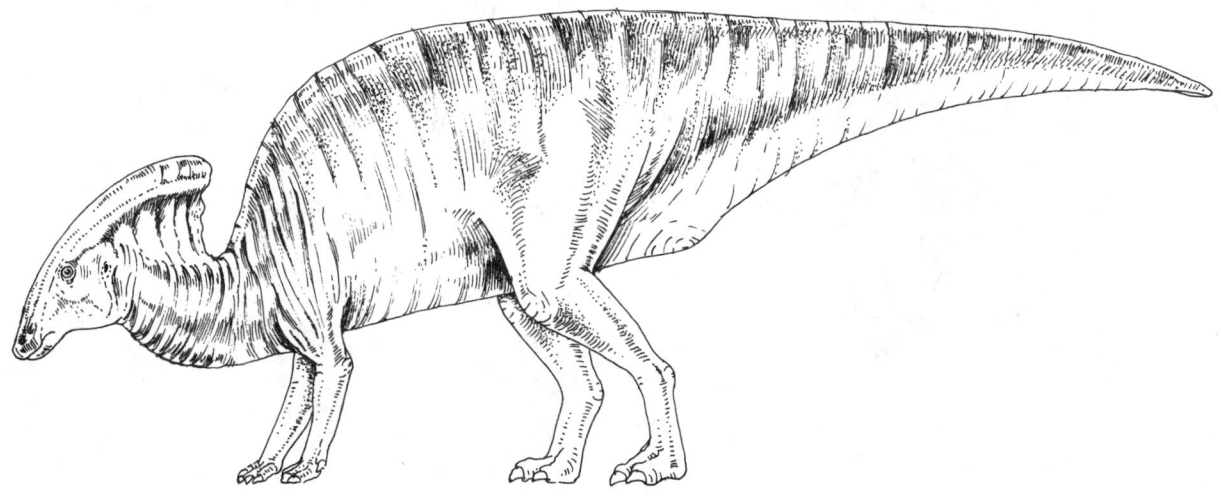

Parasaurolophus, also of the hadrosaur family, is about 30 ft (9 m) long. It has a tubular crest that is about 6 ft (1.8 m) long.

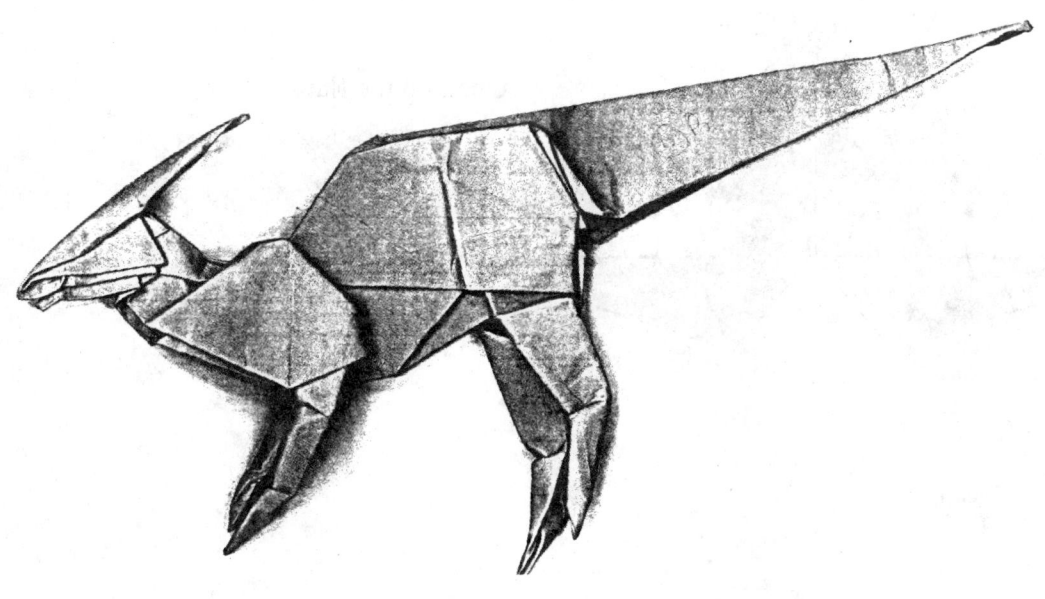

The *Parasaurolophus* Head

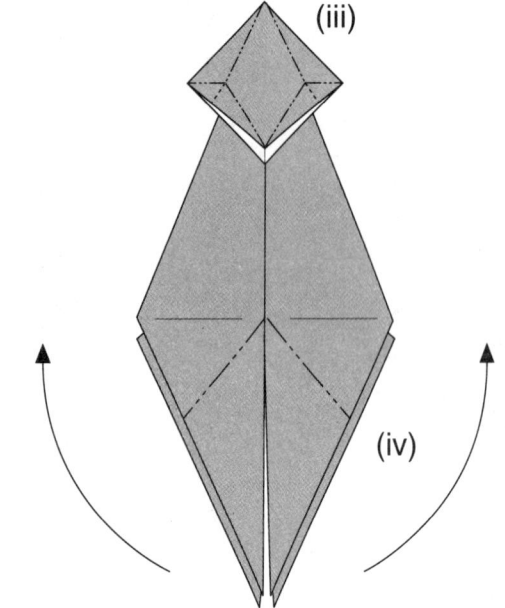

1

(i) Use a piece of 18 cm square paper.
(ii) Fold a hadrosaur base, offset 4 cm.
(iii) Frog fold the top square portion.
(iv) Reverse fold the two bottom flaps 90 degrees upwards to form the forelimbs.

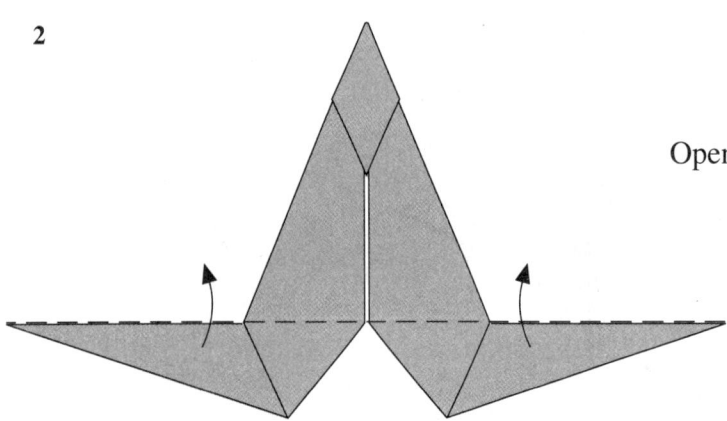

2 Open up the flaps.

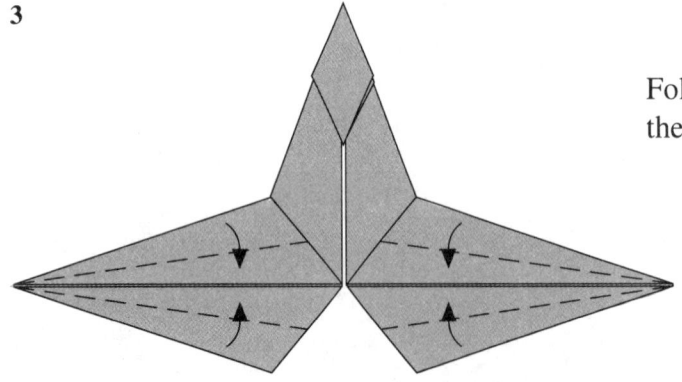

3 Fold inwards to make the forelimbs thinner. Get to the position shown in step 4.

4

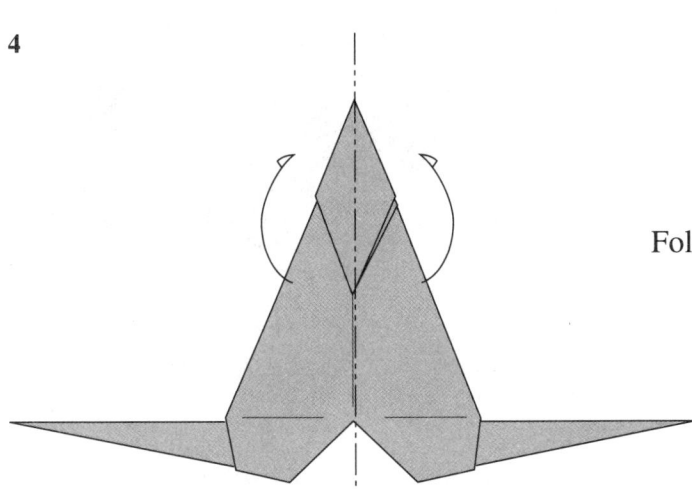

Fold the model in half.

5

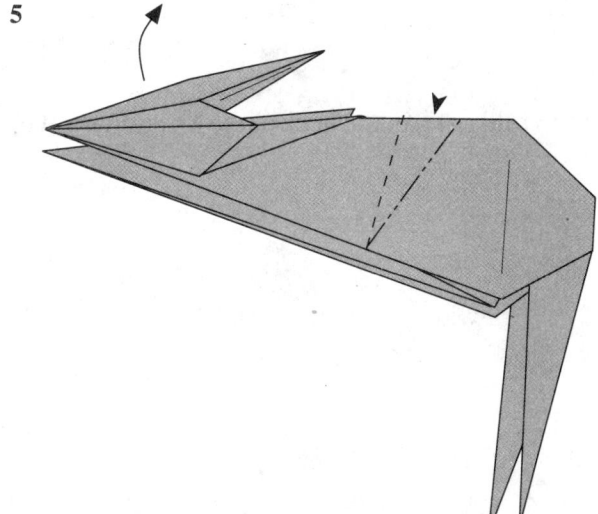

Crimp fold to form the shoulder and neck.

6

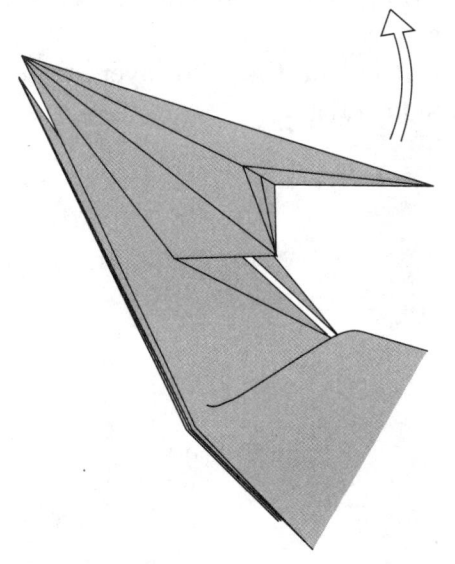

Pull the flap upwards as shown.

7

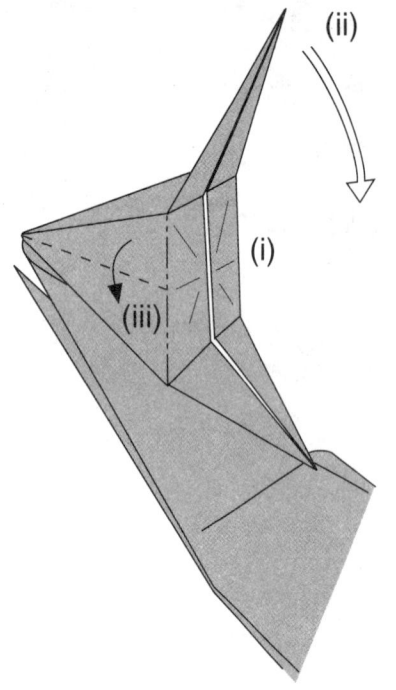

8

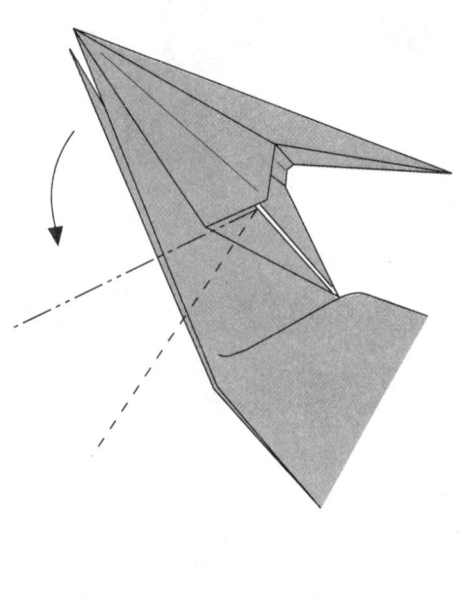

(i) You can see a box-like section. Crease the left and right edges of the "box".
(ii) Pull the top flap downwards.
(iii) The sides should close back to the position in step 6.

Crimp fold to form the neck at the location shown.

9

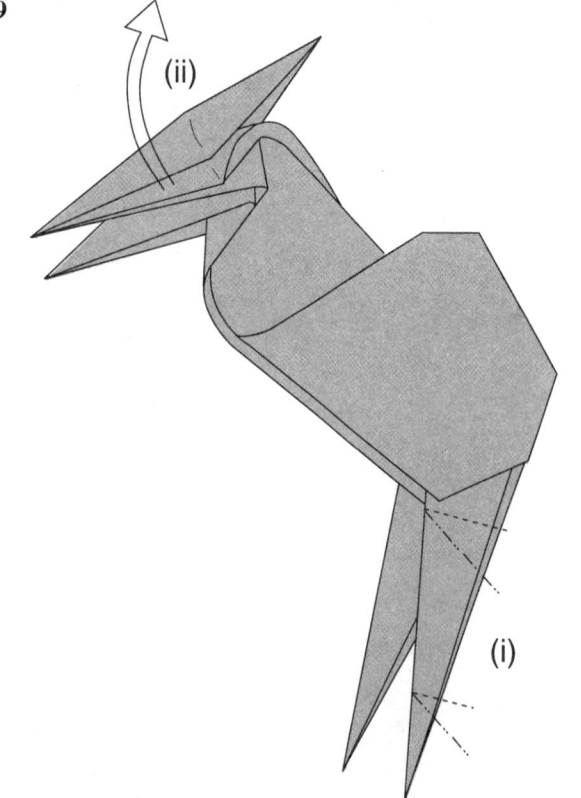

(i) Crimp fold the forelimbs to form the elbows and hands.
(ii) Lift up the first two layers to reveal the hidden flap.

10

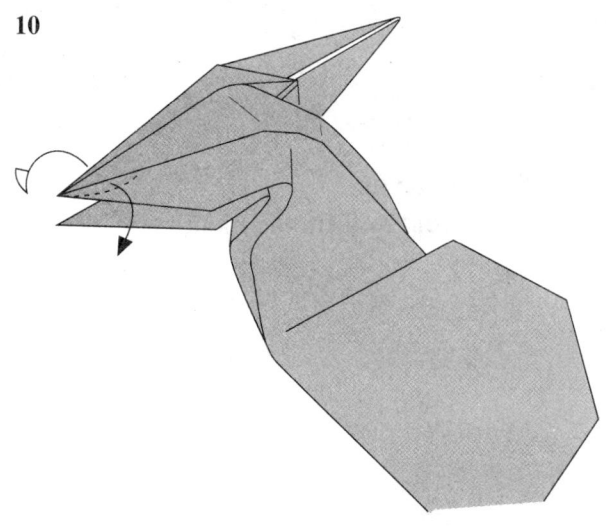

Unfold the end part of the hidden flap inside-out.

11a

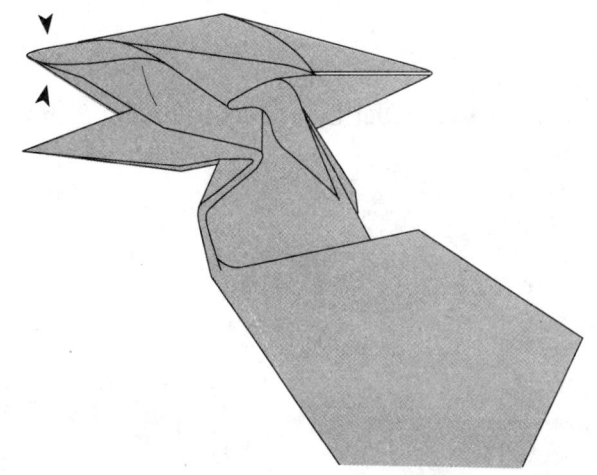

Pinch the tip and flatten the nose area with part of the hidden flap turned inside-out.

11b

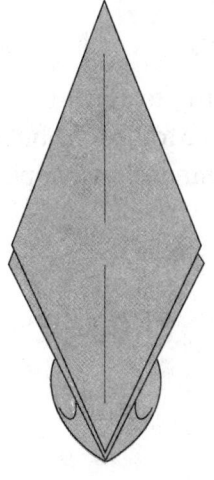

The diagram shows the head as viewed from the top, with the end part of the hidden flap turned inside-out.

12

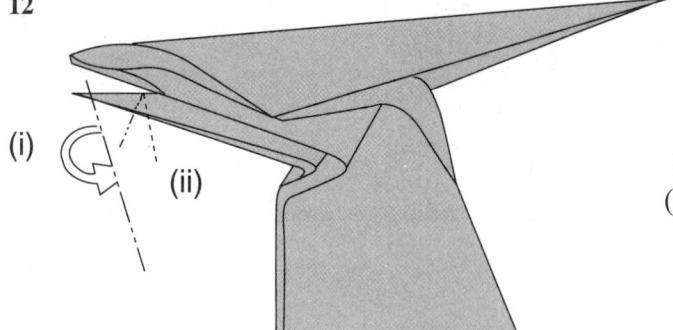

(i) Tuck in the tip.
(ii) Crimp fold to form the mouth.

13

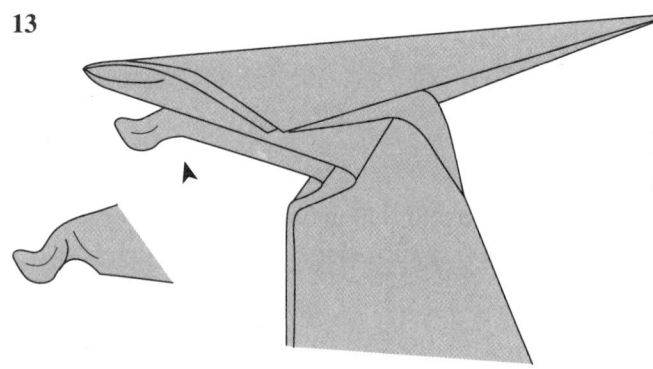

Pinch the area under the mouth to give it a small dent.

14

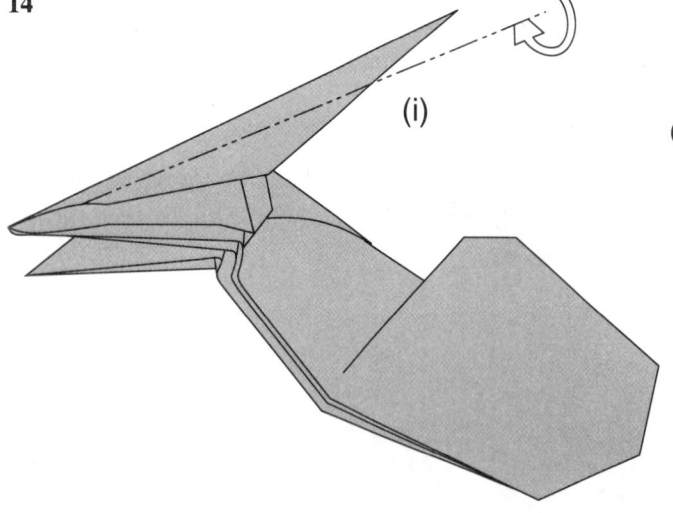

(i) Fold inwards to form the crest. The crest should not be folded flat but rounded to give it a three-dimensional appearance.

15

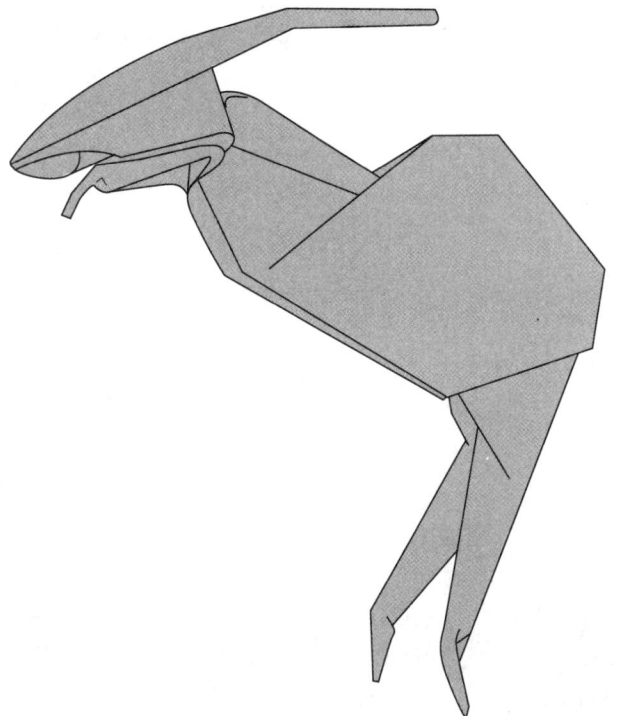

Angle the crest such that it is sloping backwards.

16

The completed *Parasaurolophus* model

The *Parasaurolophus* body is the same as the *Saurolophus* body.

Lambeosaurus

Lambeosaurus, another hadrosaur, has a hollow hatchet-shaped crest that juts forward from the skull.

1

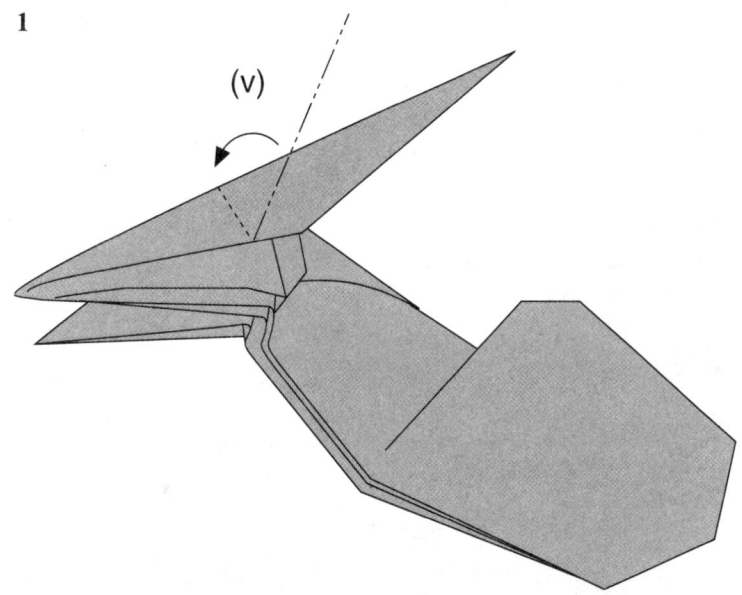

(i) Use a piece of 18 cm square paper.
(ii) Fold a hadrosaur base, offset 3.3 cm.
(iii) Do steps 1(iii) to 13 of the *Parasaurolophus* model.
(v) Crimp fold to form an upright hood.

2

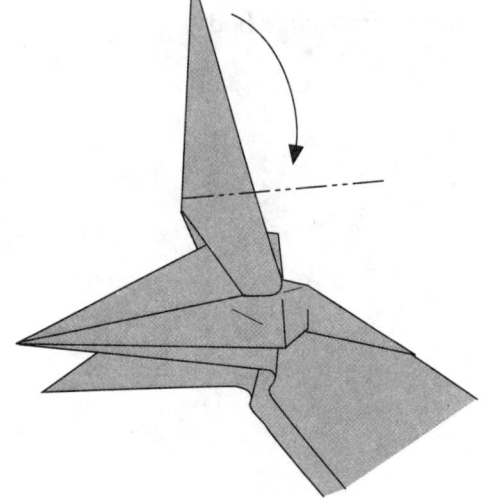

Reverse fold downwards.

3

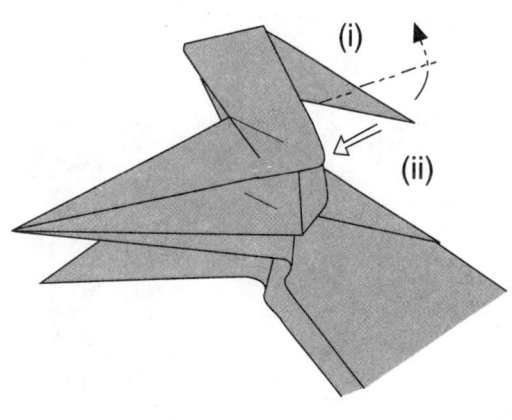

(i) Reverse fold the tip upwards.
(ii) Slide in the back portion so that the crest appears as in step 4.

147

4

The completed *Lambeosaurus* model

The *Lambeosaurus* body is the same as the *Saurolophus* body.

Iguanodon

Iguanodon (meaning "iguana tooth") was a large ornithopod which lived during the Early Cretaceous period. It is about 30 ft (9 m) long and stands about 16 ft (5 m) high. This dinosaur has four large fingers on each hand and a spike-like thumb that may have been used as a weapon or to help in its feeding.

The *Iguanodon* head

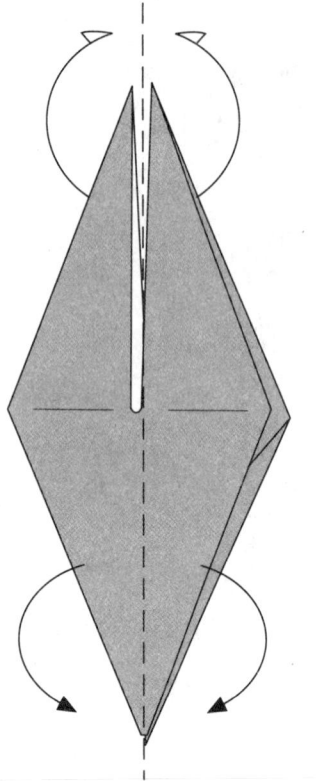

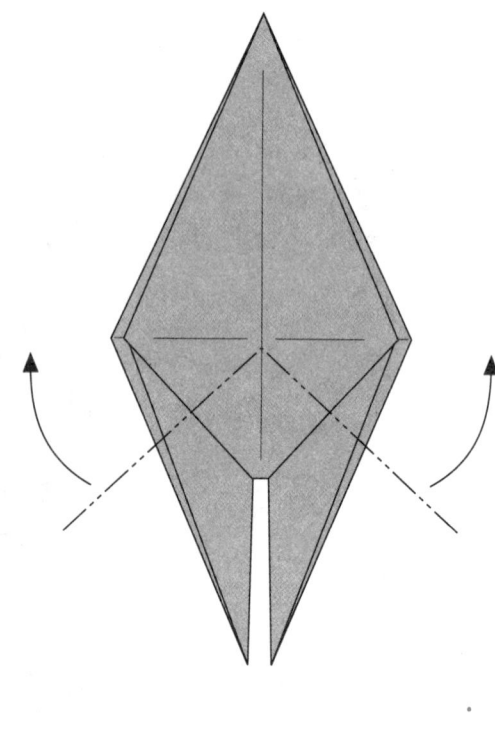

(i) Use a piece of 15.8 cm square paper.
(ii) Fold a bird base.
(iii) Fold the opposite sides together as in step 2.

(i) Reverse fold 90 degrees upwards to form the forelimbs.

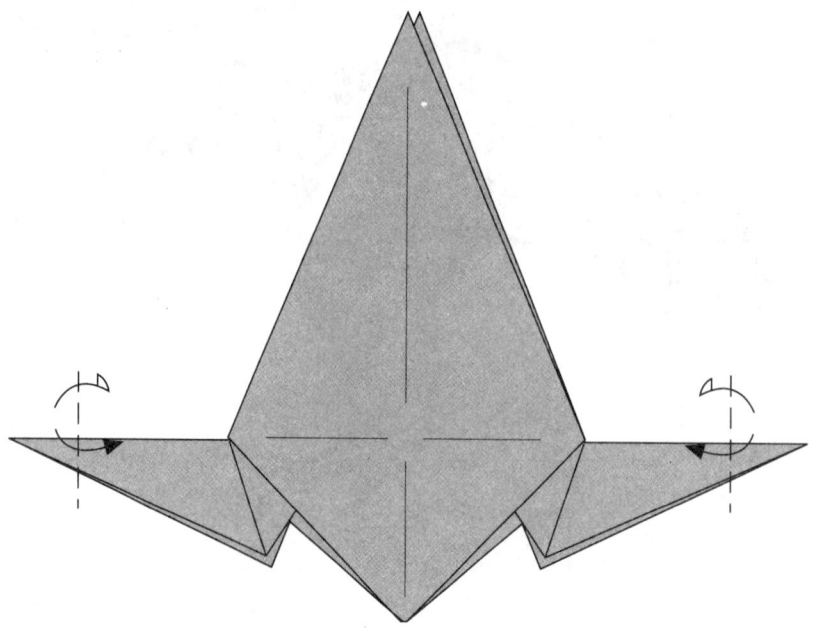

Reverse fold.

4

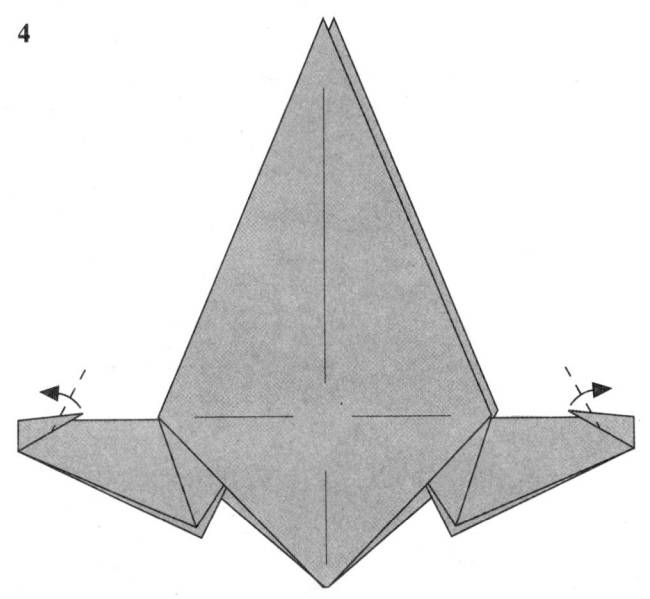

Reverse fold to form the thumb.

5

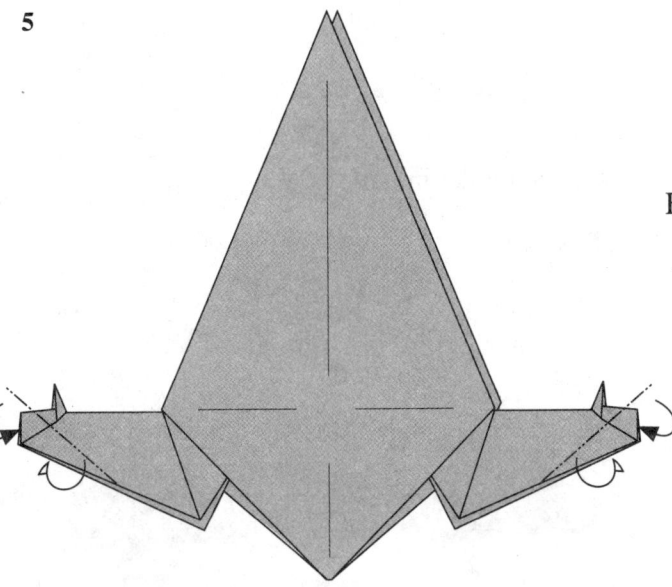

Fold inwards.

6

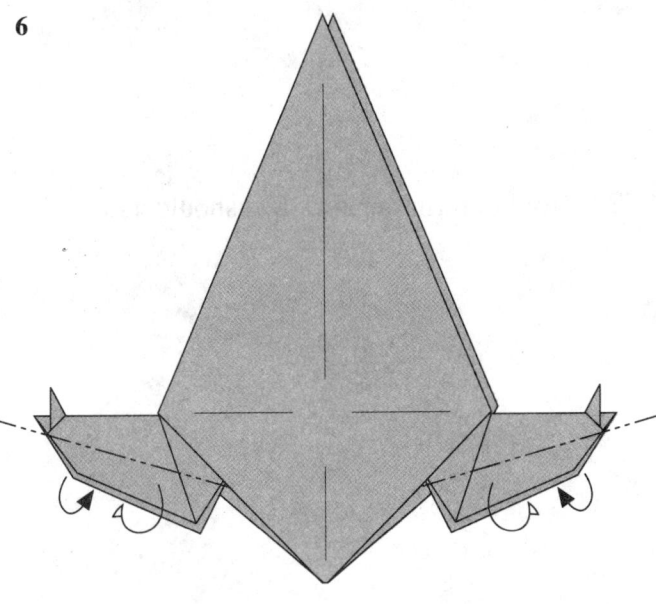

Fold inwards to make the forelimbs thinner.

7

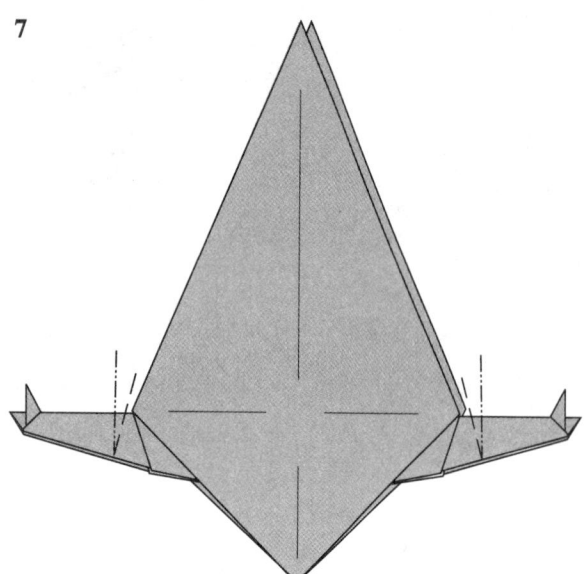

Crimp fold to form the elbows.

8

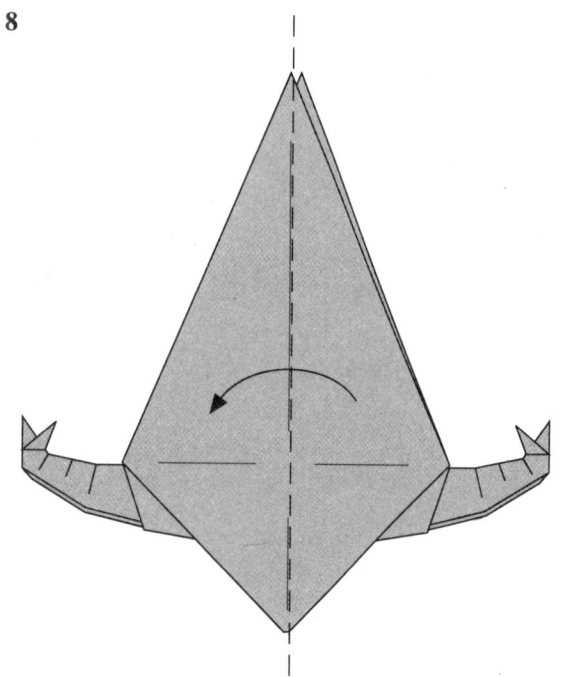

Fold the model in half.

9

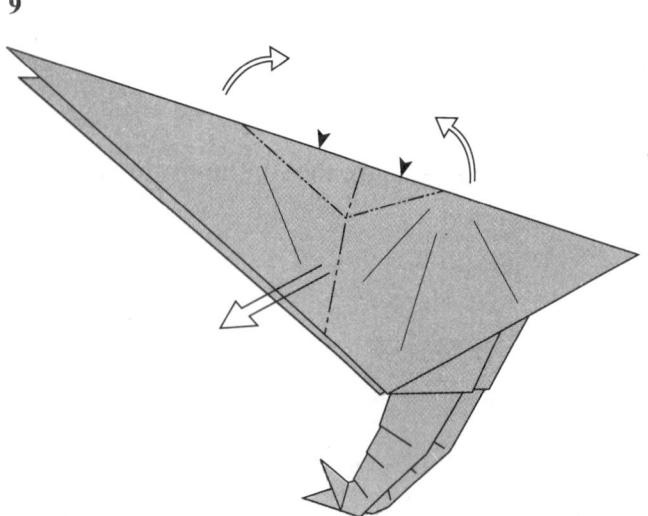

Sink fold to form the neck and shoulders.

10

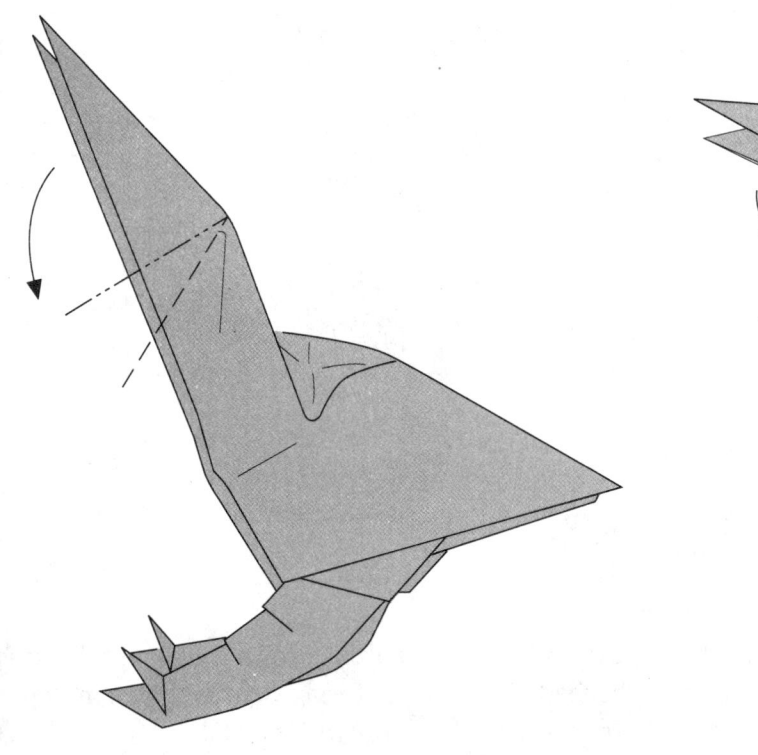

Crimp fold both layers downwards to form the head.

11

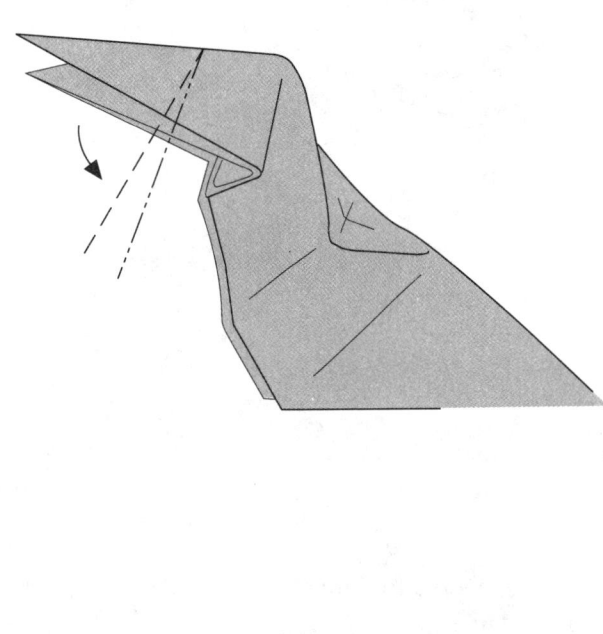

Crimp fold both layers slightly to form the cheeks.

12

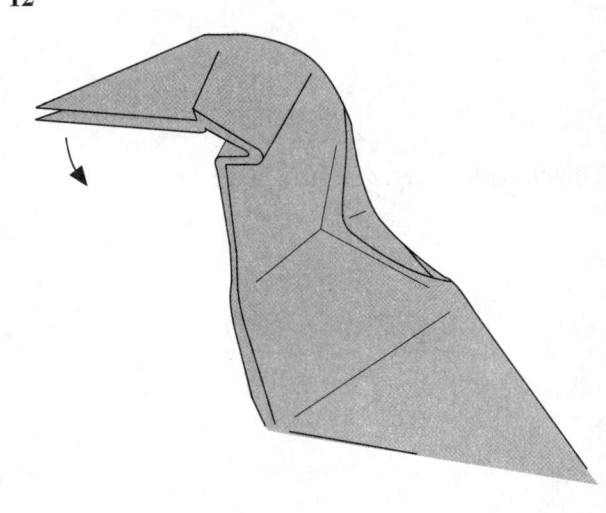

Pull the lower flap downwards to form the lower jaw.

13

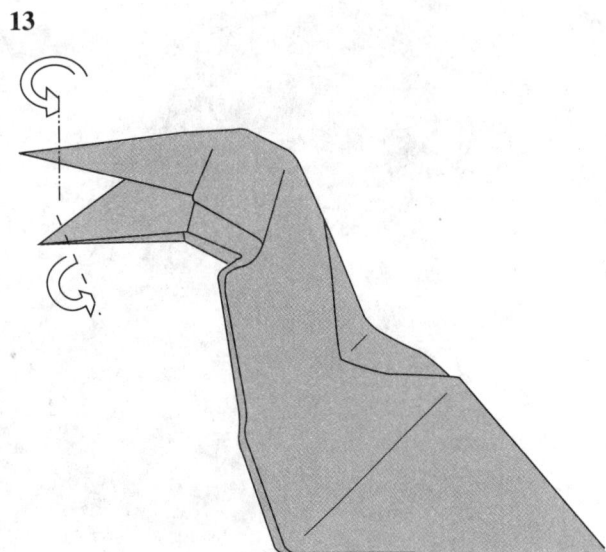

Tuck in both tips to shorten the head.

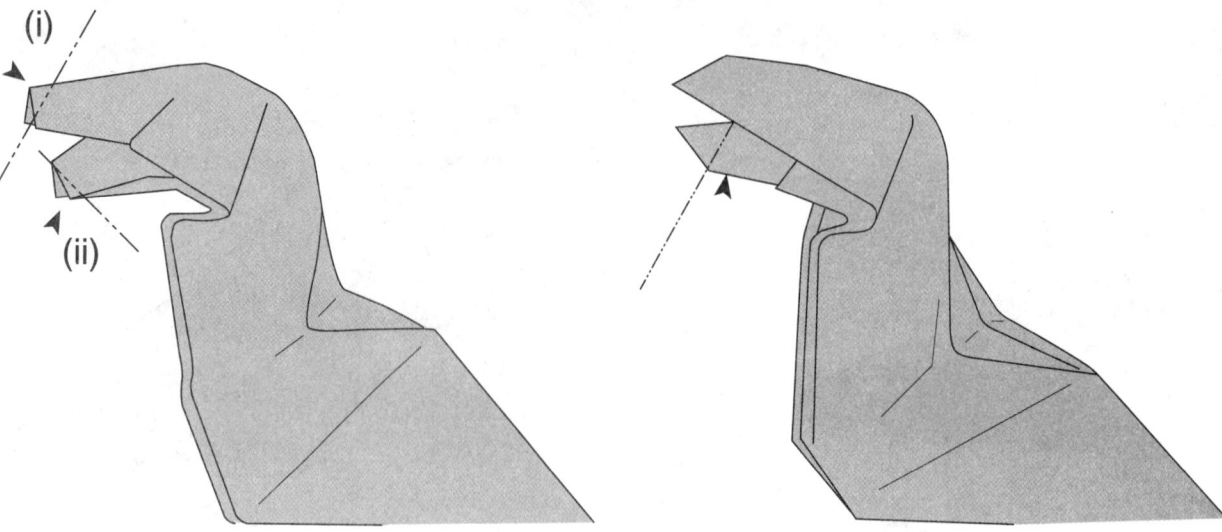

(i) Reverse fold inwards.
(ii) Tuck inwards.

Crimp fold downwards to form the mouth. Press beneath the mouth to form a dent as shown in step 16 (see also *Saurolophus* step 11).

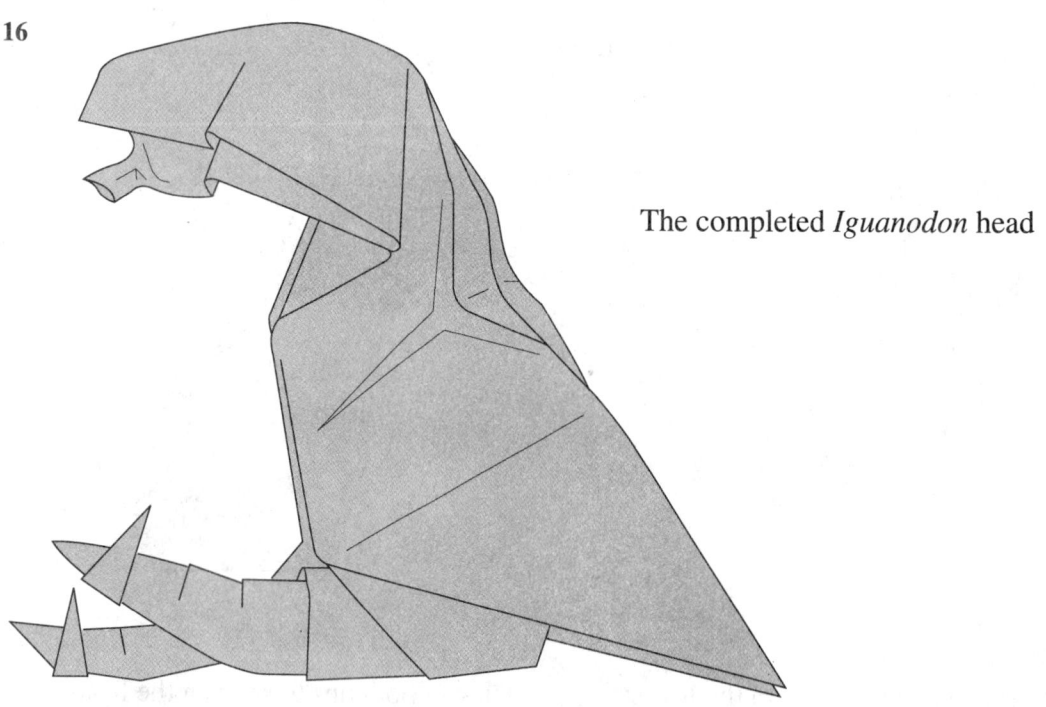

The completed *Iguanodon* head

The *Iguanodon* Body

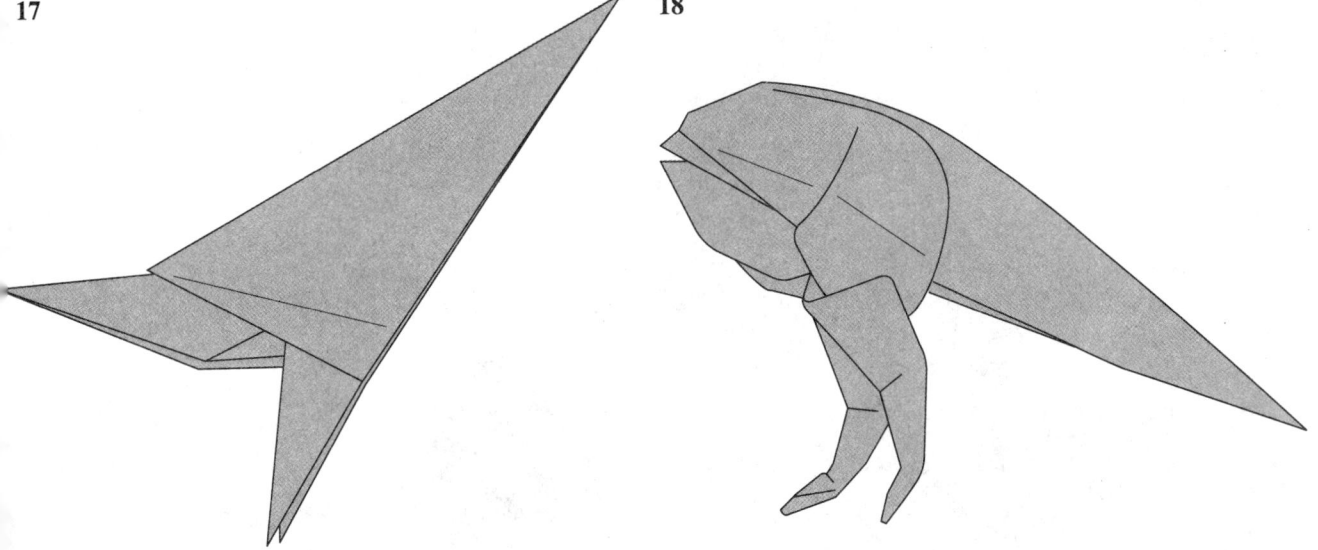

17

18 How the completed body should look

(i) Use a piece of 21 cm square paper.
(ii) Fold an offset preliminary base, offset 2 cm.
(iii) Fold a tail base A.
(iv) Follow the steps for making the *Saurolophus* body.

19 The completed *Iguanodon* model

Join the head and body together with glue.

Stegoceras

Stegoceras was a pachycephalosaur (meaning "thick-headed reptile") that lived during the Late Cretaceous period. This "bone-head" is about 6 ft (1.8 m) long, lightly built but with a massively thickened skull roof. This thick skull has given palaeontologists cause to believe that Stegoceras behaved very much like the mountain goats of today, using its head to butt each other in a display of dominance.

The *Stegoceras* head

1

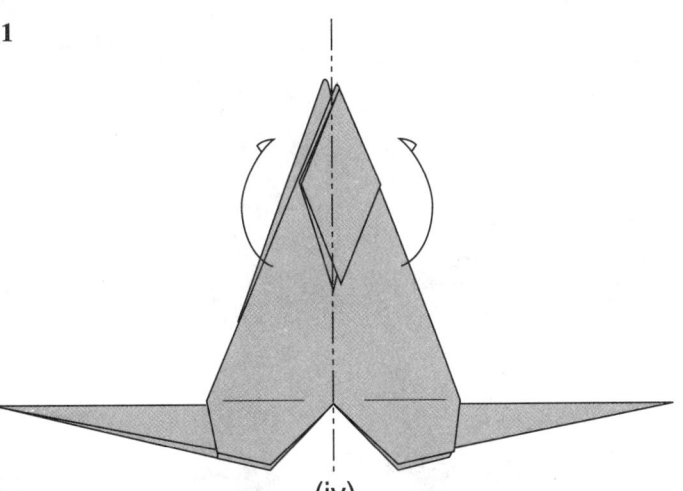

(i) Use a piece of 18 cm square paper.
(ii) Fold a hadrosaur base, offset 3.7 cm.
(iii) Do step 1 of the *Saurolophus* model.
(iv) Fold the model in half.

2

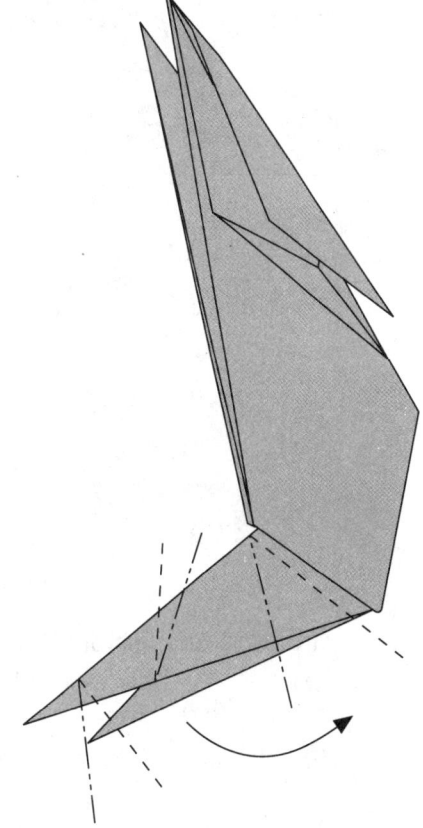

Crimp fold the forelimbs to form the shoulders, elbows and wrists.

3

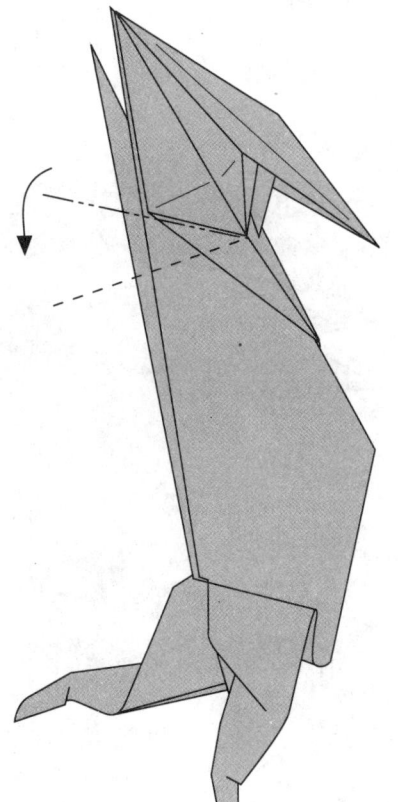

4

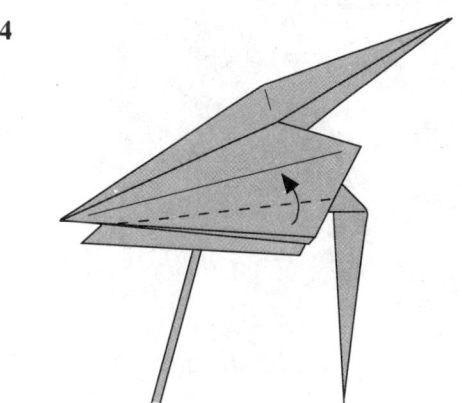

Crimp fold the neck downwards to form the head. Fold the flap upwards. Repeat for the other side.

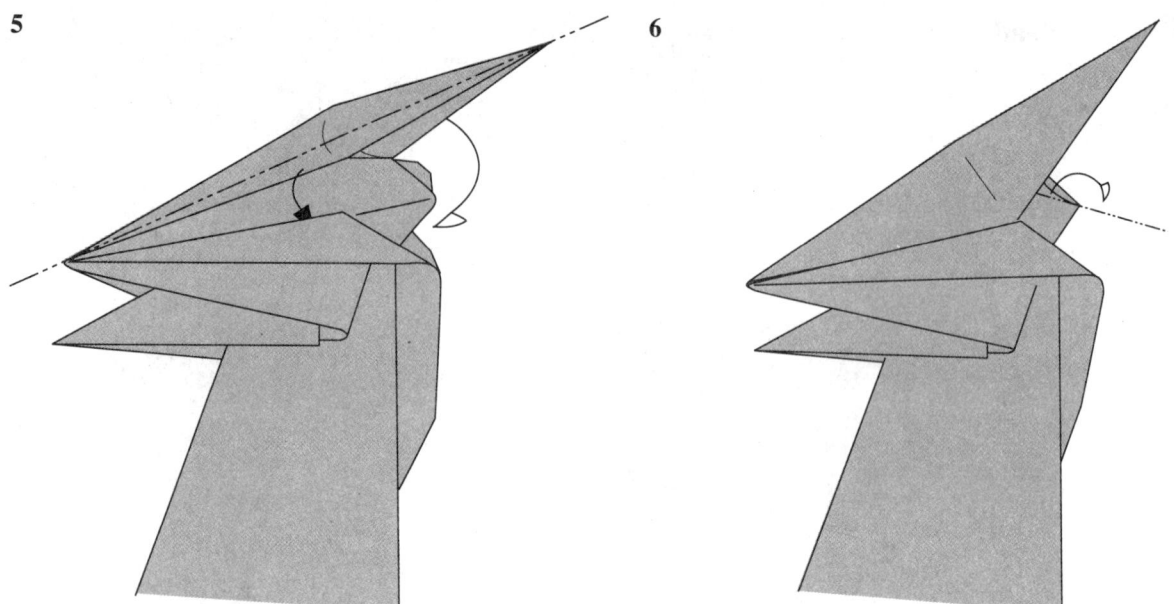

5 Fold downwards and tuck inside. Repeat for the other side.

6 Tuck in to make the flap thinner. Repeat for the other side.

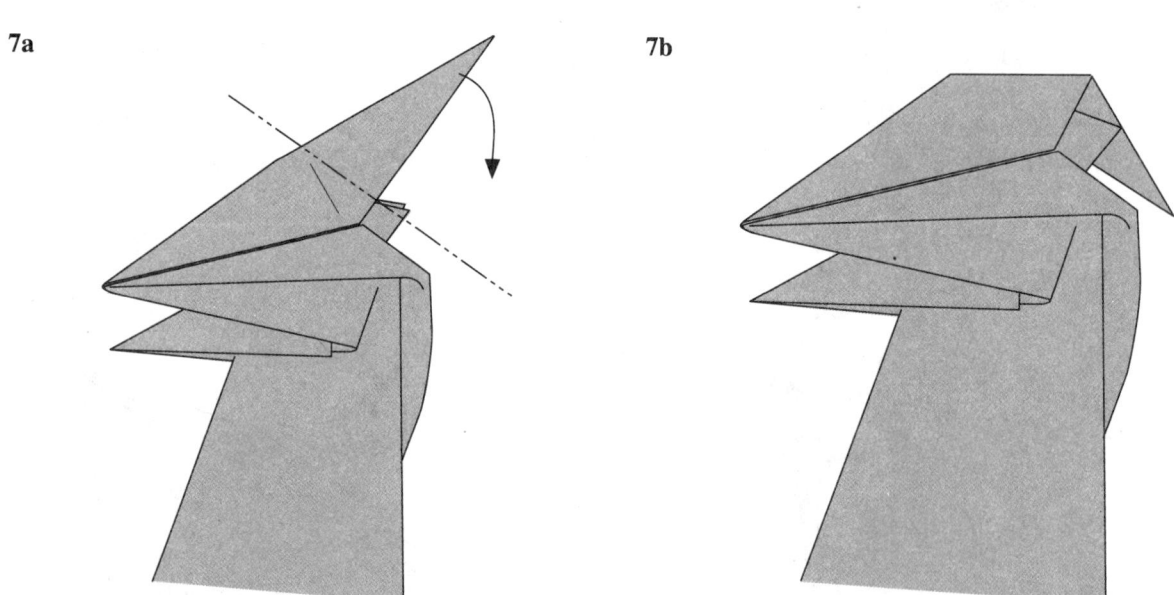

7a Reverse fold downwards as in step 7b.

8

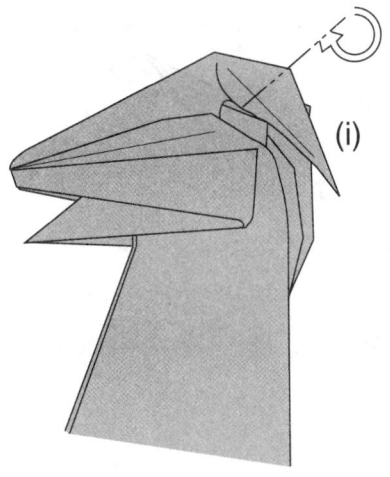

Fold tip inwards and tuck it inside.

9

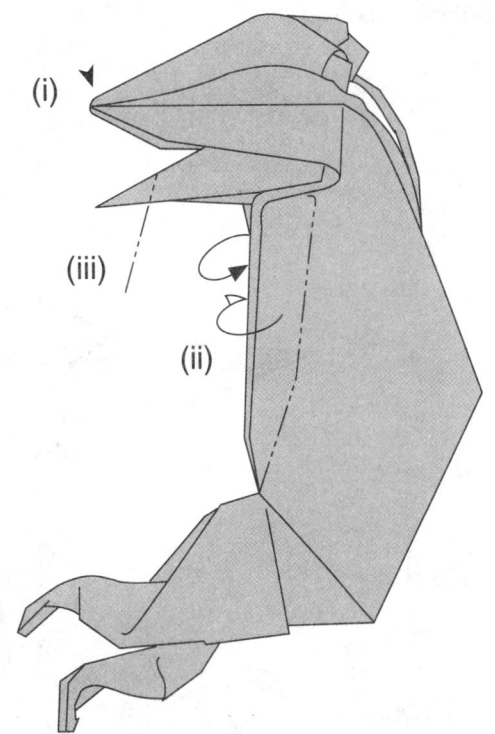

(i) Bend the nose to angle it downwards as shown in step 10.
(ii) Fold inwards to make the neck thinner.
(iii) Shape the mouth. Do steps 10 and 11 of the *Saurolophus* model.

10

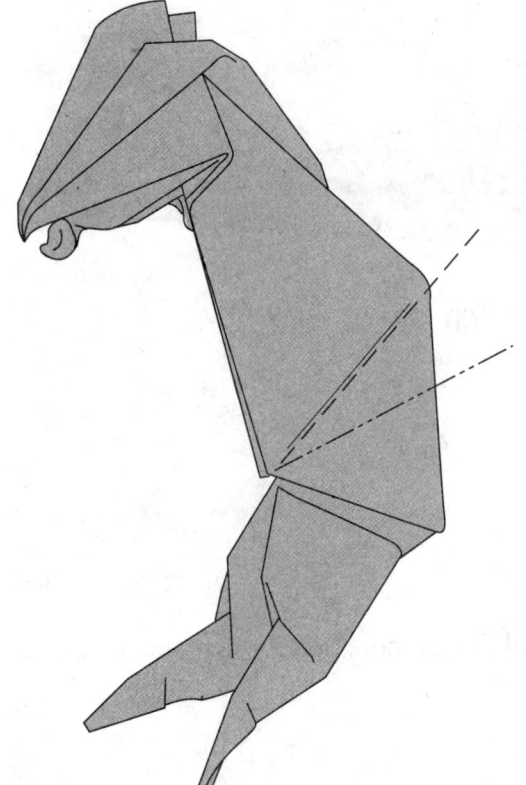

Crimp fold upwards to form the shoulders as in step 14.

The *Stegoceras* body

11

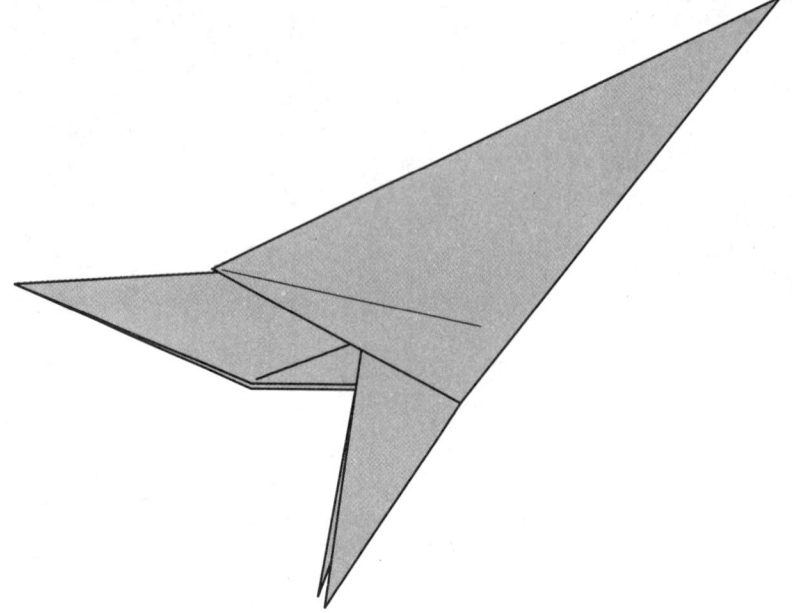

(i) Use a piece of 21 cm square paper.
(ii) Fold an offset preliminary base, offset 1.5 cm.
(iii) Fold a tail base A.
(iv) Do steps 13 to 18 of the *Tyrannosaurus* model to get to the stage shown in step 12.

12

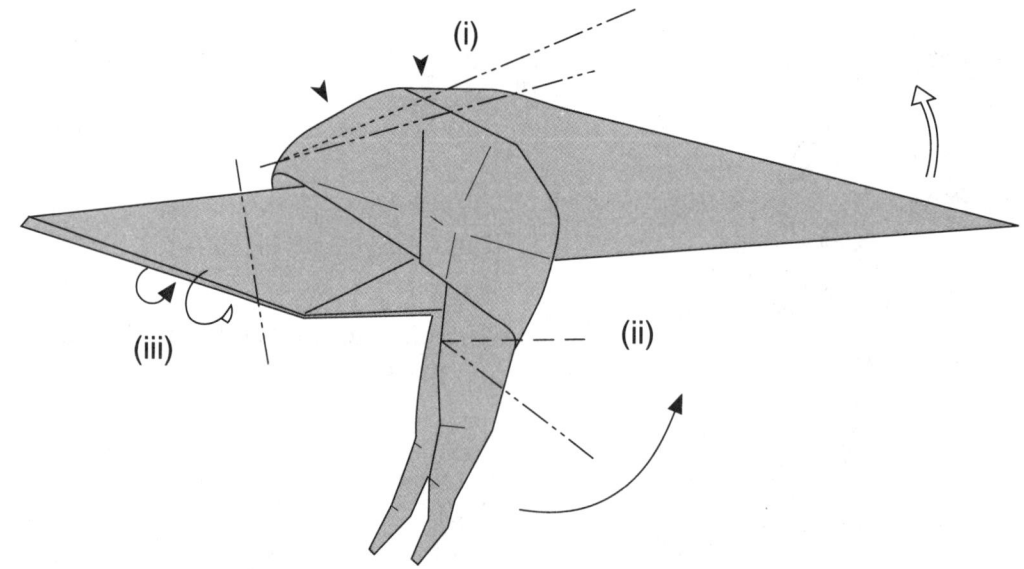

(i) Flatten the back by pulling the tail upwards and folding in more paper where the back crease is.
(ii) Crimp fold the legs to give it an upright posture.
(iii) Tuck in to hide this portion.

13

The body should look like this.

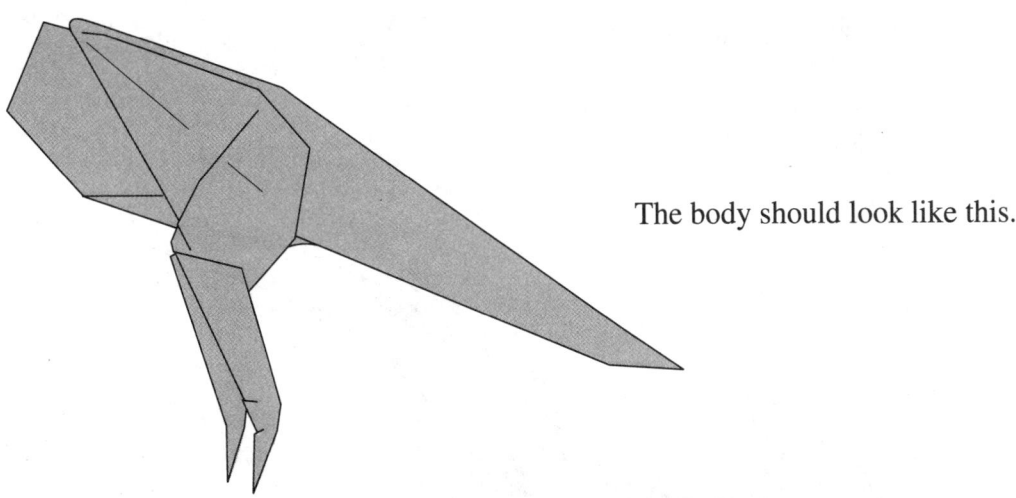

14

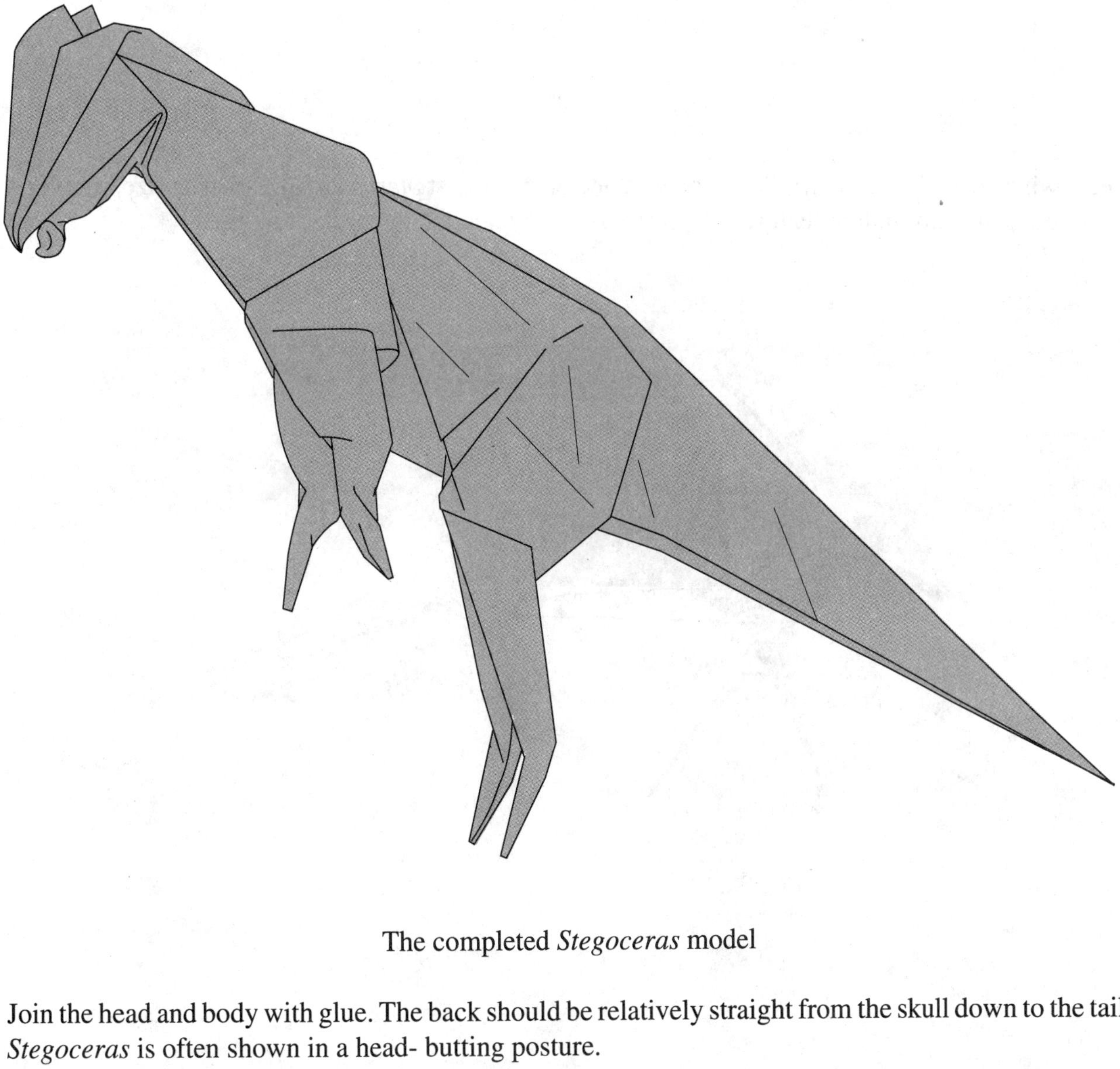

The completed *Stegoceras* model

Join the head and body with glue. The back should be relatively straight from the skull down to the tail. *Stegoceras* is often shown in a head-butting posture.

Pteranodon

With a wing span of 20 ft (6 m), *Pteranodon* is one of the largest *pterosaurs*. Despite its size, it is very lightly built. Its outstanding feature is a protruding bony hood at the back of its head.

1

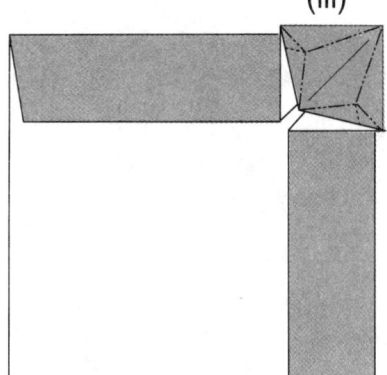

2

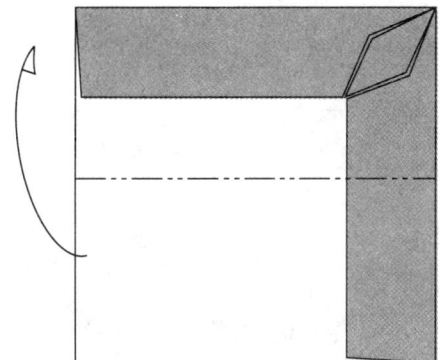

(i) Use a thin piece of 21 cm square paper.
(ii) Do steps 1 to 5 of the hadrosaur base using an offset of 4.4 cm.
(iii) At the top right-hand corner, fold the square flap by using a frog fold to get to step 2.

(i) Fold the bottom half behind (not the front!).

3

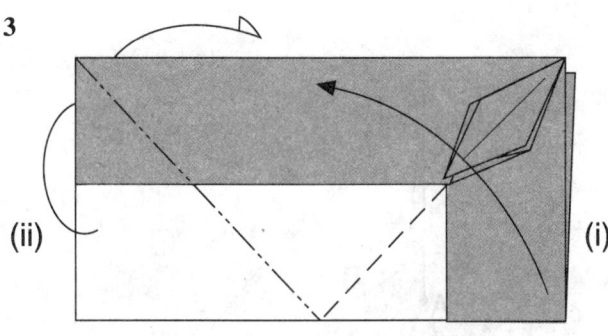

(i) Fold the bottom right corner forward to the centre top.
(ii) Fold the bottom left corner backwards to the centre top. Your folds should appear on opposite sides of the model.

4

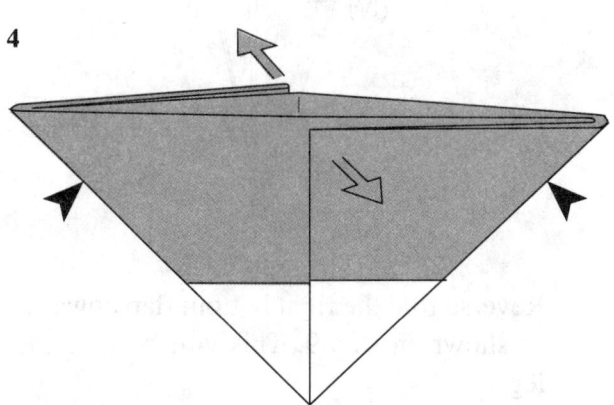

Do a squash fold to get a preliminary base.

5

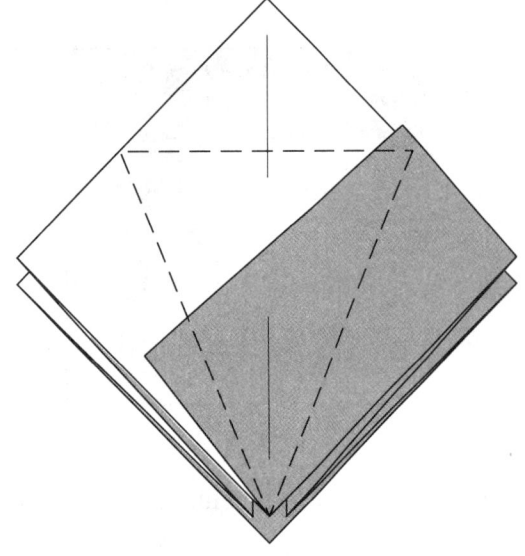

Proceed to make petal folds on both sides to arrive at a bird base.

6

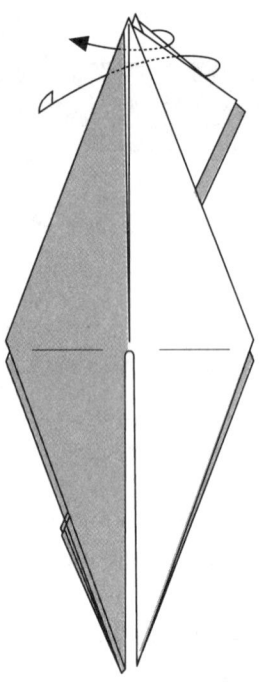

Pull out the two triangular flaps over to the right-hand side.

7

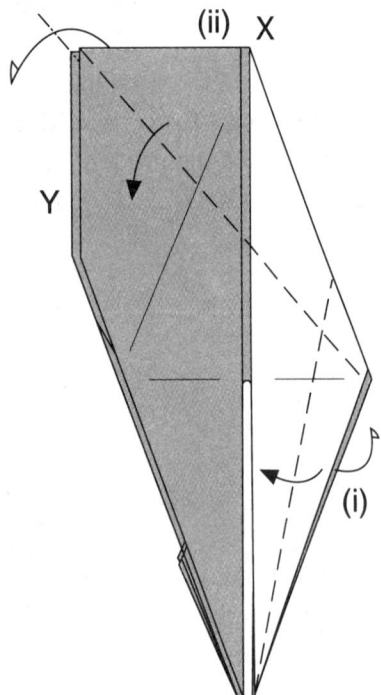

8

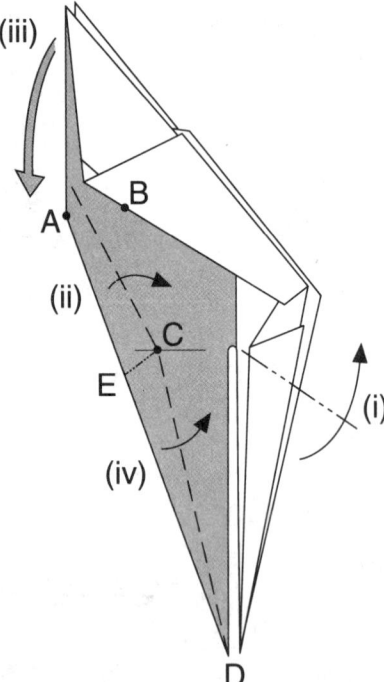

(i) Fold the right edge of the model. Repeat for the other side.
(ii) Fold the top portion, aligning X with Y. Repeat for the other side.

(i) Reverse fold the right bottom flap upwards as shown in step 9. This will become the legs.
(ii) Fold A to B up to point C.
(iii) Tilt the wings down.
(iv) Fold inwards along C to D.

9

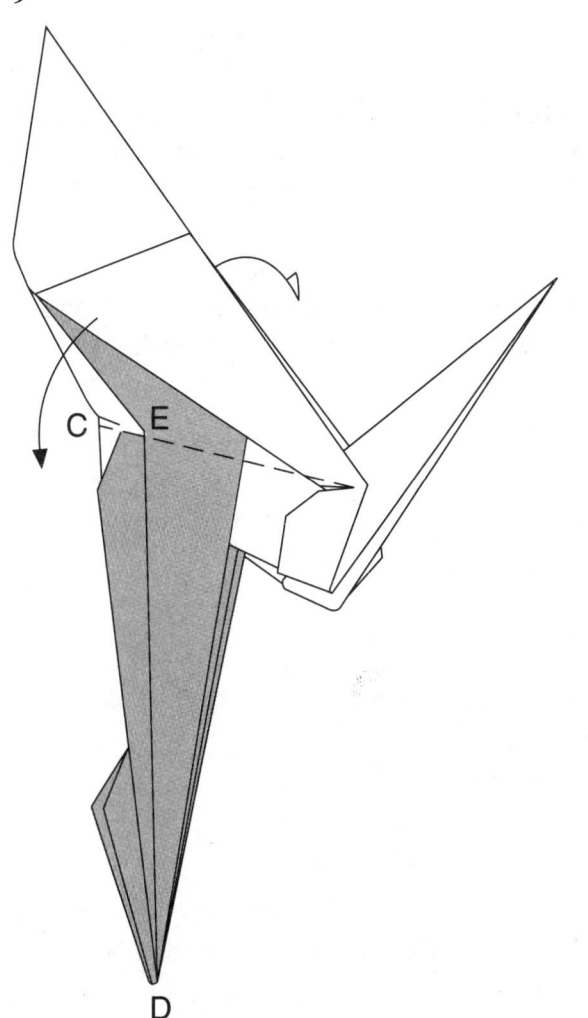

Fold the top portion downwards. It forms the wings.

10

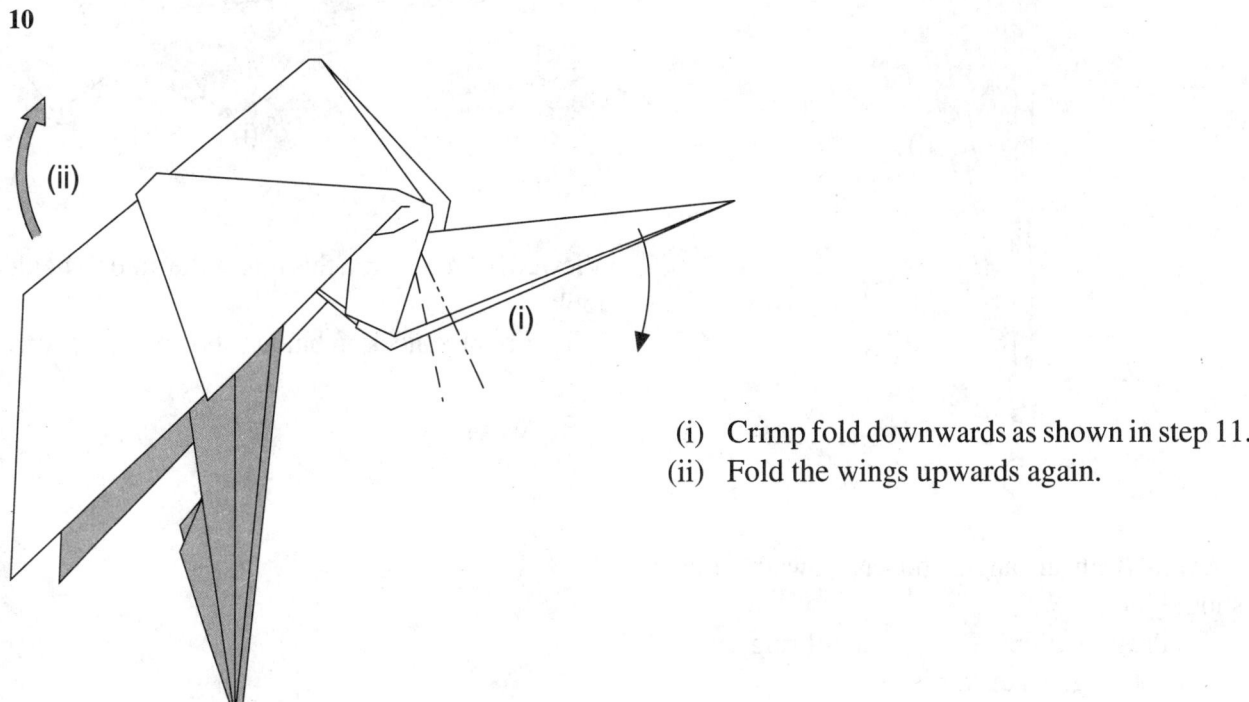

(i) Crimp fold downwards as shown in step 11.
(ii) Fold the wings upwards again.

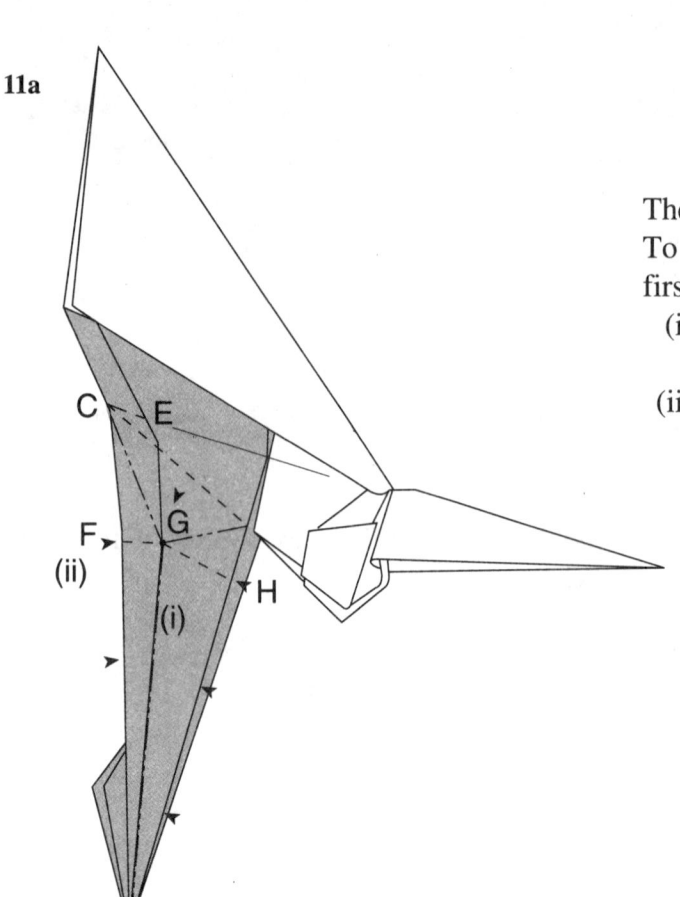

11a

The bottom left flap will form the neck and head. To make this portion thinner we need to flatten it first.

(i) Make a mountain fold crease from G to D. Repeat for the other side.
(ii) Press the right and left side edges (F and H) together to flatten this flap along the mountain fold crease (G to D).

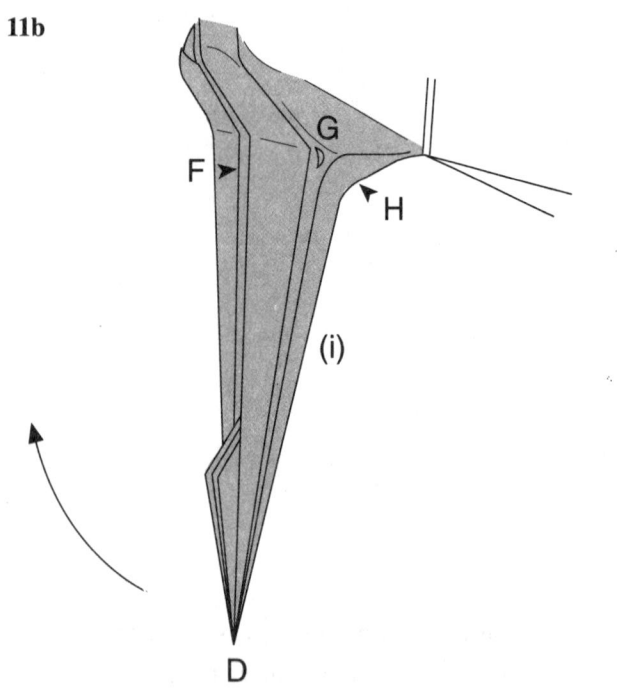

11b

Viewed from an angle, this is how the model should look.

(i) Press at points F and H and bring point D 100 degrees upwards.

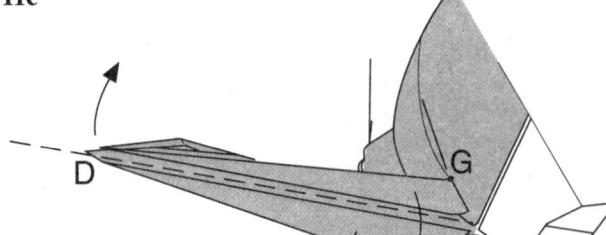

11c

Viewed from beneath, this is how the model should look.

(i) Fold the neck in half as shown in step 13.

166

12

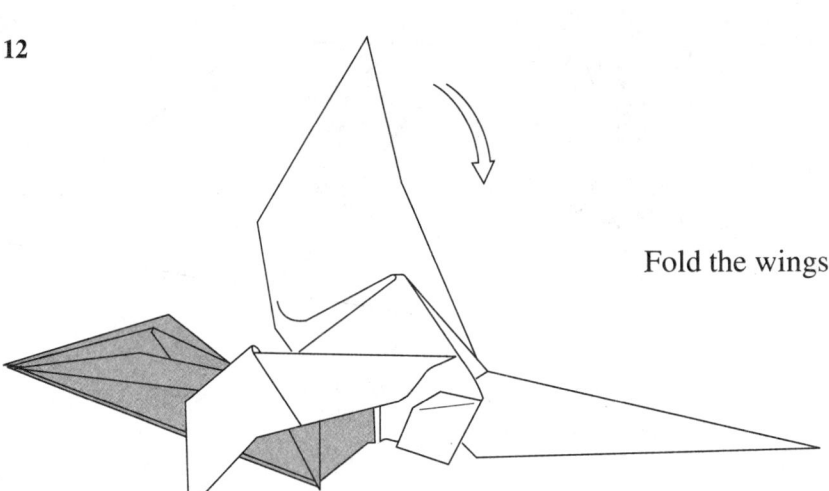

Fold the wings in a downward position.

13a

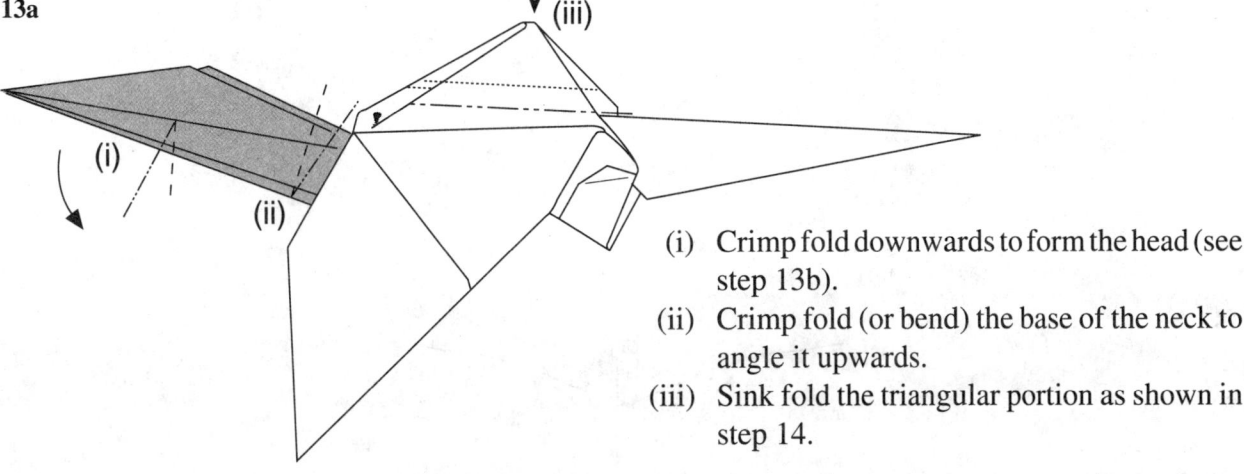

(i) Crimp fold downwards to form the head (see step 13b).
(ii) Crimp fold (or bend) the base of the neck to angle it upwards.
(iii) Sink fold the triangular portion as shown in step 14.

13b

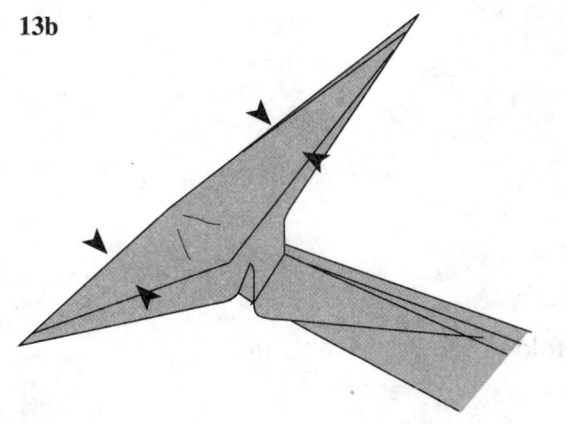

Pinch the two ends together to shape the beak and hood.

14

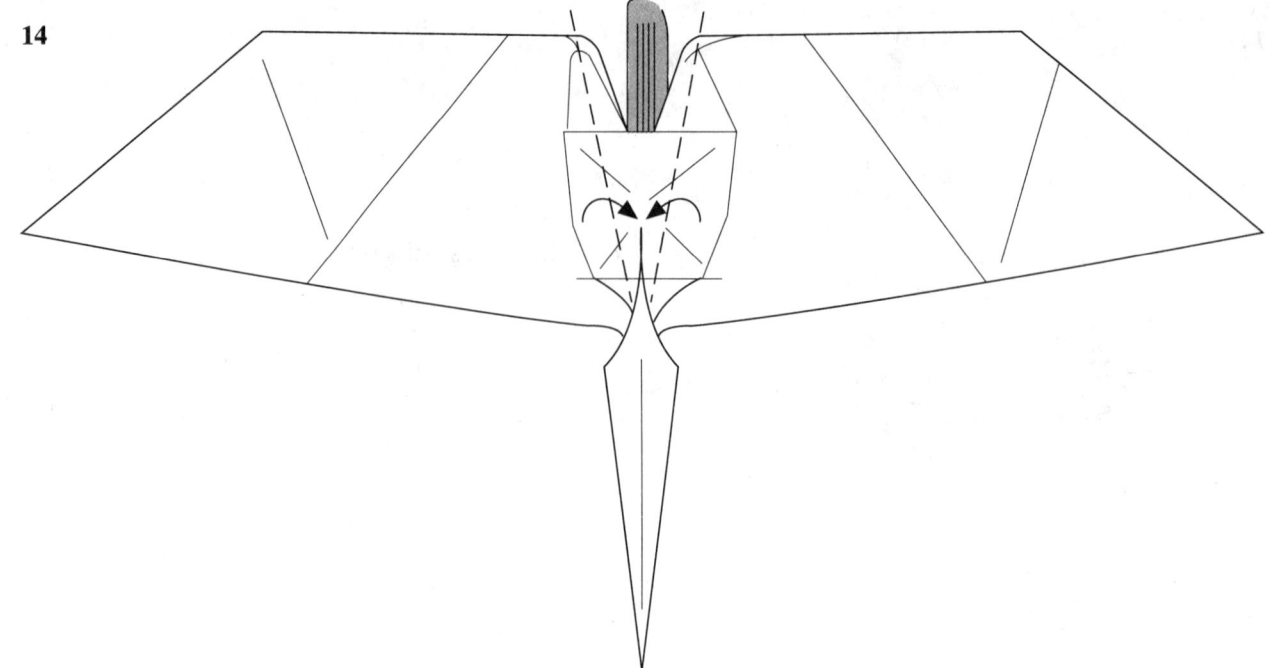

Viewed from the top. Fold inwards to get to step 15.

15

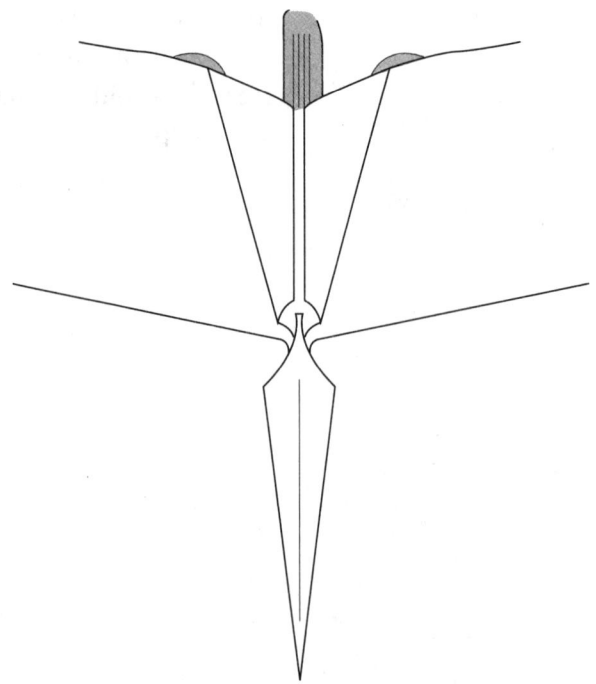

The completed fold

16

The completed *Pteranodon* model

Angle the end triangular portion of each wing downwards to give it some shape. Give the neck of your *Pteranodon* an S-shape. If you want, you can use scissors to slit the leg flap to form the legs. You can then curve the legs so that they are slightly apart.

Dimetrodon

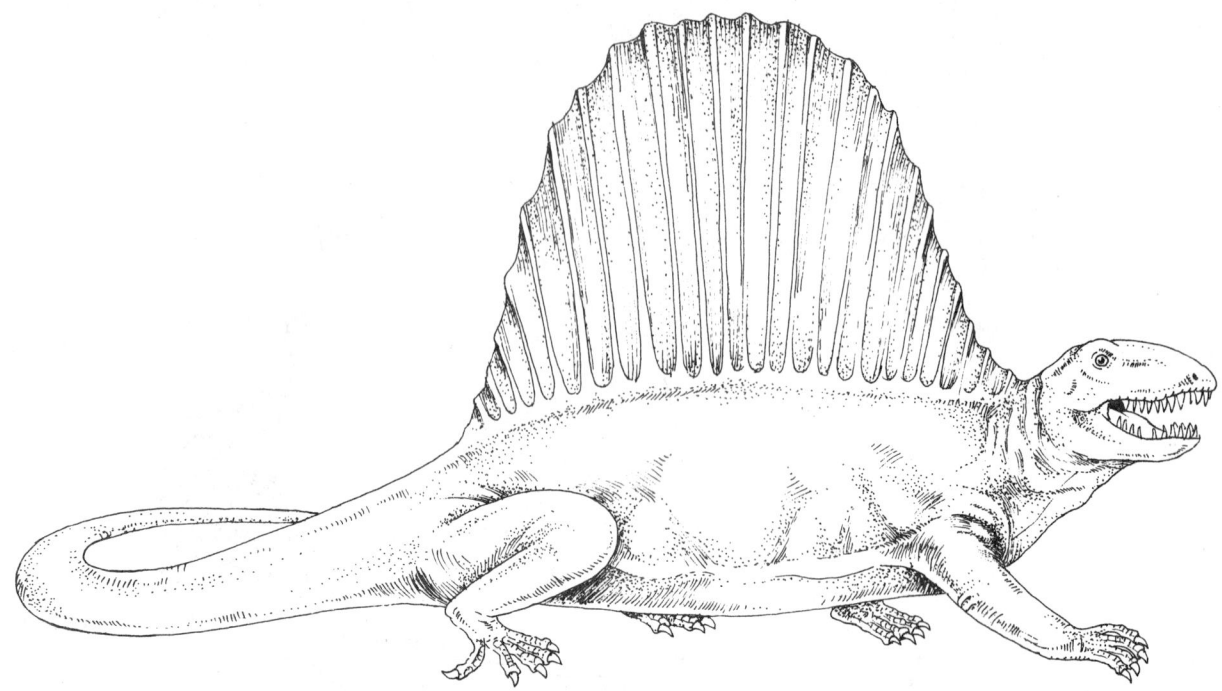

Dimetrodon is not actually a dinosaur but a pelycosaur, about 10 ft (3 m) long, living during the Permian period (pre-Triassic). This meat-eating fin-backed reptile has short back teeth and long pointed front teeth for tearing flesh. Its most outstanding feature is the sail on its back. This sail is used to absorb heat and regulate body temperature.

1

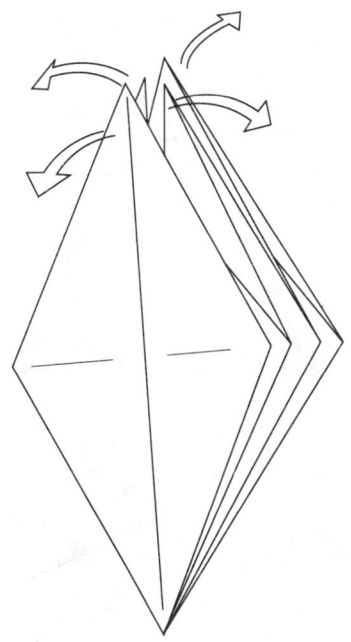

(i) Use a thin piece of 21 cm square paper.
(ii) Make a frog base.
(iii) Open up the frog base.

2

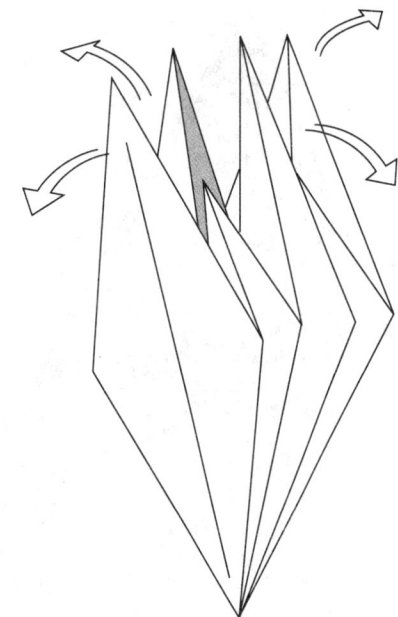

By pulling the four points apart, open up the model completely.

3 **4**

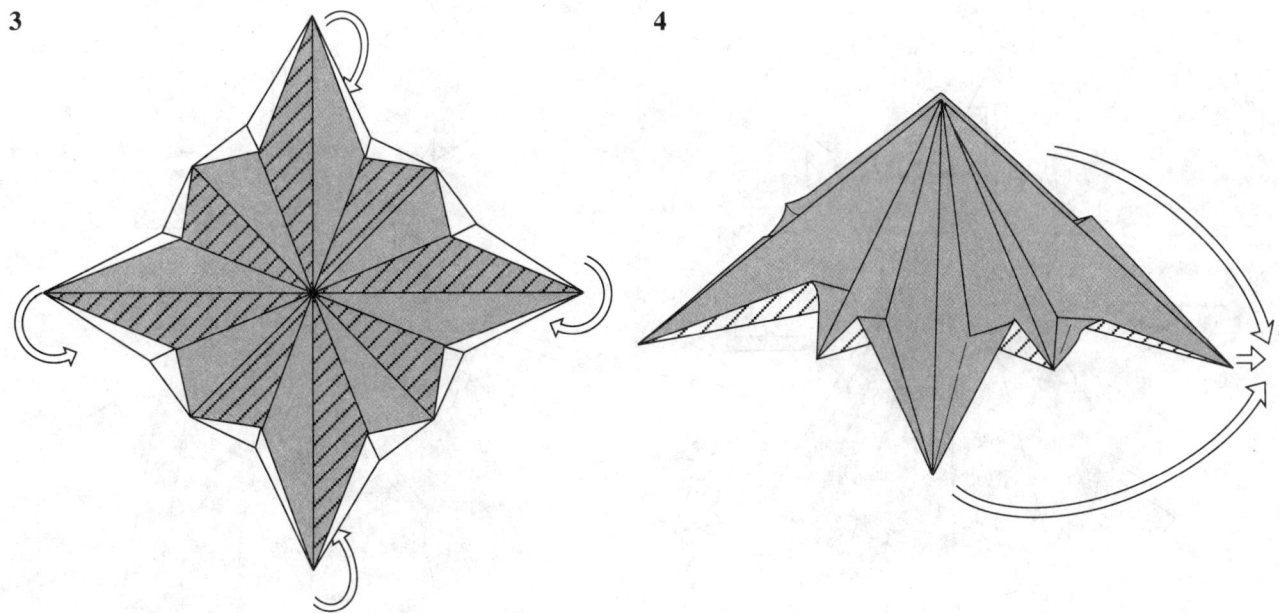

Invert the paper so that what was previously the inside becomes the outside.

Gather three of the four corners together as shown in step 5.

5

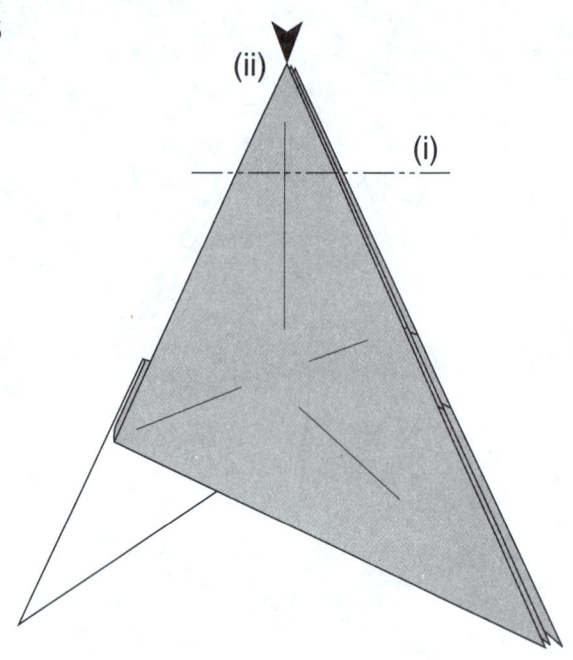

6

Make sure your model looks exactly as shown. You should have a triangular model with three flaps on one side and one flap on the other.
Fold the short flap (on both sides of the model) over to the left. Your model should look like that in step 6.

(i) Make a crease about 2.5 cm from the top.
(ii) Sink fold the top 2.5 cm portion.

7

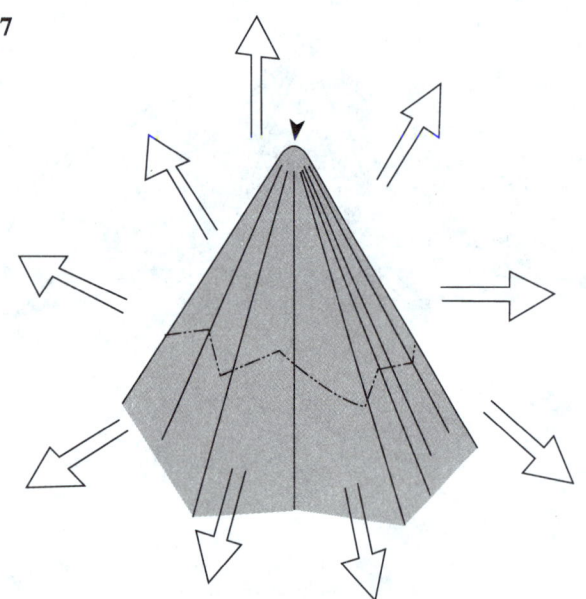

8

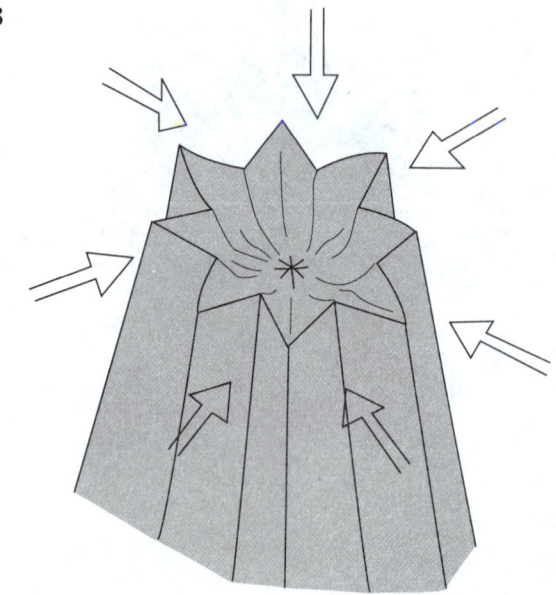

Diagram of a sink fold in progress. (Paper is pulled out in all directions and then pressed in from the top.)

Diagram of a sink fold in progress. (Once the paper is "sunk", the creases are brought in neatly to form a petal. It should then be neatly folded back as in step 9.)

9

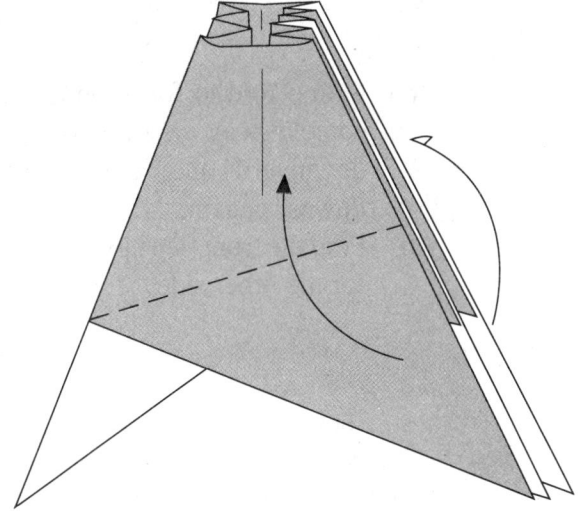

Fold upwards. Repeat for the other side.

10

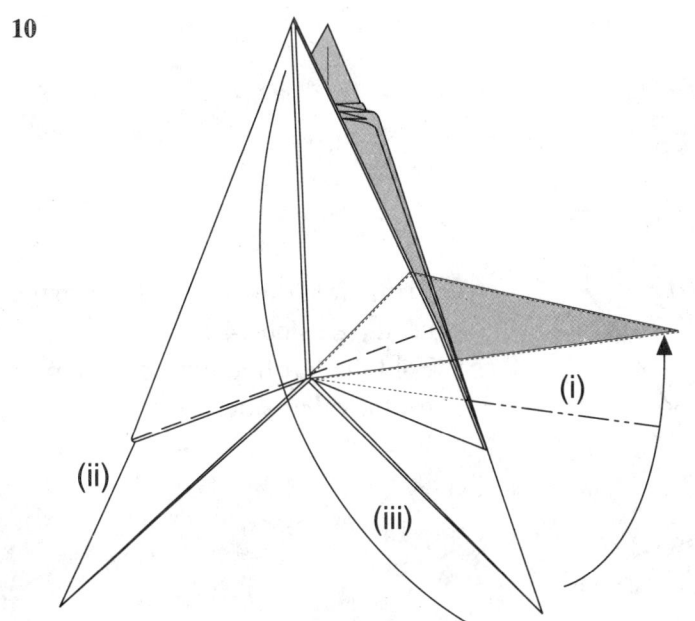

(i) Hold the middle of the model and slide the bottom right flap (head flap) 90 degrees upwards as shown in step 11.
(ii) Repeat for the bottom left flap (tail flap).
(iii) Bring the front and back flaps down again.

11

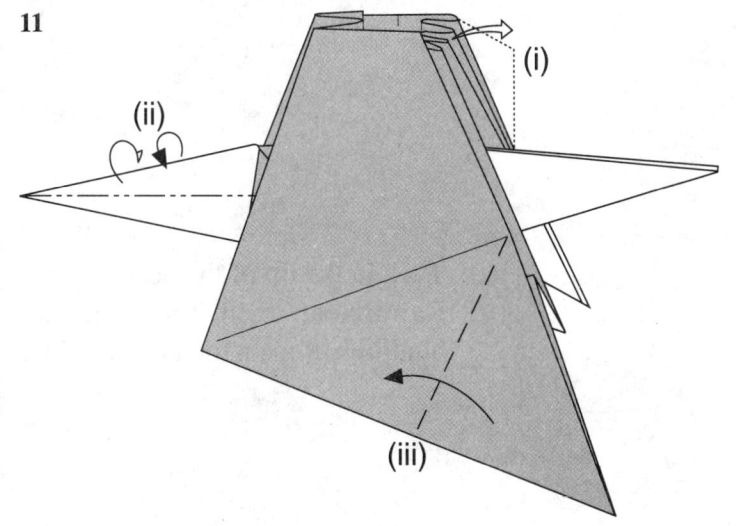

(i) From the top, pull out a fold. Readjust the head flap position if it is disturbed.
(ii) Fold the tail flap inwards to make the tail thinner.
(iii) Fold the front flap. Repeat for the other side.

12

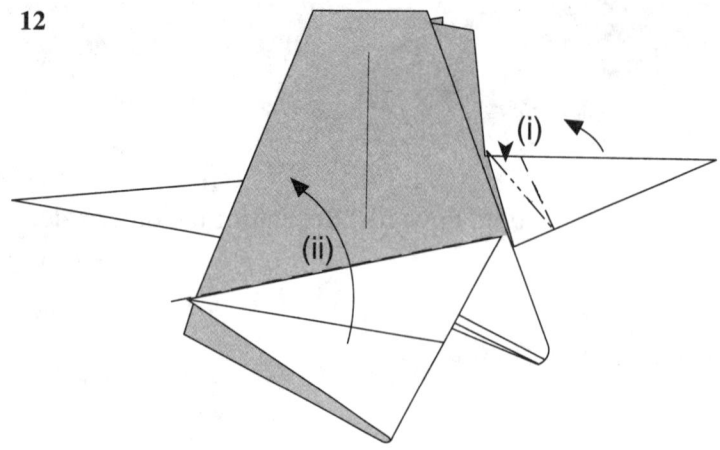

(i) Crimp fold to form the neck. The easiest way is to reverse fold downwards and then reverse fold upwards again.
(ii) Fold the front flap upwards. Repeat for the other side.

13

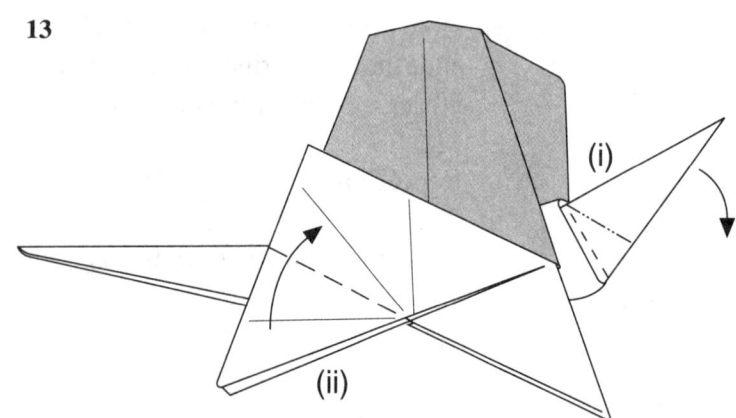

(i) Crimp fold downwards to form the head (see step 14).
(ii) Fold the left flap upwards. Repeat for the other side.

14

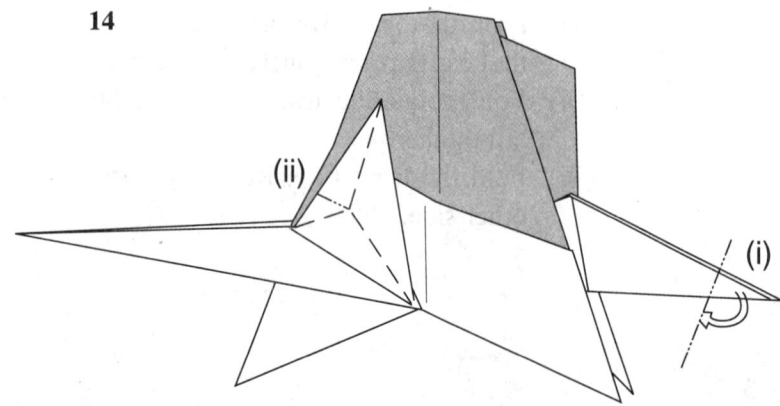

(i) Tuck in the tip of the head.
(ii) Rabbit-ear fold to form the hindlimb. Repeat for the other side.

15

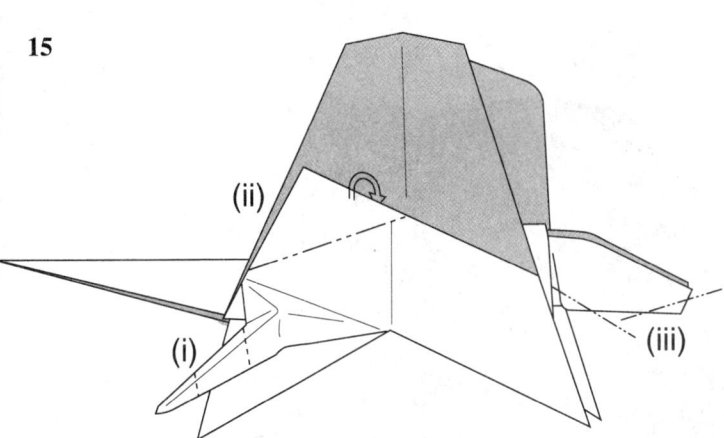

(i) Bend the hindlimb to form the foot as shown in step 16.
(ii) Tuck in the triangular portion. Repeat for the other side.
(iii) Tuck in along the creases to shape the head.

16

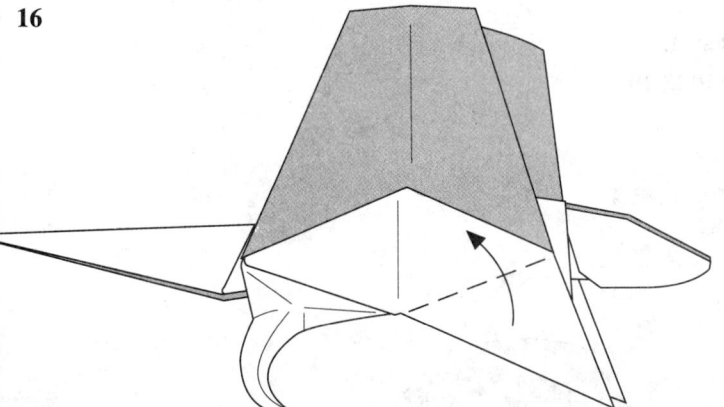

Lift up the right flap. Repeat for the other side.

17

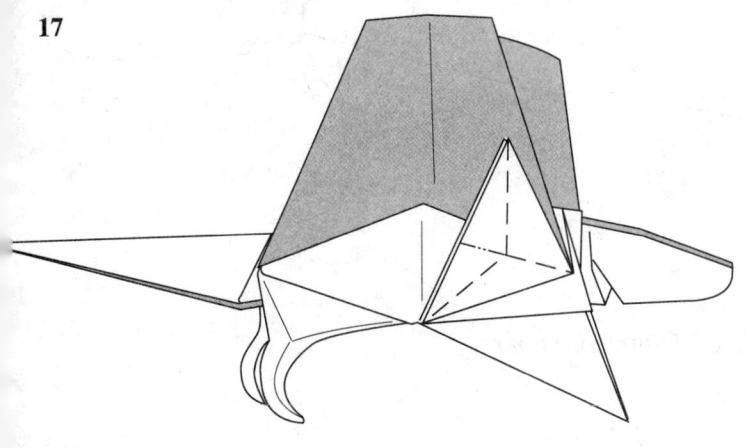

Rabbit-ear fold to form the forelimbs. Repeat for the other side.

18

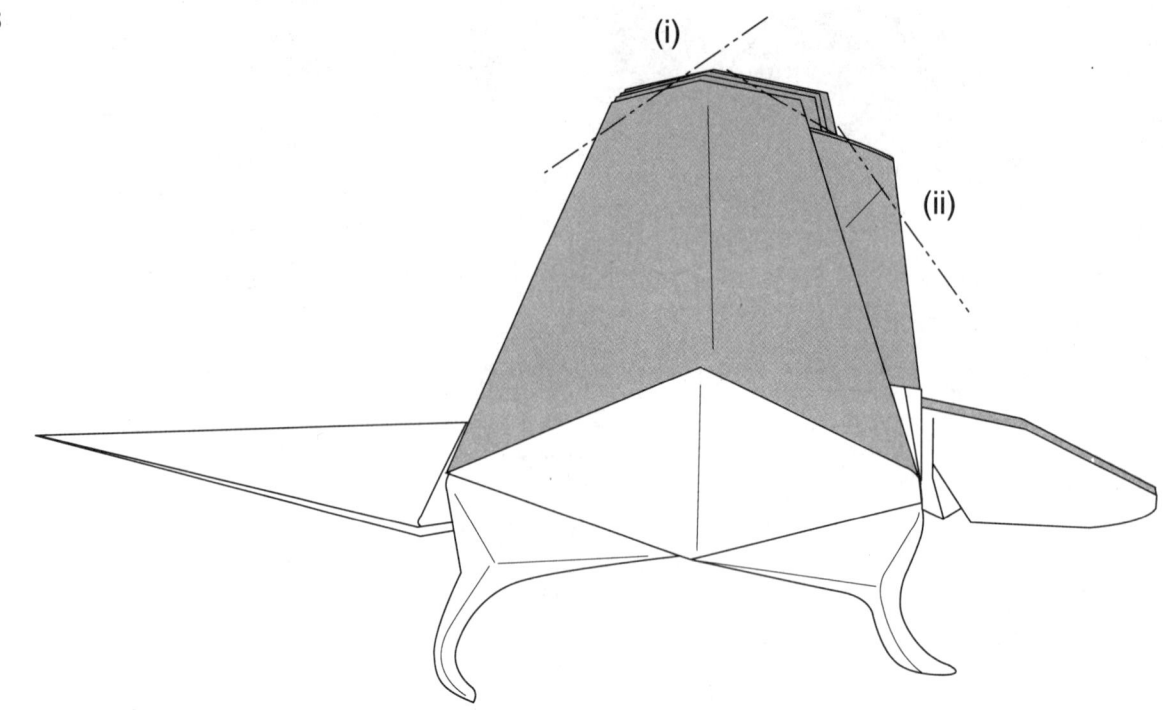

(i) Tuck in along the creases to shape the sail.
(ii) For the front portion, do a sink fold to tuck in.

19

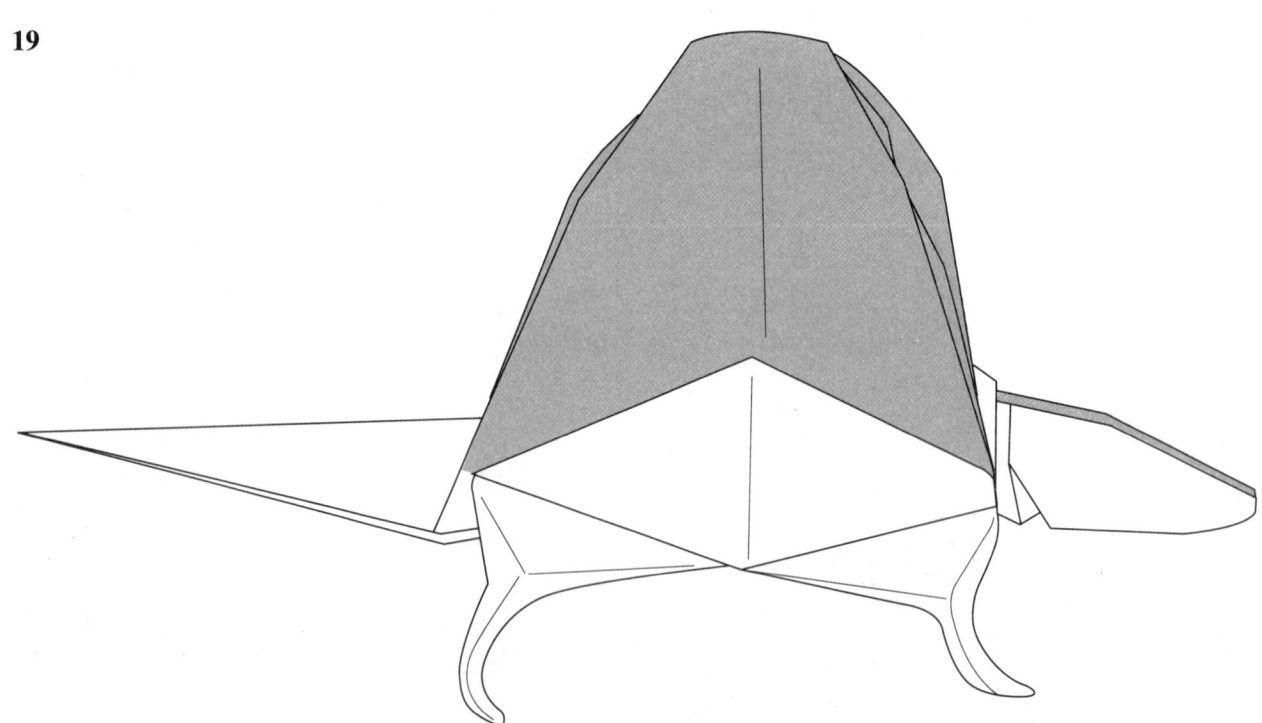

The completed *Dimetrodon* model

Making Your Own Dinosaur Park

Before making your dinosaur park, you should have some idea as to how large each dinosaur is in relation to other dinosaurs. Due to paper size constraints we will not be able to make exact scale models but only approximations. The largest model, *Brachiosaurus*, is about 40 ft (12 m) tall, i.e. as tall as a four-storey building, whilst the smallest, *Compsognathus*, is only the size of a chicken.

Follow the paper size and type given for making each dinosaur. You will want to make a model of each type of dinosaur first. Here are some tips to make your park more realistic.

1. Make more of the herd dinosaurs

The large theropods like *Tyrannosaurus* and *Allosaurus* moved about singly. However, *Compsognathus* moved about in packs. So did the vegetarians like ceratopsians, hadrosaurs and sauropods. Make more of these models to give the herd-like effect.

2. Have the right type of dinosaurs together

Do not position your meat-eaters like *Ceratosaurus* living peacefully with the vegetarians. It is like placing the lion next to the zebra.

3. Have dramatic scenes

Here, imagination is important. Try to think of a possible scenario and then arrange your models around that scenario. You can show a pack of *Deinonychus* trying to bring down a hadrosaur, or you can have a *Tyrannosaurus* fighting a lone *Stegosaurus*, or have an *Allosaurus* guarding a dead *Iguanodon* that it recently killed while a pack of hungry looking *Coelophysis* waits impatiently to scavage the remains.

Again, your choice of the models is important. A *Tyrannosaurus* will not be fighting with a pack of *Compsognathus*, and a pack of *Velociraptors* will not try to bring down a *Brachiosaurus*.

4. Give your models varied postures

By making minor changes to the steps, you can give your dinosaur a different posture or neck position. That way you can have a pack of *Compsognathus*, some running away, others looking up, and yet others looking behind their shoulders.

5. Position your models to give a three-dimensional effect

Most of the models have a three-dimensional look about them. The head of your *Tyrannosaurus* model should not be flat but shaped to show its cheeks protruding. When positioning your models do not make them stiff-looking. You can have a *Tyrannosaurus* with its head turned sideways and tilted at an angle to attack the *Stegosaurus*. Its feet should be positioned wide apart and its tail curved in one direction. The *Stegosaurus* can be trying to keep its eye on the *Tyrannosaurus* and swinging its tail towards its adversary at the same time. Its armour plate can be spread apart in a defensive move.

The mighty *Tyrannosaurus* about to do battle with a heavily armoured stegosaur, *Stegosaurus*.

The three-horned ceratopsian, *Triceratops*, rears its head against a medium-sized hunter, *Ceratosaurus*.

A pair of male pachycephalosaurus, *Stegoceras*, engage in a head-butting contest for dominance — very much like the mountain goats of today.

A male hadrosaur, *Parasaurolophus*, tries to ward off an attack by three small *Dromaeosaurus*.

An awesome flesh-eating theropod, *Allosaurus*, guards its kill against a pair of scavenging *Coelophysis*. These nippy hunters will seize the opportunity to feed on the remains once *Allosaurus* has finished with its meal.

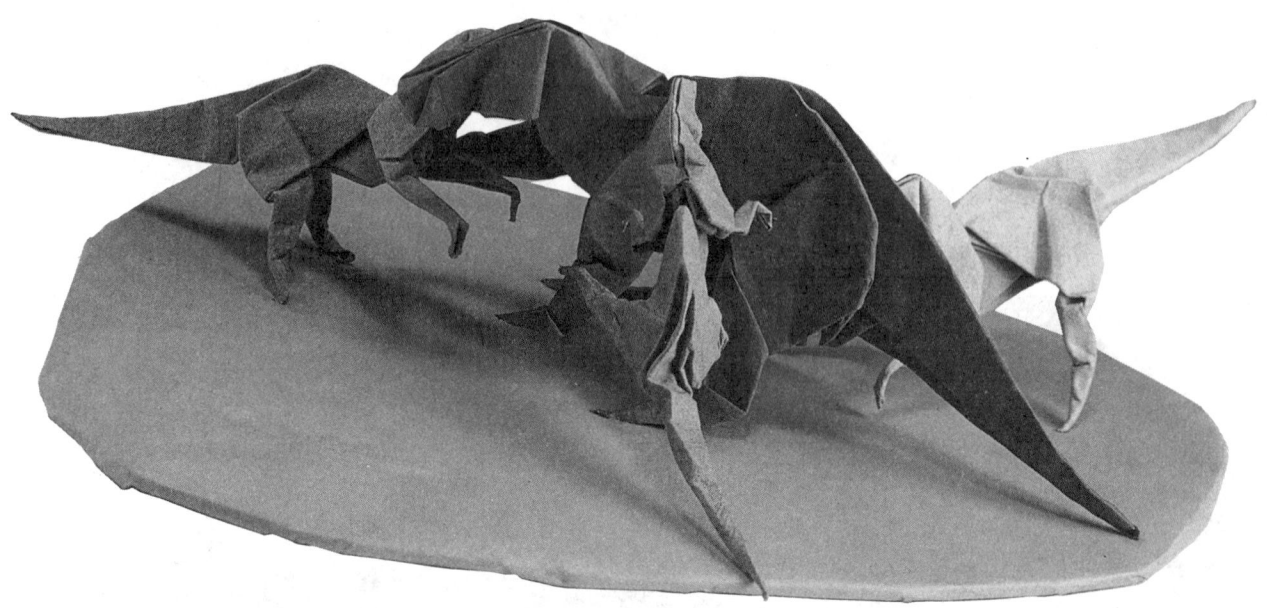

A pack of *Deinonychus* bringing down their defenceless prey, *Iguanodon*.

In this scene, the towering *Brachiosaurus* stands next to *Diplodocus*. *Pteranodon* soars high above. In the foreground, a medium-sized hunter, *Megalosaurus*, gives chase as a group of fleet-footed *Compsognathus* scatters. Grazing nearby is the hadrosaur, *Lambeosaurus*, an undergrowth feeder. *Dimetrodon* basks in the sunlight, using its huge sail to regulate its body temperature.

Approximate Dinosaur Dimensions

Dinosaur	Meaning	Standing Length	Height	Weight
Tyrannosaurus	tyrant lizard	45 ft /13 m	20 ft /6 m	6 tonnes
Allosaurus	different lizard	36 ft /11 m	15 ft /4·5 m	2 tonnes
Ceratosaurus	horned lizard	20 ft /6 m	10 ft /3 m	1 tonne
Megalosaurus	big lizard	30 ft /9 m	15 ft /4·5 m	2 tonnes
Compsognathus	elegant jaw	2 ft /60 cm	1.5 ft /40 cm	3 kg
Deinonychus	terrible claw	13 ft /4 m	6 ft /1·8 m	—
Coelophysis	hollow form	10 ft /3 m	6 ft /1·8 m	27 kg
Velociraptor	swift robber	6 ft /1·8 m	4 ft /1·2 m	—
Diplodocus	double beam	88 ft /27 m	30 ft /9 m	10 tonnes
Apatosaurus	thunder lizard	70 ft /21 m	30 ft /9 m	30 tonnes
Brachiosaurus	arm lizard	75 ft /23 m	40 ft /12 m	70 tonnes
Camarasaurus	chambered lizard	60 ft /18 m	25 ft /7·5 m	18 tonnes
Saurolophus	crested lizard	30 ft /9 m	16 ft /5 m	4 tonnes
Parasaurolophus	parallel-sided	30 ft /9 m	16 ft /5 m	4 tonnes
Lambeosaurus	Lambe's lizard	30 ft /9 m	16 ft /5 m	4 tonnes
Iguanodon	iguana tooth	30 ft /9 m	16 ft /5 m	5 tonnes
Stegoceras	covered horn	6 ft /1·8 m	4 ft /1·2 m	—
Triceratops	three-horned face	30 ft /9 m	10 ft /3 m	6 tonnes
Stegosaurus	plated lizard	30 ft /9 m	12 ft /3·6 m	2 tonnes
Pteranodon	winged and toothless	20 ft /6 m	—	15 kg
Dimetrodon	two-measure teeth	10 ft /3 m	4 ft /1·2 m	—

Paper Size To Use (in centimetres)

Dinosaur	Head	Offset	Body	Offset	Paper Type
Tyrannosaurus	25	—	35	2·5	thick
Allosaurus	24	3·8	30	2·2	thick
Ceratosaurus	19	3·0	21	2·0	thick
Megalosaurus	17·8	—	25	2·4	thick
Compsognathus	6·4	—	9	1·0	thin
Deinonychus	12·5	—	18·8	2·7	thin
Coelophysis	12	—	16·9	2·5	thin
Velociraptor	10	—	14	2·0	thin
Diplodocus	32	9·6	40	11	thick
Apatosaurus	30	8·5	40	11	thick
Brachiosaurus	45	12·3	37·7	7·5	thick
Camarasaurus	30	6	32	6·7	thick
Saurolophus	23	3·4	26·8	3·8	thick
Parasaurolophus	23	5	26·8	3·8	thick
Lambeosaurus	23	4·3	26·8	3·8	thick
Iguanodon	20.2	—	26·8	3·8	thick
Stegoceras	15.4	3·2	18	1·3	thick
Triceratops	23	—	30	2·1	thick
Stegosaurus	29	—	40	—	thick
Pteranodon	21	4·4	—	—	thin and coloured on both sides
Dimetrodon	25	—	—	—	thin and coloured on both sides

References

MICHAEL BENTON, *On the Trail of the Dinosaurs* (Crescent Books, New York, 1989)

MICHAEL BENTON, *The Reign of the Reptiles* (Crescent Books, New York, 1990)

DOUG DIXON, *The Big Book of Dinosaurs — A Natural History of the Prehistoric World* (Brompton Books Corp, USA, 1989)

DAVID NORMAN, *Dinosaur!* (Boxtree Ltd, London, 1991)